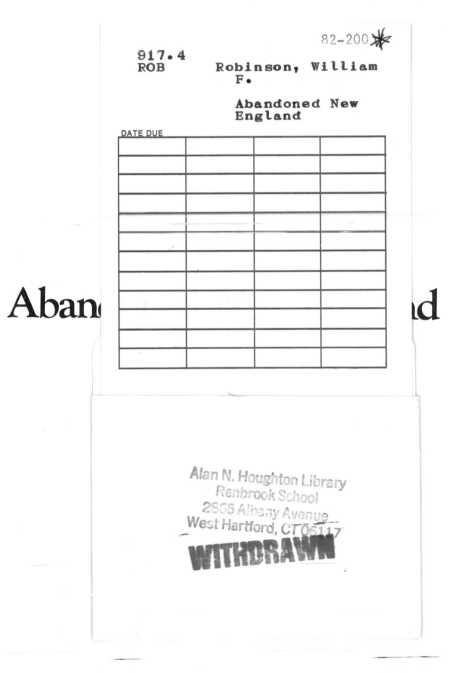

Aban... ...nd

Abandoned

Its Hidden Ruins and

William F. Robinson

New England

Where to Find Them

New York Graphic Society   Boston

Second paperback printing

Designed by Designworks

The drawings on pages 62 top, 94, and 112 are by Peter J. O'Callaghan.

Some of the material in the chapter "Town Animal Pounds" first appeared, in different form, in *Yankee*.

Library of Congress Cataloging in Publication Data

Robinson, William F.   1946-
    Abandoned New England.

    Bibliography: p. 199
    Includes index.
    1. Historic Sites—New England—Guide-books.   2. New
England—Description and travel—1951-   —Guide-
books.   I. Title.
F5.R62   917.4′04′4   75-24590
ISBN 0-8212-0654-0 cloth
ISBN 0-8212-0734-2 paper

MU
New York Graphic Society books are published by Little, Brown and
    Company
Published simultaneously in Canada by Little, Brown and Company
    (Canada) Limited
Printed in the United States of America

For Peggy

Contents

Acknowledgments

I would like to thank the great many people who aided me in my search for these places and their history. I would particularly like to thank Fran Belcher of the Appalachian Mountain Club; Mrs. Helen Hammond of Parsonsfield, Maine; John Reading of Brookline, Massachusetts; Dwight Smith of the Conway Scenic Railway; Mr. C. Whitlock of Bethany, Connecticut; the Bristol Clock Museum; the Bath Marine Museum; the Collins Ax Museum; the Peabody Museum; the Railway and Locomotive Historical Society; and the many *Yankee* readers who were so kind to write, adding to my list of town pounds.

Many thanks to Robin Bledsoe for her assistance and advice in the preparation of the manuscript.

I would especially like to thank the Boston Athenaeum and Jack Jackson for their great assistance. Finally, I would like to recognize the aid given to me by Cedric L. Robinson, my father. His extensive knowledge of New England history and historical material has been of immeasurable value.

Introduction

When the Pilgrims arrived in New England, they found a "remote,
rocky, wild-woody wilderness, a receptacle for lions, wolves, bears,
foxes, raccoons, badgers, beavers, otters, and all kinds of wild creatures,
a place that never afforded the Natives better than the flesh of a
few wild creatures, and parched Indian corn inched out with chestnuts
and bitter acorns."[1] Yet the sweat and prayers of these early colonists
soon turned this tumbling wilderness into a "New English Canaan,"
and by 1654, Captain Edward Johnson, a Massachusetts colonist,
could write in a book he called *Wonder-Working Providence* that:

*in a very little space, everything in the country proved a staple
commodity, wheat, rye, oats, peas, barley, beef, pork, fish, butter,
cheese, timber, mast, tar, soap, plankboard, frames of houses, clapboard
and pipestaves; iron and lead is like to be also; and those who were
formerly forced to fetch most of the bread they eat and the beer they
drink, a hundred leagues by sea, are through the blessings of the Lord
so increased, that they have not only fed their elder sisters: Virginia,
Barbadoes, and many of the Summer [Bermuda] Islands that were
prefered before her for fruitfulness, but even the grandmother of us all:
even the fertile isle of Great Britain. . . . Thus has the Lord been
pleased to turn one of the most hideous, boundless, and unknown
wildernesses in the world to an instant, as it were (in comparison to
other works), to a well ordered Commonwealth.*[2]

An artist's conception of "the progress of civilization in New England," showing the many sides of New England life.

New England assumed a leading role in the farming, mining, manufacturing, and shipping of the young colonies. It seemed an inexhaustible wellspring of food and goods as well as of spiritual thought. Yet for all its output, New England has never been a bountiful land. Harsh winters and rocky soil have opposed the farmer's plow. The early manufacture seemed great only in proportion to the relatively small population of the colonies. Likewise, its mineral deposits were worked because all the larger deposits on the continent lay unknown, in the inaccessible wilderness west of the Appalachians.

It was for these reasons that, as America developed westward, new areas of greater natural resources — the coal regions of Pennsylvania, the flat farmlands of the Midwest, the iron deposits of the Great Lakes region, or the cattle lands of the Southwest — gradually eclipsed New England's modest output. As these western regions began sending their products back east, the New Englanders found themselves unable to compete profitably and abandoned their old trades. As these industries and ways of life were abandoned, many of the outmoded farms, manufactories, and transportation lines were converted to new uses. Others were not, and over the years they have remained unused and empty.

Like castoffs lying forgotten in some great attic, these relics of New England's varied past lie in many corners of the landscape, untouched since the day progress ended their usefulness: a mountaintop iron furnace in Connecticut that once made cannon to fight the British; a canal lock that once lowered produce out of the New

England interior, now dry and stranded in a Massachusetts woods; great four-masted sailing ships lying aground and forgotten in a quiet Maine harbor; a Rhode Island mill town whose factory and houses stand vacant and crumbling; or a beautiful colonial church, built by a rich farming population, now desolate and surrounded by overgrown fields. The slow decay of the ages, the moss, wild flowers, and ivy have given these relics a somber beauty, a patina of wear forced upon them by the harsh New England climate, which contrasts sharply with the strong walls and meticulous detail given them by earlier generations.

They survive in many unexpected places. Their sites range from the hearts of cities, through the suburbs and rural countryside, to the forested wilderness of New England's northern border.

In itself, each relic's story is an account of an all but forgotten way of life that has disappeared with the forces of progress. When taken together, however, these stories blend to form a mosaic of New England history that traces the region's metamorphosis from a rural farming region connected by primitive roads and interspersed with a few craft industries to the great urban-suburban megalopolis it is today.

Some of these relics of New England's past have been gathered into museums or reconstructed as historic sites, but hundreds upon hundreds more have been left untouched because of their great number or physical size. Only in the case of the seacoast — the buildings, wharves, forts, and lighthouses that have escaped demolition — has any one subject been systematically preserved. Most others, with the exception of the grist mills, have only a few preserved and restored examples. It is these mostly forgotten and unattended places that are the subject of this book. For continuity, they are grouped by general topic: transportation lines, rural life, early industries, mining, large manufacturing, and the sea. These subjects are arranged roughly in order of their appearance and prominence during New England's history to give the reader the best historical perspective.

Not covered in this book are the objects that have been preserved for the most part, such as the seacoast sites, the more significant or ornate examples of colonial architecture, and the many sites of specific historical interest. Also not covered are relics that have long since vanished or have become totally inaccessible, such as the old rural towns that today lie beneath the many large New England reservoirs.

However, the reader will find that a few preserved or still-operating sites have been included in the book where doing so adds a better understanding of the many other places like it that stand unused.

At the back of the book are included a selected bibliography and site lists. The first is to aid those who wish to research specific sites and subjects. The second is for travelers who might want to visit the relics mentioned in this book and the hundreds more like them that cover the New England countryside. Driving directions are given where necessary as well as a short description of what the visitor can expect to find.

The New England 1 Landscape

While the story of the people who came to settle New England, the Pilgrims and Puritans, is familiar to us all, the character of the land they settled is less well known.

Geologically, New England is quite old. Its rolling hills and modest mountain ranges, the Green Mountains in Vermont and the White Mountains in New Hampshire, are the worn-down stumps of mountains that could have once rivaled the Himalayas.

Like the mountains, New England's areas of flat lowlands are also quite modest in size. For the most part they are found in a few large valleys inland and in a thin ribbon along the coast. The only large areas of tillable flat land are in eastern Massachusetts, in the Connecticut River Valley from the Massachusetts–Vermont–New Hampshire border south to Long Island Sound, and along the region's western edge in the Berkshire and Vermont valleys.

Much of the rest of New England is rolling countryside, an endless repetition of narrow valleys, long steep hillsides, and flat hilltops. They march northward from Long Island Sound in wave after wave of ever increasing height to the foothills of the White and Green Mountains.

Overlaying these mountains, hills, and lowlands are the effects of New England's Ice Age. The glaciers left a legacy of disrupted drainage patterns that forced old streams into new beds, creating many falls and rapids yet to be worn down by time. The glaciers also scraped flat the hilltops and churned the rocks broken loose into the soil. Every year

Opposite: An 1838 view of the Connecticut River Valley near Middletown. Early settlements in accessible lowlands prospered from an ability to ship goods by water. In the distance are the rolling uplands that edge to the valley.

The New England Landscape

a portion of these stones and boulders are forced to the surface by the winter's freeze. The early colonists piled them up each spring into the familiar stone walls and, not understanding their origin or the reason for their appearance, believed them the work of the devil, attempting to break their faith.

Though not the most attractive landscape to the early colonists, New England had the good fortune to be the closest to Europe along the sea-lanes. Despite this strong link with Europe, the Hudson River, lying twenty-odd miles to the west of the New England–New York border, weakened New England's link with the great American interior to the west. The Hudson, and its tributary, the Mohawk, served as a ready-made route to the interior and channeled all commerce downriver to New York, bypassing New England and leaving it in many ways a closed, self-contained community.

It is these facts of geography, coupled with the nature of the people who settled New England, that determined its history: the story of a region of modest resources that, by the efforts of its people, has time and time again discarded the old and embraced the new in order to maintain a prominent position in the life of America.

A 1789 view of the Green Woods, as the wilderness area of northwestern Connecticut was called. The rolling hills are typical of much of the New England uplands. The plumes of smoke come from early iron forges (see Chapter 12).

2 Paths, Post Roads, and Turnpikes

The first white settlers traveling inland through New England used the trails laid out long before by migrating Indian tribes. "It is admirable to see what paths their naked hardened feet have made in the wilderness in [the] most stony and hardened places," remarked Roger Williams in 1643, seven years after an overland flight along Indian paths took him from religious persecution in Massachusetts to the founding of Rhode Island.[1]

These "trodden paths," as the colonists called them, grew over the next centuries into the main overland roads. Little improved from Indian days, they were rocky, poorly drained, and breached by an army of unpredictable streams. Summer dryness turned them into avenues of choking dust, and the first shower sunk the unfortunate traveler to his knees.

By 1700, three of these paths were the main roads from Boston to New York. Running west from Boston, the Bay Path connected Worcester and Springfield. Farther south, the Connecticut Path ran from Boston to Hartford. The Lower Path cut overland from Boston to Providence before following the shoreline to New York.

In the more settled areas the roads were wide enough for wheeled traffic, but for the most part they were fit only for horseback or foot travel. These three paths were also called post roads after 1673, when riders began carrying mail between New York and Boston once a month.

In the fall of 1704, an intrepid lady named Madame Sarah Kemble Knight traveled the Lower Path from Boston to New York with a post rider guiding her part of the way. Her diary of the journey not only gives us a feeling for the hazards of eighteenth-century travel but also stands as a tribute to the lady's fortitude:

About Three [in the] afternoon went on with my Third Guide, who Rode very hard: and having crossed Providence Ferry, we came to a River which they Generally Ride through. But I dare not venture; so the Post got a Ladd and Canoe to carry me to the other side, and he rode through and Led my horse. The Canoe was very small and shallow, so that when we were in she seemed ready to take in water, which greatly terrified me, and caused me to be very circumspect, sitting with my hands fast on each side, my eyes steady, not daring so much as to lodge my tongue a hair's breadth more on one side of my mouth than the other, nor so much as think on Lott's wife, for a wry thought would have overset our wherey.

Once across the river, Madame Knight remounted her horse and rode into the night to reach the inn ahead.

Here we found great difficulty in traveling, the way being very narrow, and on each side the Trees and bushes gave us very unpleasant welcome with their branches and boughs, which we could not avoid, it being so exceedingly dark. My Guide, as before so now, put on harder than I, with my weary bones could follow; so left me and the way behind him. Now Returned my distressed apprehensions of the place where I was: the dolesome woods, my Company next to none,

Mr. Hooker and His Congregation Traveling Through the Wilderness. *In 1636, about seventy-five of the eighty-five households of Newtowne (later Cambridge), Mass., abandoned their homes en masse to make one of our nation's first westward migrations. Led by friendly Indians, they traveled the Indian paths overland to the Connecticut River Valley to settle at Hartford.*

Main Overland Routes
of the Colonial Period

Going I know not whither, and encompassed with Terrifying darkness;
The least of which was enough to startle a more Masculine courage.[2]

Those colonists who ventured off the trodden path into the wilderness faced even worse difficulties. The forests grew dense overhead, and the ground was choked with brush and fallen trees. Horses were useless and the hardy pioneers were forced to crawl under or over each obstruction as they met it.

During the colonial period, the New England frontier was slowly pushed north and west out of Connecticut, Massachusetts, and Rhode Island; and in the more settled areas a system of so-called county roads, and King's highways developed to supplant the original Indian paths. At first they were trails connecting individual farms. As villages began appearing, the connections between towns became more important. Since the towns did not usually lie along straight lines, travelers going any great distance along county roads followed a zigzag route.

American stagecoach of post-Revolutionary times. Passengers sat three abreast on hard wooden benches.

As early as 1639, the General Court of the Massachusetts Bay Colony examined their roads and decided:

In some places they are felt too straight, and in other places travelers are forced to go about, it is therefore, ordered, that all highways shall be laid out . . . so as may be with most ease and safety for travelers; and for this end every town shall chose two or three men, who shall join with two or three men in the next town . . . to lay out the highways in each town where they may be most convenient . . . notwithstanding any man's property, or any corne ground, so as it occasion not the pulling down of a man's house, or laying open any garden or orchard.[3]

The colonial pioneers took little notice of these laws. For them, the survival of their family in a new land took precedence over the "ease and safety of travelers." Hazarding a rotted log bridge or a miry, root-entwined roadway and scrambling around rocks and fallen trees were trifles to people who daily faced Indians, wild animals, and possible starvation.

Even in the more settled sections of New England, the roads fared little better. The Yankee farmers ignored the concept of a right-of-way and used any nearby road for their own purposes. Laws be damned — the road was just another part of their farmland and too valuable as open land to leave untouched. Nocturnal travel was most dangerous on these roads, as the wayfarer faced woodpiles, pigsties, or fences.

In some towns the only road was the county road, the rest a continuous patchwork of farms. Families not on the county road were allowed to cut across each other's land for Sunday church services. In 1732, some farmers in Lebanon, Connecticut, complained that to get to church they must cross "particular men's properties as tresspassers and through thirteen or fourteen fences and many miry places as well as over bad hills and be troublesome to our neighbors."[4]

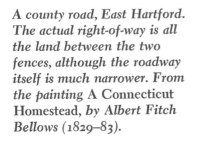

A county road, East Hartford. The actual right-of-way is all the land between the two fences, although the roadway itself is much narrower. From the painting A Connecticut Homestead, *by Albert Fitch Bellows (1829–83).*

One of the worst states of affairs existed in Plainfield, Connecticut, as late as 1712. Here even the county road did not exist, and the traveler was forced to copy the Lebanon farmers by making his way across farm after farm to reach the county road in the next township. As a result of this inattention, few colonial roads could bear heavy traffic, and the farmer wishing to move a loaded wagon needed at least half a dozen oxen for the task.

The one great contribution the colonial age made to America's road system was the milestone. These stone markers were placed along the highways to tell travelers the distance to their destinations.

The Boston area, with its comparatively large population, was the first to have milestones along its major routes. At first they were placed not by the government but by wealthy public officials. While today people may serve their community in the hope that they will be someday memorialized with a school, road, or park, colonial men took matters into their own hands as they erected milestones with their names upon them.

In 1707 Chief Justice Samuel Sewall left the Boston Town-House, the seat of the colonial government, to roll a wheel along the one road out of peninsular Boston (Boston was then connected with the mainland by a narrow strip of land) to measure out the first two miles of the route. Sewall records in his diary:

July, 14th 1707. Mr. Antram and I, having Benj. Smith and David to wait on us, Measured with his Wheel from the Town-House Two Miles, and drove down Stakes at each Mile's end, in order to placing Stone-posts in convenient time. August, 7th 1707. Peter Weare set up

*the Stone Post to shew a Mile from the Town-House ends: Silence
Allen . . . and a Carter assisted, made a Plumb-Line of his Whip.*[5]

Today, Sewall's milestones have long since vanished and he is famous
only for condemning the "witches" brought before him. In the 1720s
and 1730s others extended the line of stones begun by Sewall and today
they can still be found along the streets of metropolitan Boston. In
Harvard Square, Cambridge, busy traffic passes within a few feet of one
of these stones. Originally its inscription read

*A milestone typical of the
colonial era.*

BOSTON

8 MILES

1734
A I

The initials "A I" were those of Abraham Ireland, who had the milestone erected. Behind the stone lies Cambridge's Old Burying Ground,
where Ireland himself has lain since 1753.

While a direct route from Boston to Cambridge is far short of
eight miles, the trip in those days took the traveler out of Boston south
down the one road out of the city, then west around the old "back bay"
(now filled in) before turning north to cross the Charles River at Cambridge. In 1786 a new bridge was built directly across the back bay that
shortened the distance between the two communities. After a second
bridge opened in 1793, the people of Cambridge revised the old milestone by turning it around and giving the back a new inscription:

CAMBRIDGE–

New Bridge

2¼ Miles

1794

This is one of the few New England milestones with a double
inscription.

By this time laws had been enacted giving each town the responsi-
bility of erecting milestones. A Connecticut order of 1767 read:

*Be it enacted by the Governor and Council, and House of
Representatives, in General Court assembled, That it shall be the
duty of the Select-men in the Several towns, on the Several Post Roads
in the State, at the expense of Such Town, to erect and keep up
Mile-Stones, at least Two Feet high, near the side of the common
traveling Road, marked with the distances from the County Town of
the County where such Town lies.*[6]

In Massachusetts a similar order of the same year caused ninety-nine
milestones to be erected on the Bay Path between Boston and Springfield. Forty remain today. Within range of the large cities along the
route they have been virtually annihilated by highway expansion, but

Joseph Wait's milestone in Springfield, erected to keep travelers from wandering off the Bay Path as he did in a 1763 storm.

in the rolling farm country east of Springfield the motorist can mark off mile after mile of the old way by the stumpy, weatherworn stones.

Despite town laws, private citizens still contributed to the placing of milestones. In the winter of 1763, Joseph Wait, a merchant returning from Springfield along the then-unmarked Bay Path to his home in Brookfield, became lost in a blizzard when he wandered off onto a side road. Afterward, determined that neither he nor anyone else repeat the experience, he placed a milestone at the junction to set travelers on the right path. Over five feet high, it is decorated with the Masonic symbols of sun, moon, and stars. For more than two centuries the milestone stood its ground as Springfield grew up around it; a few years ago it was moved inside the nearby Springfield Armory Museum to protect its sandstone faces from further destruction by the elements.

Other milestones were erected by innkeepers, for they were considered a necessary ornamentation of any wayside inn. In Sutton, Massachusetts, on a colonial highway to Boston, a Colonel Bartholomew Woodbury, innkeeper, erected such a stone. It was 1771 and the county commissioner was putting up milestones along the highway. Woodbury realized that these new stones would miss his inn by a few hundred yards. By hook or crook he convinced the commissioner to skip a stone and allow Woodbury to erect it instead. Since that date, a five-foot granite slab has stood before the site of Woodbury's inn to misinform the traveler: 48ML to Boston 1771 — B.W.

The Revolutionary War brought home to the colonies the poor state of their roads. With the British men-of-war patrolling the seas, the Continental army was reduced to dragging itself overland along these poor highways. In some cases they were forced to build roads where none had been before. One of these was the Bayley-Hazen Military Road in northern Vermont. It was part of Washington's plan that the Continental army invade Canada, and this road was to be the invasion route. The road began at Newbury on the Connecticut River and ran northwest to Westfield near the Canadian border. The road was started in 1776 under the direction of General Jacob Bayley, but was soon abandoned. In 1778 Washington ordered its resumption and it was completed by Colonel Moses Hazen. Though only a few raiding parties ever used it during the Revolution, afterward it became the main artery for settlers headed for the rich flatland of northern Vermont. Today, much of the old route is abandoned, and one can find markers identifying the old stretches in the towns of northern Vermont.

After the Revolutionary War the new nation decided that the best way to improve the roads was to grant charters to private companies who would improve the roads in return for tolls collected on them. These were the turnpikes. Each state incorporated its own turnpike companies and, so long as they kept the road in good condition, the companies could collect tolls until they had regained their investment plus twelve percent. Exempt from these charges were:

Persons traveling on the Lord's Day and other public days to attend public worship, persons travelling to attend society, Town or Freeman's Meetings, Military exercizes and Funerals, and persons going to and returning from mill, and farmers belonging to the town where any gate shall be established, passing through the same to attend their ordinary farming business.[7]

Stagecoach travel and its hazards in the early nineteenth century.

Persons also passed free if the tollkeeper were not on duty or the gate left open. If the road were allowed to fall into disrepair, however, it would automatically revert back to a free, public road.

The routes of the turnpikes were laid out in two ways. Some were simply bad stretches of existing highways "improved" into turnpikes. In areas where travel between cities was accomplished by zigzaging over roads connecting intervening towns, turnpike companies were authorized to build new roads straight overland.

The difference between the miry free road and the "improved" turnpike was sometimes slight. The old roads were cleared of roots and rocks. Ditches were dug on each side to improve drainage. Abrupt rises in ground were graded, but few turnpike companies improved the roadbed itself beyond laying planks or gravel in the marshier sections.

The first New England turnpike, the second in the nation (the first was a road west out of Alexandria, Virginia), smoothed out twelve

Corduroy-Bridge, Mount Mansfield Road. This roadbed of rough logs was the best a traveler could expect before the days of graveled roads.

miles of rough road between Norwich and New London, Connecticut. Four years after the pike was incorporated in 1792, Timothy Dwight, president of Yale College, traveled the road and commented, "Few persons formerly attempted to go from one of these places to the other [Norwich to New London] and return on the same day. Pleasure carriages were scarcely used at all. The new road is smooth and good, and the journey is now easily performed in little more than two hours."[8]

The actual work of building the turnpike was done with pick and shovel by local people hired along the way. In Connecticut, however, individual towns often paid for the new roads. The state legislature

simply passed a law requiring the individual towns to build a road along
the proposed turnpike route. Once the road was cleared and the bridges
built, the legislature turned around and granted a charter to a turnpike
company to take over the new road. This did not sit well with the
Connecticut townsmen, who felt a double injury in having to pay to
use what they had paid to build.

The turnpikes laid over new routes followed one basic maxim: "The
shortest line is a straight one and can not be rivaled, and as such
merits the first consideration."[9] In many cases there was never a second
consideration, as turnpike companies went bankrupt digging over mountains and filling in marshes in their remorseless fight to keep their
route straight.

Since before the days of Madame Knight, travelers on the Lower
Path from New York to Boston hugged New England's southern shoreline east to Narragansett Bay at Wakefield, Rhode Island, then turned
north and followed the bay's shore to Providence. In 1816 the Providence
and Pawcatuk Turnpike Society was incorporated to build a road
diagonally across this L-shaped route. Starting in the city streets of
Providence, the pike would cut southwest to meet the Lower Path
where Connecticut and Rhode Island meet at Long Island Sound. In-
between lay rolling hills and bogs, the whole covered by rocks, sand, and
scrub pine.

Three years after work began, the state legislature gave the company
permission to erect a tollgate *as soon as it completed* six miles of road;
additional gates could be built at the end of additional six-mile sections.
The countryside was simply too rough. In 1820 the Providence and
Pawcatuk Turnpike Society decided that they could not complete the
pike. They turned the route's last eleven and a half miles to the
Connecticut border over to the newly formed Hopkinton and Richmond
Turnpike Corp.

When the completed pike finally opened, it revolutionized travel
between New York and Boston. The shortest route became a steamship
from New York to New London, then a stagecoach overland along the
Connecticut and Rhode Island portions of the turnpike, and on the
old Lower Path from Providence to Boston.

The new pike's importance was short-lived, as in 1830 the steamships out of New York extended their run to dock at Providence,
bypassing the New London–Providence overland route. Suddenly outmoded, the old turnpike company still held on, though by the 1850s its
revenues were so low that they couldn't clear the road of winter snow.
By the late 1800s the Providence and Pawcatuk Turnpike Society was
bankrupt and the pike became a public road, serving as the main route
through southwestern Rhode Island.

In the 1920s the state began improving its roads for automobile
traffic. Taking a lesson from the turnpike builders' experiences, they
wisely avoided rebuilding the worst sections of the pike. Today, in
Wyoming, Rhode Island, near the place where the Providence and

Pawcatuk Turnpike Society ran out of funds, Rhode Island Route 3 leaves the old turnpike route and parallels it a few miles west. Twelve miles closer to Providence it swings back to join the old pike again. In between are twelve-odd miles of gravel and dirt road, straight as an arrow, but marshy, rocky, and up and down all the way.

In the sixty years between the first turnpike in 1792 and the gradual bankruptcy of the pike companies in the 1850s, over three hundred turnpikes collected tolls in New England. A hundred more were incorporated, but there is no record of their ever opening. Maine had the fewest, with only five. The greatest concentration was in Connecticut, with 102 different roads under private control. Here the mania for turnpike building reached its height.

In Voluntown, Connecticut, on the Rhode Island border, lies a classic example of the early nineteenth-century belief that any road built anywhere would turn a profit. Although a chain of turnpikes already accommodated travel between Norwich, Connecticut, and Providence, Rhode Island, "to a greater extent than it was able to pay for, certain optimists found encouragement to believe that a rival route, having no advantage beyond a mile or two, would provide a saving investment."[10] In 1829 the Shetucket Turnpike was incorporated and in 1832 was opened from Norwich to the Rhode Island line. Everything fell flat when the Rhode Island legislature refused permission to continue the pike through the state. So the Shetucket Pike was left to peter out into local roads at the state line.

The citizens of Rhode Island, it seems, were most vehement against turnpikes. Timothy Dwight, traveling on the Providence to Norwich Turnpike in 1796, complained that the Rhode Island legislature had refused the turnpike company permission to expend more money on the pike than was originally allowed, leaving the pike half finished, the legislature's philosophy being:

Turnpikes and the establishment of religious worship had their origin in Great Britain, the government of which was a monarchy and the inhabitants slaves; that the people of Massachusetts and Connecticut were obliged by law to support ministers and pay the fare of turnpikes, and were therefore slaves also; . . . but that freeborn Rhode Islanders ought never to submit to be priest-ridden, nor pay for the privilege of traveling on the highway.[11]

In 1805 the Rhode Island section of the Providence to Norwich Pike was finally completed and, Dwight observed, "freeborn Rhode Islanders bowed their heads to the slavery of traveling on a good road."[12]

Though they accepted the "slavery" of the turnpike, they still balked at the tollhouses. As the old Providence to Norwich Pike today winds its way through Johnston and Scituate, Rhode Island, under the modern designation of Route 14, it is crisscrossed a number of times by a meandering gravel road still known as Shun Pike. On this and similar

roads, the old Yankees would loop off the highway to bypass the tollgates before sneaking back onto the pike again. Old legislative dockets overflowed with petitions by turnpike companies for permission to relocate their tollgates because roads had sprung up around them.

While the turnpike companies were constantly worried about shunpikes, it was another bypassing route that ultimately proved their downfall: the railroads. As line after line of track was built the competing turnpikes quickly went bankrupt and reverted to public ownership.

The tollkeepers' houses reverted to private homes while most of the little shacks that were the tollhouses themselves slowly disappeared. One tollhouse that still stands lies by the terminus of the Mount Washington Summit Road in New Hampshire's White Mountains. This road, opened in 1861, still collects tolls from tourists wishing to drive up a winding eight miles to the top of New England's highest mountain.

Traffic still lines up on the Mount Washington Toll Road to pass by the tollhouse. It was built in 1860, a year before the road to the summit of New England's highest mountain opened. The tollhouse was used for over a hundred years before a newer building replaced it in the mid-1960s. In the background rise other mountains of the White Mountains Presidential Range.

The Great Arch, put up in Brookline in 1810 to mark the starting point of the Boston to Worcester Turnpike (the present Route 9).

The tollhouse itself was built in 1860 and was used continuously for over a hundred years until it was replaced by a larger structure. Today it can be seen just off Route 16 in Pinkham Notch; motorists waiting to pay their toll can pause to look inside the 1860 building to see a typical tollhouse of the last century: a simple shack with a desk, chair, clock, and potbellied stove.

While the Mount Washington Summit Road still brings in a profit, it is an exception to the typical fate of the New England turnpikes. Most never broke even, and fewer ever collected the twelve percent profit allowed them by law.

Many of the old turnpikes have been improved and widened into our modern highway system. Yet in places where the old pikes have been bypassed one can still find the old "trodden ways" and pikes much as they were two centuries ago.

In 1801, the State of Connecticut chartered the Farmington and Bristol Turnpike Company. This pike, "nineteen miles, fifty-six rods, and twenty-one links,"[13] began at the west door of the Old State House in what is today downtown Hartford and ran west to connect with the Litchfield and Farmington Turnpike Company in the Litchfield Hills. Only five years after its first charter it was back for permission to move its tollgates because of shunpikes. In 1819 the company gave up its charter without ever repaying its investors the original building cost of $15,232.10.

Today the old route is a study in contrasts. Beginning in Hartford, as Route 4, west, it is the main traffic artery of Asylum Street and Farmington Avenue. Moving west, it is lined by expensive homes as it passes through the fashionable suburbs of West Hartford and Farmington. Once beyond Farmington, a beautiful town of splendid colonial mansions, the old pike and Route 4 separate. Route 4 heads due west to pass through the river valley mill towns that sprang up after the pike was created, while the old pike becomes a country lane through fields of rich bottomland. Finally it enters the Nassahegon State Forest and reverts to a dirt road, little improved since the turnpike days.

This road combines the dual fate of the old turnpikes: some bypassed to lie untouched in New England forest preserves; others, like the Farmington and Bristol's eastern end, still bustling arteries of traffic where, "if the old corporation could collect its tolls today it would be but a few days before it had recouped its $15,232.10."[14]

3 The Canals

As post-Revolutionary America began improving its overland routes, there were those who favored another form of transportation — the canal boat. "Shall we begin with canals, which will carry the farmers' produce cheap to market, and return him merchandize at reduced prices? Or shall we first make roads to accommodate travelers, and let the produce of farms, mines, and forests labor under such heavy expenses that they cannot come to market?" asked Robert Fulton in 1807, pointing out that even with the improved turnpikes it took ten four-horse wagons to carry what could be towed in a canal boat by one horse.[1]

The advantages of water-borne travel were not new to America. Since early colonial times, the settlers had relied on navigable rivers and protected harbors for the movement of bulk goods. Indeed, it was the coastal packets sailing from anchorage to anchorage transferring news and cargo that did the most to bind the colonies into a connected whole.

From the little harbors of the Maine coast to the settlements along the Connecticut River, New Englanders were prosperous because they could load their produce aboard a ship to be sold in a nearby city or across the ocean.

In the larger seaports the merchants, though they dealt in this intra-colonial trade, were uninterested in expanding it because of their more profitable overseas trade. But with the start of the Revolutionary War they were suddenly thrown into chaos. The British men-of-war that had once protected them now considered their ships fair game. The hazards of overseas trade and the post-Revolutionary expansion of the cities

A canal boat on the Middlesex Canal. The boatman at the prow holds a pole for guiding the boat into the locks.

(towns like Boston, with some 16,000 inhabitants in 1734 and about 18,000 in 1790, jumped to over 33,000 by 1810), created a situation in which local farms could no longer supply the needs of the urban population. The cities were forced to find a way to reach inland for goods without having to pay prohibitive overland hauling charges.

One answer was the construction of canal locks around the falls and rapids that had previously defined the headwaters of river navigation. In this way the river valley upriver would be opened for trade as far as the next rapids.

At the turn of the century three New England rivers had locks built on them. The first, in Hadley Falls, Massachusetts, was opened in 1795; it carried flat-bottomed boats around a 53-foot falls to open up the fertile Northampton-Amherst section of the Connecticut River Valley. Other canals opened around Millers and Montague Falls, Massachusetts, in 1800; Bellows Falls, Vermont, in 1802; and Sumners Falls and Olcott's Falls (both near White River Junction, Vermont) in 1810 to make over 250 miles of the Connecticut River navigable.

On the Merrimack River, the power canals of the city of Lowell grew out of a canal opened there in 1797, and on the St. Georges River in Maine a comparable project was begun in 1793 but abandoned in 1806.

The plans of these short canals were almost all similar. Upriver from the falls a canal bed was created by digging along the bank or by building a wall in the riverbed parallel to the bank. Here boats entered to be safe from the currents of the river. They were then towed or poled to the locks where they were lowered to the level of the river below the falls. Another short stretch of canal was then passed through to leave the boat in calm water a safe distance downriver.

At first the locks were built entirely of wood, the gates simply flat wooden doors and the lock walls closely spaced timbers driven into the ground. Water was let in and out through small windows that could be opened and closed in the gates. These wooden walls were not reliable, as water could leach between the timbers into the surrounding soil and around the gates, undermining the whole lock.

Later the locks were built of granite blocks, which prevented the water from getting through them. Constant emptying of the lock,

A primitive canal boat enter-ing a lock on the Middlesex Canal. Such boats were often broken up and sold for lumber at the journey's end.

This 1826 watercolor shows a boat on the Middlesex Canal crossing the Concord River by means of the floating towpath. The canal boat entered the Concord River from beneath the bridge on the river's far bank and will reenter the canal proper at lower left.

Canals of the Nineteenth Century

however, produced a continuous fluctuation of pressure on the banks
of soil behind the walls, and soon loosened them. The vertically driven
timbers could withstand this soil creep, but the freestanding granite
blocks often fell from the weight of the soil, to be pushed to the center
of the lock, crushing any boat that might be there.

Other hazards came from the canals' proximity to the rivers. Winter
ice jams and spring freshets often overflowed into the canal to carry
the locks downriver in pieces. These problems and hazards kept the
early canal builders constantly repairing their works.

River ports downriver from interior lands opened to trade by means
of the canals quickly prospered. The New England harbor cities,
however, began to fear that their lack of a nearby river would cut them
off from the new profits. What was worse, they would have to buy their
staples through a middleman in one of the river ports.

To rectify the problem, the harbor cities laid plans for canals of
their own. These would not be simple locks, but canals 20 to 80 miles
long, whole waterways to take the place of the rivers the harbor cities
lacked.

Boston investors were the first with the Middlesex Canal, connecting Boston Harbor with the Merrimack River to the north, just above
Lowell. Laid out in 1794 and opened in 1803, it began in Charlestown
and made its way northwest for 22 miles to its highest point at the
Concord River. Here the 30-foot-wide, 4-foot-deep canal was 107 feet
above mean tide. To cross the Concord River, which had been dammed
just below, the canal builders had laid a dirt embankment partway out
into the river as a towpath. The remaining section of the river was
spanned by a floating wooden boardwalk. Though this floating towpath
is long gone, the great iron rings set in a granite slab that anchored
the towpath to the shore can still be found on the Concord's northern
bank in North Billerica. Once across the river, the boats reentered the
canal and descended 27 vertical feet over a 5¼-mile distance to meet

the Merrimack River. In making the full 27¼-mile journey, the boats passed under fifty bridges, over seven aqueducts, and through twenty locks. When it first opened, the canal was considered the "greatest work of its kind which has been completed in the United States."[2]

The Middlesex Canal immediately became an important artery of trade. Seven days a week, from dawn to dusk, boats carried raw materials from the New Hampshire backwoods down to Boston and finished European finery back up to the inland settlements. By 1805, 9,400 tons of goods, 8,000 tons of it lumber destined for the shipyards of Boston Harbor, were traveling the canal each year. An inkling of the volume of this traffic can be realized in the face of a large boulder in the Wilmington Town Forest, where the canal made a tight bend around a small hill. At the inside of the curve, just at the edge of the towpath, stood a rock too large to be moved. Because of its position, the towline of every boat on the canal rubbed against its side, furrowing out a series of deep horizontal grooves that can still be seen today.

The towpath and dry bed of the Middlesex Canal in Wilmington. The great rock at left is grooved from the many towropes dragged across its face.

*A canal-river boat descending
the Merrimack River.*

The 2½ mph speed limit for freight (3 mph for passenger boats) made the canal trip a full day's journey. Though the tow animals could easily have pulled the boats faster, anything over 3 mph would have set up a wake that would quickly wash away the packed dirt canal banks. However, the canal was not built to save time, but rather to save costs. An oxcart pushing cross-country along the canal route had charged $5.60 a ton when the canal boats were charging $1.25 a ton for the same trip.

While the prices of produce were reduced by the canal, the question of profits of the Middlesex Canal Company itself was quite a different matter. The original estimate of the canal's cost was $200,000, to be raised by selling eight hundred shares of stock to form a closed corporation called the Middlesex Canal Company. All profits would be divided among the shareholders and no further shares would be sold. If more funds were needed, these shareholders would be assessed on pain of losing their shares. By 1803, when the canal opened, these shareholders had each been assessed for additional funds seventy-nine times.

There had simply never been such a vast canal project in America before, and its designers and engineers had no experience to fall back on. When rocky and marshy soil forced half of the canal to be built above ground level, they relied on packed dirt embankments lined with clay to hold the water. This was soon washed away by heavy rains, undermined by burrowing muskrats, and punctured by eddying water and boatmen's poles. Locks and aqueducts were constantly rebuilt with "improved" designs as the previous one gave way. Such problems continued well after the canal's opening in 1803, and it was not until 1819 that yearly revenues exceeded repair costs. By this time two generations of Bostonians had poured $1,164,200 into the canal. While the Middlesex's shareholders lost money on the canal proper, they made it up ten times over in the profits they gained from the trade it brought down the Merrimack.

The Blackstone Canal at Millbury, Mass., in 1841. Except for variations in size, most canal boats after 1825 resembled the one shown here.

In 1812, to expand this trade, the Middlesex Canal Company sponsored the construction of a number of short canals around obstructions in the Merrimack. In all, nine canals were built, from just above the end of the Middlesex Canal near Lowell to Sewall's Falls north of Concord.

The boats that made their way downriver and through the canals were of simple design. Flat-bottomed barges with knee-high gunwales, they measured 70 by 10 feet to fit the locks they passed through. Henry David Thoreau described many of these boats in his *A Week on the Concord and Merrimack Rivers*. While on the river,

they are managed by two men. In ascending the stream they use poles fourteen to fifteen feet long, shod in iron, walking one third the length of the boat from the forward end. Going down, they commonly keep in the middle of the stream, using an oar at each end; or if the wind is favorable they raise their broad sail, and have only to steer.[3]

Because the price of lumber was so high, and as most freight moved downriver to Boston, many boats were broken up after one trip and sold for their lumber, the boatmen then returning upriver with their profits to build another boat. The life of these boatmen, cut off from daily contact with the rest of society, developed into a rough independence much admired by Thoreau in his youth:

It was inconceivable by what sort of mediation any mere landsmen could hold communication with them. . . . We used to admire unweariedly how their vessels would float, like a huge chip, sustained by so many casks of lime, and thousands of bricks, and such heaps of iron ore. . . . The men appeared to lead a kind of life on it, and it was whispered that they slept aboard.[4]

While the boatmen were admired by the children, the local farmers and townsmen objected to their brawling, swearing, and general im-

Worcester, 1838. At lower left a freight boat is being drawn up the Blackstone Canal into the city.

piety. What was worse, the reverence they created among the children often tempted youths to run off from their dreary farm chores and become boatmen themselves. Yet for Thoreau each of these complaints about the boatmen was an argument in their favor:

One can hardly imagine a more healthy employment, or one more favorable to the contemplation and observation of nature . . . it seemed to us that as they glided noiselessly from town to town . . . they could comment on the character of the inhabitants with greater advantage and security to themselves than the traveler in a coach, who would be unable to indulge in such broadsides of wit in so small a vessel, for fear of recoil.[5]

The populace along the Middlesex-Merrimack waterway and the Connecticut River were not the only recipients of boatmen's observations. By 1839, when Thoreau was making his trip up the Concord and Merrimack, there were a number of other places in New England where canalmen's profanity broke the Puritan stillness.

These canals had been constructed during the 1820s. In Maine, the Cumberland and Oxford Canal connected Portland with timber-rich Sebago and Long lakes, 20 miles to the north. The Blackstone paralleled the river of the same name to cover the 45 miles between Providence and Worcester; and the grandest of all, the Farmington, lay 80 miles long, from the tidewater in New Haven to the banks of the Connecticut River in Northampton. Plans for these canals had been made in the 1790s but were stymied by the Boston-dominated Massachusetts legislature, as it refused charters for the sections of these canals to be built on Massachusetts soil (Maine was still a part of Massachusetts).

The first to get a green light was the Cumberland and Oxford Canal. It was chartered by the fledgling Maine legislature at its first session in 1820. Construction did not begin until 1825, but by 1830, the *George Washington*, 60 feet long, 10 feet wide, and drawing 3 feet, made the first trip up the completed canal. It ran from tidewater on the Fore River in Portland Harbor, up the west side of the Presumpscot River, to the south end of Sebago Lake, 26 locks and 20½ miles to the north. Here the boat dropped its centerboard, raised a folding mast, and sailed across the lake to a lock on the Songo River, running between Sebago and Long lakes. On nearing the lock, the boatmen would blow a trumpet announcing their approach, giving the lock tender time to ready the lock. By the time the boat arrived he would have the upriver gate closed and the downriver gate open. If there were only one boat to lock through, the matter was over quickly. The towline would be cast off and the boat would be poled into the lock and the great doors closed. Water was let in through small apertures in the upriver gate until the water level in the lock matched that of the upriver side. The gates were then swung open, the tow animal given a few choice profanities and some small stones thrown at it to get it going, and the boat continued on its course. The whole operation took only five minutes. It was often lengthened, however, if two boats arrived at the same time. Then, canal etiquette required all crews involved to engage in a short brawl to determine who would lock through first.

The boats themselves were as gaudy as the red shirts that were adopted as a uniform by most C&O boatmen. Unlike the one-use Middlesex boats, the C&O boats were built more substantially. They were high and blunt at both ends, with an open hold and a little living cabin to the rear, and resembled miniature versions of our present ocean tankers. Their owners spared no expense in having gaudy paint and expensive carvings adorn the bow and stern. They were given such names as *Waterwitch*, *Boisterous*, *Sebago*, *Honest Quaker*, and *Speedwell*.

Like every other New England canal company, the C&O did not own the 150 boats that traveled the canal. While a few merchants owned a fleet of five or ten boats, most were owned by their captains. The company's sole revenue came from locking charges and cargo

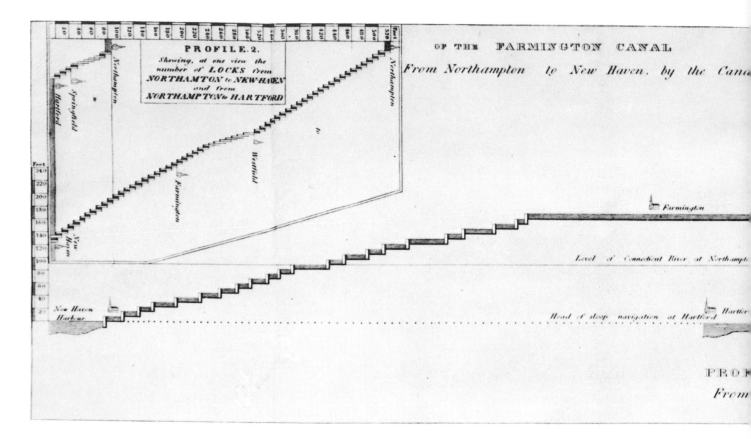

An 1830 plan of the New Haven–Northampton Canal and the lower Connecticut River canals. The Hadley Falls Canal was completed in 1795; the Farmington, in 1835; and the Enfield Falls, in 1829.

tariffs: Apples, 3/10 of a cent per mile per barrel; molasses, 2 cents per mile per hogshead; staves and shook (barrel parts), 3 cents per mile per thousand; passengers, ½ cent per mile; and locking charges, 6 cents per boat per lock.

Another canal project stymied by Boston, which wanted to be the only seaport terminus for New England's canals, was the Blackstone, from Providence to Worcester. Before the canal opened in 1828, Worcester was so isolated that a Boston merchant could ship goods 3,000 miles to Liverpool cheaper than 40 miles overland to Worcester.

The Blackstone Canal, dropping 451 feet through forty-eight granite locks in its 45-mile length, differed from the Middlesex and C&O canals in that, while the latter were only transportation arteries for areas at each end of the canals, the Blackstone lay in the midst of its customers. These were the dozens upon dozens of textile mills that had grown up along the Blackstone River since 1790, when Samuel Slater built the first successful cotton spinning machinery at Pawtucket Falls. The problem was that both the canal and the mills depended on the waters of the Blackstone River, one to fill its canal bed, the other to turn their waterwheels. As the canal reduced the cost of bringing up raw cotton from Providence and sending back finished goods, more and more mills sprang up. Soon any slack in the river's flow from lack of rain meant that either the canal or the mills had to go without sufficient water to

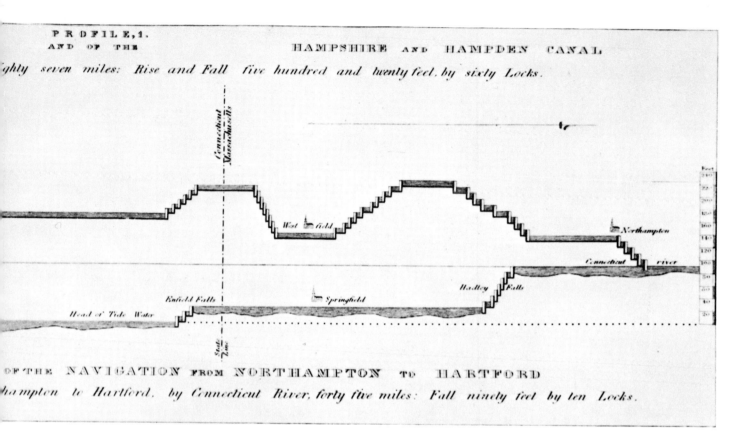

operate. Open violence flared as the mill faction dumped boulders into the locks to make them impassable, and the canal faction hatched plots to burn every mill in the valley.

This conflict lasted until 1835, when a new element settled the matter in favor of the mills — the opening of the newly completed Boston to Worcester Railroad. This undercut use of the canal's northern end as Worcester began to trade with Boston. The canal hung on for another decade, but by 1847 the Providence to Worcester Railroad was chugging up the valley on tracks laid over sections of the old canal bed.

In 1835, just as the Blackstone Canal was beginning its wane, New England's greatest canal venture was completed. This was the Farmington Canal, running eighty miles from New Haven, Connecticut, to Northampton, Massachusetts. Though there were many ostensible reasons for its creation — the success of the Erie Canal in New York, the need to open the isolated Farmington River Valley to trade, the need to bypass the unimproved sandbars and rapids on the lower Connecticut River — the real reason was the realization by the people of New Haven that, "having no river flowing into our waters, and cut off from the places above us, and around us, unless we can unite ourselves with those places by artificial means, our business must remain local in character and limited in extent."[6]

A lock on the Farmington
Canal at Cheshire, as it
appears today. At right, the
railroad bridges the canal,
switching its roadbed from
one bank to the other. At left
is the old locktender's house,
now a private residence.

The swampy, trash-filled lock
on the Blackstone Canal at
Millville, Mass. Here boats
were lifted from the river
some 10 feet to the canal bed
at the far end of the lock.

With New Haven investors supplying the major capital, work began in New Haven in 1825, reaching Farmington in 1828, Westfield, Massachusetts, in 1829, and finally the Connecticut River at Northampton in 1835. Through its journey, the canal rose 292 feet and descended 213 feet by means of sixty locks. It leaped small valleys on giant dirt embankments and crossed eight rivers on aqueducts. One old embankment still stands in Milldale, Connecticut. Here the dry bed still crosses the Ten Mile River 60 feet above the streambed.

The canal's great length forced its builders to pinch pennies as they went along. Though granite locks had been found best, the Farmington builders used wood, which later had to be replaced at greater expense. The soil along the route was rocky and porous, but the builders spent as little as they could in making the canal bed leakproof. The result was a fiasco. Unending washouts stalled traffic and cut off toll revenue. In addition to rebuilding costs, the canal company also faced court action from irate farmers whose crops suffered water damage.

Although a boat could feasibly travel the canal end to end in twenty-five hours, droughts, floods, accidents, breakouts, collapses, and malicious damage by local farmers usually lengthened the trip.

Though this did not bother the movement of bulk goods, it did little for the tempers of the travelers on the leaky and damp passenger boats. Even without breakdowns, the boats traveled at a snail's pace, and passengers often alighted to shake out their cramps by exploring the surrounding countryside or sauntering on ahead to await the boat in some warm tavern. The attitude toward passenger travel on the canals is best summed up by this excerpt from *The Northern Traveler*, an 1826 guidebook which, though it deals with the Middlesex Canal, held true for them all: "Besides these [previously listed overland routes] there is a boat on the MIDDLESEX CANAL, which leaves the upper lock at Charleston (2 miles from Boston,) three times a week, and goes to Chelmford in about nine hours: 28 miles passage 75¢. This mode is not particularly recommended."[7]

Nevertheless the canals, while they operated, did much to encourage the movement of goods and helped to change many a sleepy farming town into a bustling "canal port."

But as the canal towns prospered, the Farmington Canal itself went deeper into debt, and by 1838 the company was spending $20,000 a year on repairs to keep the canal open. Finally heavy floods in 1843 and a severe drought in 1845 left the canal with little water and no means to contain what there was.

In a desperate move to recover its losses, the Farmington Canal Company entertained a proposition from railway entrepreneurs to lay railroad tracks along the canal's banks for their "mutual benefit." "But since the banks are to be occupied by the railway, will not the engines and their trains, it may be asked, interfere injuriously with the towing path for the use of canal boats, — especially in the part through which that travelled path will be entirely occupied [by the railroad]?" asked the

The doors of the Songo Lock, Naples, Me. Originally constructed around 1830, they were rebuilt to their present form in 1911.

Opposite: The two lower locks of the series of three on the Enfield Canal at Windsor Locks. While still operated for pleasure boats, the canal has taken a backseat to the Interstate highway that crosses the river just below.

railway advocates before answering with ominous overtones, "The interruptions will be but momentary and without dangerous or serious hindrance to the boatmen, who knowing the established passages of the trains, will time their progress to avoid an encounter on these sections where interference could take place."[8]

The canal owners acquiesced and the railroad started north up the valley.

By 1847 the railroad had put the canal out of business, and no train running north from New Haven was ever again bothered by towhorses on the right-of-way. In Cheshire, Connecticut, a water-filled section of the old canal still passes beneath the railroad tracks that outmoded it.

Bankruptcy by railroad was to be the fate of almost all the New England canals as one after another was given up around 1850. On April 23, 1849, three small advertisements appeared in the *Providence Manufactures & Farmers Journal*. One gave public notice "to all manu-

facturing companies and individual mill owners interested in the waters of the Blackstone River and its tributaries . . . that they [the Blackstone Canal Company] are prepared to receive proposals for the sale and transfer of . . . the waters . . . which have been used in connection with the Canal belonging to said Company." The two remaining ads listed the merchandise to be sold at two public auctions: four canal boats, one canal storehouse, two lockhouses, seventeen locks, and miscellaneous adjoining land — the canal company's remaining property. In the same day's paper five larger ads with woodcuts and ornate bordering listed the timetables for the Stonington, Boston and Providence, New Bedford and Taunton, Worcester and Nashua, and Providence to Worcester railroad lines.

One lock was never sold; it still stands in Millville, Massachusetts. This giant, 10 feet wide by 70 feet long, once locked boats out of the canal and into a slackwater section of the river. Other interesting remains can be found just north of Uxbridge, Massachusetts. Here the traveler can stop on a side road to look south down a mile-long stretch of the old canal. Turning and looking north, the traveler can see the canal channel snaking along the shoreline of a large lake. Here the canal is actually in the lake itself, bounded on one side by the shoreline, on the other by a dirt towpath embankment built up in the lake.

In Maine the C&O was able to hold on twenty years longer because it could outdo the railway by servicing every hamlet on the lakeshores, but it too was abandoned in 1870. Though most of the C&O's locks have long since fallen into ruin, the Songo Lock still operates between Sebago and Long lakes. Rebuilt in 1911 for the use of lake steamers, it today serves the pleasure boats that line up to experience the once-common procedure of "locking through."

The wholesale obsolescence of the canals with the arrival of the railroads was not entirely due to the railroad's greater speed in the movement of goods. There was also the lure of greater possible profit to its builders. While the canals operated like modern toll roads, the railroads owned the rolling stock and dealt directly with the people whose freight they carried. The canals divided any profit between the canal company and the individual boat owners, but with the railroads all profits went directly into the pockets of the railway company.

As the railroads took over, the canals were broken up and made into power canals for industry. Their lower locks were replaced by dams, where turbines used the difference in water level between the canal and the river to power factories and mills along the old towpath.

The old Enfield Canal, while primarily a power canal, still locks boats through on the Connecticut River in Suffield and Windsor Locks, Connecticut. This comparatively small, 5¼-mile canal was built around the Enfield Rapids to lure boats from turning off the Connecticut River at Northampton onto the soon-to-be-completed Farmington Canal. When it opened in 1829, the already large river traffic lined up to ascend its three tiers of locks, pass up the 80-foot-wide canal bed, and cross over an aqueduct before clearing the northern locks to reenter the river. The Enfield was successful, and the town of Windsor Locks that sprang up at its southern end became a favorite haunt of rivermen as it mushroomed into the gamblingest, drunkenest, bawdiest town in New England.

The coming of the railroad in 1845 put an end to all this. Outmoded, the canal fell into disuse until it was repaired later in the century for use as a power canal for local factories. Today, a few boats every year still lock through New England's most impressive remains of the canal era, the flight of three locks at the canal's southern end. Moving up the canal into Suffield, they pass over New England's last complete canal aqueduct, standing 60 feet wide and 104 feet long, as it carries the canal bed high above the rushing waters of Stony Brook below.

While the Windsor Locks Canal is one of the few operating canals in New England, there are many spectacular remains of abandoned canals. Besides those listed in this book, there are many others to be found by means of the U.S. topographical maps that still show the old canal routes. Yet for the most part the old canals are now best described in this 1895 eulogy to the Cumberland and Oxford Canal:

Its channel, where once floated a queer navy, is dried up, and in most places overgrown with trees and bushes; its locks, and the shanties built to accomodate the lock tenders, are crumbling in the dust. The sturdy red shirted boatmen . . . have long since joined the "silent majority," and their ringing voices are heard no more along the old towpath.[9]

4 The Farms on the Hills

Opposite: Old stone walls mark the site of a hillside settlement in Ledyard, Conn. They are the most common relic of New England's past, and can be found almost everywhere in the rolling countryside.

Driving the back roads of upland New England anywhere from Connecticut to Maine, the traveler will crest a rise in ground to find the road suddenly lined by century-old oaks. Behind these patriarchs the land is wooded with birch and pine, with old stone walls crisscrossing among them. Entering the woods, one can find a gnarled, aged apple tree and perhaps a shallow, square depression in the ground. All these are signs that, maybe a century ago, this was the house, yards, and orchard of a New England hill farm.

Once New England was almost completely covered by small farms. During the nineteenth century, great population migrations and economic changes left in their wake an entirely different New England from that of the colonial period.

Today we tend to imagine old New England as compact little villages, great colonial homesteads, wooden-pillared churches, and town halls gleaming white in the sun. Few realize that the real old New England was a continuous patchwork of little farms, their modest houses clumped in little groups in each township. Today's rural New England is not so much a replica of colonial times as it is the reflection of those events that conspired to change it.

In 1770, a group of settlers from Pomfret, Connecticut, migrated north to establish a town of the same name in frontier Vermont. Like the founders of the original Pomfret in 1713 — and all those who came too late to grab pieces of the few large lowland areas — they chose to clear and farm the hilltops and ridge crests rather than the nearby valleys.

Farm tools of 1790. Except for a few blades, they are entirely of wood. The plow shows an iron tip, but many farmers used wooden tips for fear that iron might poison the soil.

For the steep hills veiled the dells in gloomy shadow, reducing the growing season. The farmers feared the lowland's "vapors": the chilling damps and mists that hung in the valleys to sap their strength and spread insect-carried diseases.

The hills, on the other hand, were sunny and posed no threat of floods, meandering streams, or backup from beaver dams. The upland bedrock never lay too far below the surface, keeping the water table within the grasp of crop roots. It made little difference if the farms were steep and rocky. The ox and back muscle that tilled the fields could as easily cut a slanted, curved furrow as a straight, level one.

What mattered most to the Pomfret settlers was their feeling of companionship in the wilderness. Today, a person standing at Pomfret's little meetinghouse, in a saddle between two higher rises, can look across the windswept hills to see houses and fields hanging off the slopes, much as the early settler could from his farmhouse door. Though the frontier might have been only a few ridgelines away, the constant sight of his neighbors on the pastoral hillsides kept the New England farmer from the loneliness and depression that struck the isolated wilderness cabins.

The hill farms were primitive by modern standards. With the poor colonial roads, little thought was given to producing surplus goods to be sold elsewhere. This could be done closer to the cities, but in the hill towns of the high backwoods, the farmer had no incentive to improve his efficiency or raise more than was necessary to feed his family and livestock for that year.

A field of Indian corn, with a border of potatoes, a few fields of the small grains, turned at the intervals of a few years into grass lands,

*formed the whole system; and the only part of this that was performed
with neatness and care, was the cultivation of Indian corn. This
commonly received two or three ploughings and hoeings, was kept free
from weeds. . . . No root crops were thought of for the sustenance
of animals; indeed, with the exception of working oxen, if the others
were kept from starving through the winter, the farmer was satisfied.*[1]

So read a report on New England farming in 1820.

The food from these crops was similarly primitive. A grease-filled
frying pan served as the main kitchen utensil. It cooked the meat pies,
pork pies, fruit pies, and doughnuts that were the hill farmer's staple.
Leftovers went into a stewpot to simmer into the next meal's soup. This
diet and the boring subsistence life made up hill farm living. Only hard
cider, drunk often and heavily, lifted the gloom from this existence.

While the men worked in the fields, the women

*picked their own wool, carded their own rolls, spun their own yarn,
drove their own looms, made their own cloth, cut, made, and mended
their own garments . . . made their own soap, bottomed their own
chairs, braided their own baskets, wove their own carpets, quilts and
coverlids, picked their own geese, milked their own cows, fed their own
calves, went visiting on their own feet . . . and this last frequently
accomplished barefoot, carrying their only pair of shoes in their hands
to save wear until they approached the meeting house.*[2]

The children also worked at assigned chores. At first they relished
their responsibilities, but as they grew into their teens, they too recognized the monotony of the life and took on the indifferent attitudes of
their parents.

In the winter the family worked at hearthside industries, occupations that took up slack time and provided a small amount of hard cash
for the few items not obtainable on the farm. Tack- and buttonmaking
were two common occupations.

*The industrious and frugal descendants of the Pilgrims toiled providently
through the long winter months at beating into shape the little nails.
. . . A small anvil served to beat the wire or strip of iron into shape
and point it; a vice, worked by the foot, clutched it between jaws
furnished with a gauge to regulate the length, leaving a certain portion
projecting, which when beaten flat by a hammer, formed the head.
By this process a man might make, toilsomely, perhaps 2,000 tacks
per day.*[3]

All this was done from wintry dawn to the last flickering of the firelight.
It was this total effort of each member of the farming family pulling
for the whole that allowed the farm families to survive in the New
England upland farms.

An 1880 comic sketch of a
colonial New Hampshire
farmer in his wide-brimmed
hat. While intended to be
humorous, the picture of the
pioneer raising a few plants
among rocks and Indians was
all too accurate.

Winslow Homer's **The Dinner Horn.** *The pot over the fire usually held simmering leftovers for the next meal.*

The hill farm population reached its peak around 1800 in southern New England; by this time over eighty percent of Connecticut had been cleared for farms. After this, a slow decline began that has continued to this day. (In New England's three northern states, the decline set in about thirty years later.)

Even as the hill farms were being cleared during the seventeenth and eighteenth centuries, the grist-, saw-, and other mills springing up in the valleys below were luring the settlers off the heights. Many of the community names within one township reflect the tension between the settlements on the hilltops and in the valleys. For instance, in lower New Hampshire, not far from the Connecticut River, stands the little village of Alstead Center, settled around 1772. Once it was simply Alstead, but as the population grew around the paper mill that appeared in 1793 in the nearby valley, the old center lost its right to be recognized as the town proper. What was once Alstead Mills in the valley became simply Alstead, and the sterile community on the hilltop, Alstead Center. Throughout the New England countryside one can find a town hall, a church, and a dozen colonial homesteads bearing the name of a bustling valley town nearby, but distinguished from it by the addition of the word "Center": towns like Groton Center, only a few miles from Long Island Sound and the great navy submarine base of its namesake; Cornwall Center, Connecticut, high in the Litchfield Hills and surrounded by Cornwall, Cornwall Hollow, and Cornwall Bridge; Chester Center, Massachusetts, in the Berkshires, which was eclipsed by the valley town that grew up around an emery mine; and Wilton Center, New Hampshire, dwarfed by the great mills along the Soughegan River downhill in Wilton.

With the proliferation of canals and turnpikes in the early 1800s, the hill farms closer to the cities felt another blow. Stagecoaches brought news of the easy life in the infant industrial towns then forming in southern New England. Though this new urban population needed the farmers' produce, the hill farmers could not supply it. They had built their farms small, and on marginal soil. They had to abandon these farms and descend into the valleys to the flat hollows, or "intervals," to find sufficient land to supply the market garden trade.

As the turnpikes wound their way up the valleys, they usually passed through the mill communities but bypassed the old centers on the heights, creating an even greater shift in importance between the two.

Even more threatening were the tales of better lands west that came with contact with the outside world. The Yankees looked at their own agricultural journals to see advertisements for western lands of "unsurpassed fertility" and "inexhaustible depth."[4]

Slowly the New England farmers began leaving their homesteads in search of these new lands. The exodus increased with the opening of the Erie Canal in 1825, and the advent of the railroads in midcentury raised the migration to epidemic proportions. Whole towns were now packing up and moving westward.

Winslow Homer's A Winter-
Morning, — Shovelling Out.
*"Out" was usually only as far
as the barns to feed the
animals.*

In the township of Stratton, high in Vermont's Green Mountains, today there stands a monument on the site of Daniel Webster's 1840 election campaign address, when he spoke to 20,000 Vermonters. A few decades later Stratton had reverted to rugged wilderness; Webster's audience had moved west to found towns such as Vermontville, Michigan, and Vermont, Illinois. By 1860, a count of the nation's 414,000-odd Vermont-born citizens showed that almost 175,000 of them no longer lived there.

Some on their way west never made it. One group bound for "Kansas or Bust" just got through Stratton to the west side of the Green Mountains before they "busted." Here they settled, forming a little hamlet they appropriately named Kansas.

It was in the upper highlands of the Green Mountains, the Appalachians, and other New England mountain chains that the settlements first fell back into wilderness. Here the air was coldest, the growing season shortest, and life the hardest.

The Appalachian Trail, following the ridge crests through New England on its Maine to Georgia route, passes many of these abandoned settlements. Quite literally, a walk down this wilderness route takes one along the main streets of these old hamlets.

Just west of the White Mountains, the trail leads down the main street of what was once Quinntown, New Hampshire. Never large, in 1830 this hamlet boasted about fifteen houses, a couple of sawmills and shops, two schoolhouses, and a country store. Today only cellar holes and a hunter's cabin remain.

This whole area — bounded by the Connecticut River on the west and the White Mountains on the east — is crisscrossed by old roads and

An 1857 cartoon of the "hopeful" and "disappointed" emigrant. The caption reiterates the "fever and ague" warnings of Easterners opposed to western migration.

THE HOPEFUL EMIGRANT EN ROUTE FOR THE WEST—THAT LAND WHICH HE INNOCENTLY SUPPOSES TO BE FLOWING WITH MILK AND HONEY.

THE DISAPPOINTED EMIGRANT RETURNING FROM THE WEST, HAVING FOUND FEVER AND AGUE ABUNDANT AND CORN THREE DOLLARS A BUSHEL—THINKS IT ALL GAS ABOUT THE MILK AND HONEY.

turnpikes that passed through hamlets like Smart's Mountain, Acorn Hill, and Hardscrabble. Only downhill on the plain of the Connecticut River do farming and a way of life continue.

One hill town of the area that has not completely reverted to woodlands is Dorchester, New Hampshire. Here the traveler can turn off the paved state road onto a dirt lane through the woods to visit its old center: a small clearing with a few still-inhabited houses, a church, a grange, and a one-room schoolhouse, all surrounding a little green. In 1840 this whole area was completely covered by farms; today only a few dirt roads and the old center remain.

Long-abandoned communities are not restricted to northern New England. In Cornwall Bridge, Connecticut, the Appalachian Trail leads down another overgrown main street of what was once Dudleytown. Sitting on a small plateau above the Housatonic River, the old hamlet was doomed from the start. High mountains surrounding the village cut out almost all sunlight, making it poor land for farming. Settled in 1747, the life and luck of her residents were so bad that "The Dudleytown Curse" became a familiar phrase in this part of Connecticut. By 1900 the last citizens had given up, leaving Dudleytown a wilderness.

As New Englanders moved west, there were those who attempted to stem the tide with dire warnings of western life:

One would suppose that the fertility of the western prairie could offer little temptation to the farmer who might produce such a crop, and remain among his own paternal fields; especially when the contrast is made between the healthiness of a northern climate, in a high hilly region, pure water flowing plentifully, all facilities for happily training a family; and a country where, indeed labor is comparatively light, land cheap, and winters lose much of their rigor and length; but fever and ague sap the constitution, and send back the adventurer a lean sallow invalid for life, or lay him prematurely in the grave.[5]

Westerners laughed at such dire predictions and replied:

Stay the Niagara, or stop the tides from coming into Boston harbor; but don't be so fool-hardy as to try to stop the most enterprising of your sons, and the most beautiful of your daughters from coming West, by mere Fourth of July orations, or County Fair addresses.[6]

The westward movement snowballed as the McCormick reaper and other machines readily adapted to the wide, flat midwestern farms but proved useless in the small, stone-fenced New England fields. The Midwest now began shipping grain back to New England cities at a price so low that even the added shipping costs did not bring it above the lowest price that the nearby New England farmers charged. Even in the river plains there was no area large enough to carry on farming as it was done out west. Now even the farmers in the intervals and river plains went west, as they chose migration over falling back into marginal, self-sufficient farming.

An 1840 view of the sad state of many New England farms.

While many were thus forced west, others went voluntarily, enticed by "western fever." This "affliction" did not strike randomly but took New England's pride: her strongest, most adventuresome citizens, leaving behind the weak, the timid, and the aged, who shrank from the challenges and possibilities of the frontier. As a writer in 1869 bewailed: "We are ever felicitating ourselves that the West is being peopled in great measure by the hardy citizens of Maine, but we are continually forgetting what sort of effect this is likely to have upon Maine."[7] Or, as put more succinctly in an 1876 article on the same problem: "What is fun for the boys is death to the frogs."[8]

The farmers left behind were a poor lot to meet the problems facing the survival of the hill farms. They were content simply to live by the beliefs of their ancestors, planting by the phases of the moon and using primitive wooden plows because they believed an iron-tipped plow would poison the soil.

The worst blow to the hill farms came in the latter half of the nineteenth century. As migration west slackened in the 1870s, New England's industries began to mushroom in size. Imported western produce made it hard for the isolated hill farmer to sell produce to the industrial cities at a profit, but it was easy for him to give up his fields and move to one of the great textile mills as a factory hand.

The farming areas worst hit were those on the outskirts of the mill towns. In the mill region of southwestern New Hampshire, only 4 miles from the industrial and college town of Keene, lies the now-overgrown hamlet of Roxbury Center. To find it today the motorist leaves the outskirts of Keene to zigzag up a mountainside on a road that quickly reduces to a dirt lane. At the crest of the hill stands a small clearing, the site of the Roxbury Center church. Only the clearing and miles of stone

An empty farmhouse in Tinmouth, Vt. Its small acreage was long ago consolidated into a much larger farm.

fences through the woods remain; the Roxbury citizens have long since moved downhill to the better life at the mills.

Farther into the hills, remote from the mill towns, the burgeoning industries attracted the hill towns' young. Teenaged girls looked at their prematurely aged mothers and fled for the dormitory life of the factory girl or the attic room of the domestic.

Like the produce sent back from the West that undercut the New England economy and increased migration, the letters of town life sent back to friends on the farm did more to increase the exodus. These letters told of good clothes, an evening's entertainment, a bit of pocket money, and the chance of improving oneself. It was this last, above all, that struck the most bitter blow to the New England hill farms. How could a monotonous, bare, subsistence life that promised only an early grave compete with the stories of cities where only the lack of ambition and diligence kept one from wealth?

By the last years of the nineteenth century, the old Yankee stock still holding out on the hill farms were a pathetic lot: aged parents whose children had long since deserted to the cities or the West, young men and women reduced to degeneracy through interbreeding among those without the fortitude to leave their ancestral homes. In 1899 a visitor to the New England hill town of Auburn, Massachusetts, observed:

Nearly everyone you meet is a Glenn-Glenn: so were his parents, and theirs, and theirs. Accordingly the town abounds in "characters." . . . One of our families is "muffle-chopped" [harelipped]. Another whole family is deaf and dumb. The proprietor of the sawmill stands three feet two and one-half inches with his boots on. Israel Glenn is a giant, measuring seven feet in height. . . . Glenns should stop marrying Glenns. . . . What has happened in the hill country of Alabama and Tennessee is happening in the hill country of New England.[9]

Those who did remain often moved from the isolation of a house surrounded by empty fields to the community of the central village. As they did, the outlying mills and shops were likewise abandoned. This accounts for today's tight New England rural villages circled by fields that run into forests.

Often the central village itself fell into abandonment.

Midway between Williamstown [Massachusetts] and Brattleboro [Vermont; the town was reputed to be Whitingham, Vermont] I saw on the summit of a hill against the evening sky what seemed a large cathedral. Driving thither, I found a huge, old-time, two story church, a large academy (which blended in the distance with the church), a village with a broad street, perhaps 150 feet wide. I drove on and found that the church was abandoned, the academy dismantled, the village deserted. The farmer who owned the farm on the north side of the village lived on one side of the broad street, and he who owned the farm on the south lived on the other, and they were the only inhabitants. All of the others had gone — to the manufacturing villages, to the great cities, to the West. Here had been industry, education, religion, comfort, and contentment, but there only remained a drear solitude of forsaken homes. The deserted village was the old-fashioned "Center" of the town, on a high hill, remote from railways and millstreams, unknown to summer boarders — an agricultural village, dependent upon the agriculture around it, and from which it sprang.[10]

Turn-of-the-century magazine and newspaper reports such as this began a new economy that has sustained the New England hill country to this day: the tourist trade. City people became attracted by these stories of "the abandoned farms of New England." They read booklets like that put out in many revised editions during the 1890s by the State of Massachusetts, entitled *Farms in Massachusetts Abandoned or Partially Abandoned,* or the federally published *Report of the Commission on Country Life.* With all this hoopla, it became fashionable to spend a summer on a "deserted farm." In actuality, few of these farms were without owners; some had been divided at auction, others had passed on to children living elsewhere.

In the early 1900s the New England states, New Hampshire especially, realized the potential of these summer boarders, who journeyed into the isolated hill settlements rather than take a train to one of the great resort hotels and began improving their roads to better attract them.

Today many an old upland town still stands only because its houses have been purchased as summer homes. In the warmer months, the little villages bustle with activity, breathing life into the local economy. Come winter, the houses are closed up and the "old centers" assume a most eerie air. Their neat appearances contrast with the strange, foreboding stillness of the empty town. And on a winter's night, "Where no house has stood, there the stars and the friendly moon suffice, but where a human habitation rears a blind and deserted bulk, the passer-by shivers and hastens his steps."[11]

Outside the hill town centers, the more isolated houses fell into ruin, particularly the smaller, less appealing farmhouses. Some simply collapsed and disappeared into the forestland growing up around them. Other farms became pastureland for the dairy industry that grew up as better roads connected the hill country with the cities. Often small lots were bought up and converted into one great farm.

In Tinmouth, Vermont, south of Rutland, halfway up the side of a mountain is a group of small farms amalgamated into one great farm. Tinmouth was the seat of Rutland County when it was settled in 1770, but in 1784 it lost that title to Rutland, down in the valley. Today little farmhouses dating from that era stand empty in the midst of hayfields, with weeds and wild flowers grown over their doorsteps.

One can still see all the phases of the slowly receding tide of farms that has ebbed from the New England highlands since the early 1800s. The first stage is usually some timeworn homestead occupied by aged parents long since deserted by their children (who have probably tried to get them to come live with them in the city). When these old folks pass on, the house, if it is in good repair, might go to summer vacationers. If it is not salable, it will see a succession of tenant families who do little to prevent its slow collapse. Soon the house becomes uninhabitable, its floors rotted and the wind flowing freely through cracked insulation. Windows are broken and suddenly the elements have free rein inside. Death comes swiftly now. The beams rot, the chimney collapses, and the old homestead slowly sags to the ground. Finally there is only the cellar hole, which in turn will be slowly obliterated by the creeping weight of the surrounding earth.

The pastures and fields undergo similar stages. In grazing land it is

almost always the low junipers and other evergreen shrubs, previously kept in check by the farmer, that spread across the old cowlots. In cultivated fields small plants first predominate, next come weeds, then tall grasses, and before long the field is covered by great banks of wild flowers. Evergreens and birches then shade out this low vegetation. In the far north the evergreens are the final stage. Farther south, fifty years to a century after the trees first appeared, the now-past-mature birches and evergreens begin to be pushed out by the hardwoods. Finally the fields become a forest of stately oaks, hickory, and maples, with only rubbled lines of old stone walls running here and there to bear witness that this land once supported human habitation.

In Connecticut, fifty percent of the land has undergone this process in the last 150 years.[12] Farther north the percentage is similar. Most of it is poor, marginal land, able to support only a few years' growth before falling barren, land that, "had the Puritans gone up the Mississippi and settled on the rich lowlands of the Middle States . . . would still be largely given up to forests."[13]

An unused farmhouse in Union, Me. It shows additions built over the years by succeeding generations.

5 Rural Schools and Churches

An 1888 view of the Parsons-field Baptist Seminary. The building on the right is now the town's public school.

As New England's population shifted westward, downhill, and to the cities, often the community buildings of a depopulated town stood long after its users had vanished. These churches, meetinghouses, schools, and stores remain as testimony to the former size and vibrancy of the old towns.

In southern Maine, along the New Hampshire border, the towns of northern York County still show this ebbing tide. Founded in the Revolutionary period, they reached their greatest population during the 1830s. Since then they have undergone a steady decline.

On the northern edge of this area lies Parsonsfield. A town of ponds and rolling hills, its present population of about 1,000 is only half its 1850 figure. Today the township is divided into a group of hamlets separated by forests, much as it was originally. Though only a few of the homes stand empty today, other traces of its former self are found in the more than 150 little family cemetery plots that lie everywhere to mark the sites of long-vanished homesteads. A traveler driving through the town cannot fail to see them by the roadside, overgrown in the woods, or starkly outlined in the midst of an empty field.

In North Parsonsfield stands the abandoned Free-will Baptist Church. Built around 1853 to replace an earlier structure, its congregation slowly dispersed until it held its last service in the mid-1960s. This was not the only denomination to worship in Parsonsfield. In the 1880s Congregationalists, Baptists, Old School Free-will Baptists, Free Baptists, Christian Advents, and Quakers all had their own churches or meetinghouses.

It might seem peculiar that such a small place as Parsonsfield had so many different denominations, but this was generally the case in many northern New England towns. In Massachusetts and Connecticut, it was law that all townspeople pay taxes to support the town church. Those who disagreed with the established religion often headed for the frontier, where they need support only their own church. Though the dissenters splintered off into many differing sects, they often settled side by side in the same village. Each built its own church and supported its own minister. This worked while each denomination had sufficient parishioners to support it, but as the population dropped each congregation quickly went into financial distress. By 1900 rural ministers complained that on a Sunday morning they could see from their pulpit more churches out the window than parishioners in the pews before them.

To deal with this problem, many small congregations of only slightly differing philosophy compromised and merged. Other sects stayed separate but shared the same church building. Still others stayed independent. Unable to support a minister of their own, they regressed back to pioneer days, relying on a circuit-riding minister to hold services.

With the decline of their flock, congregations often had little money to encourage the spread of their religion. A beautiful old example of this stands just up the road from the North Parsonsfield church, its Baptist Seminary. Built in 1855, it gave Parsonsfield and other youth knowledge beyond the rudiments taught in the country schools. This old academy, as they were called between the Revolutionary and Civil wars, was similar to a high school in that it prepared youths for entering college, but also acted as a teachers' college for those who wished to become schoolmasters. Unlike the public schools, the seminary charged tuition. If the enrollment was not enough to pay costs at any given time the seminary was closed. The first seminary building was erected in 1833, but by 1846 "the buildings were in bad condition, the institution was largely in debt, and the Seminary building was patched with a variety of colors."[1] Through local effort, a larger classroom building was built, and later dorms, offices, and a gym were added. In 1880, however, the seminary again went under. For a while, the high school held classes here before moving to a new building. Finally, in 1949, the seminary's doors closed for good; the classroom building became the town grammar school and the rest of the seminary fell silent.

Many New England towns of the nineteenth century had schools similar to the Parsonsfield Seminary. With the rise of public schools they either became the town high school, stayed private and developed into one of the exclusive New England "prep" schools, or passed into oblivion.

Just a stone's throw from the old seminary in Parsonsfield stands another relic of early American education: the white-wooden, one-room Blazo Schoolhouse. Once the children of North Parsonsfield studied here. Today it is vacant as children attend a larger and better equipped consolidated school.

An abandoned farmhouse in Parsonsfield.

Interior of the North Parsonsfield Baptist Church.

One of the over 150 family cemeteries in Parsonsfield. This is one of the smallest, with only one gravestone.

*Unused building of the
Parsonsfield Seminary today.*

*Interior of the Blazo School,
North Parsonsfield's one-room
schoolhouse.*

A typical one-room school-house of the nineteenth century — in disrepair, windows broken, and at the edge of a crossroads.

During the colonial period town schools were of two types: the grammar school, which prepared boys for college; and the dame school, a combined nursery school–kindergarten–elementary school that received its name from the elderly "dame" who ran it. No town had more than one of each of these schools, and the dame school sometimes rotated from place to place throughout the township.

Colonial farmers had strongly complained that although they were taxed for the upkeep of the village schools, the distance to them often made attendance a hardship. From this problem grew the concept of the district country schools, which appeared in the 1800s. Towns were divided into many small precincts, each responsible for building, maintaining, and staffing a small school. Due to poor roads, the districts were quite small; for instance, the township of Parsonsfield once had seventeen country schools.

As the schools were supported solely by their districts, their condition depended directly on the magnanimity of the citizens. This was usually minuscule. For the most part they built the school near the center of their district on the cheapest piece of land they could find. The lot was as small as possible and the school itself often projected into the public road, which was often the students' only playground. In the ancient hamlet of South Acton, Maine, a few miles south of Parsonsfield, one of these little shacks still stands, not more than a few feet from the old main road of the town.

While the country schoolhouses were small, about 20 by 30 feet, the wooden benches inside were jammed with students. Come wintertime, the proximity of one's schoolmates was welcome, as it offered the best warmth in the drafty building. Although each school had a fireplace or stove, it only served to bake the children nearest it, leaving those farther away to freeze. The students' parents provided firewood, and woe betide the poor scholar whose father missed his turn at supplying wood. He would have to sit farthest away from the hearth and could not approach the fire to warm himself.

Color illustration 1

A 5-foot-high milestone erected in 1787 by Oliver Prescott near his home in Groton, Mass. The slate stone is in almost perfect condition, except that the "Esq." after Prescott's initials has been chiseled out.

Color illustration 2

*New England's most spec-
tacular canal remains; the
Enfield Canal's aqueduct over
Stony Brook in Suffield,
Conn., built between 1827
and 1829.*

Color illustration 3

The North Parsonsfield Baptist Church, built in 1853 and abandoned in the early 1960s.

Color illustration 4

Hill farm ruins at Salisbury Heights, N.H.

Color illustration 5

The entrance to the Chester, N.H., town pound, built in 1804.

Winslow Homer's The Noon Recess. *Low pay, no privacy, and boredom characterized the life of the country schoolteacher.*

The Hockanum school during a spring freshet, ca. 1890. Today a nearby marker shows that floodwaters have often lapped the building's eaves.

In the early nineteenth century, two semesters were held, one summer, one winter, each lasting about four months. A woman taught the summer session, which was really only an extension of the early dame schools. Children no more than three or four years of age attended this session as much to be tended while their mothers worked at home as to be educated. Few older boys attended in summers. They worked beside their fathers in the fields and could not be spared. The winter session began about the first of December. Now the older children attended, but not the young ones; winter weather made it unsafe for them to leave the farm. A male teacher presided over winter classes, as the pupils were usually quite spirited.

The youngest children sat on benches at the front of the class. Many could not yet read or spell and were a constant source of giggling and poking. Farther back sat the older youths, boys on one side, girls on the

One of the hundreds of old one-room schoolhouses that stand idle across the New England countryside, this one in Goffstown, N.H.

other, ranging in age up to their mid-teens. These were the most troublesome students. The girls relied on their sex to escape punishment for their infractions and were often surprised to find the schoolmaster's whip did not discriminate. The older boys were usually rowdy and sometimes able to overpower the unfortunate schoolmaster, at which point the district went in search of a stronger replacement.

The curriculum was extremely basic: spelling and stitching in the summer session, and little more than the three R's for the "advanced" winter session. The teachers received little pay for their attempts at education. The thrifty Yankees avoided paying food and lodging money by having the teacher "board round." Here the poor schoolmaster was shuffled from house to house as each family with a school-age child took turns providing bed and board.

By the latter half of the nineteenth century the rural schools began to improve. Teachers received better pay and the curriculum improved. High schools and academies drew the older students to the more accessible central villages, so only the younger children now attended the district schools.

In Hockanum, Massachusetts, a hamlet wedged on a flood plain between the heights of the Holyoke Mountains and the banks of the Connecticut River, lies a beautiful district school of this later era. Unlike its rude wooden cousins in the hills, this one-room schoolhouse is of substantial red brick. Yet even here the wily hand of the old Yankees can be seen, for the school is built on a spot often inundated by the flooding Connecticut River. A less substantial edifice would probably have been washed away each year, while solid brick needed only to be dried out after each flood.

Its young pupils also found their own use for the brick. It was common practice to sharpen one's pencils on the rough surface, so the little school always showed a dappling of gray on its red sides.

Inside, the rows of tight benches common to the early schools had by the turn of the century been replaced with sixteen box desks. Due to the steady migration of its students to the grammar and high school, even this small number was never filled. Before the desks stood a box stove, two chairs for use while reciting, the teacher's desk, a blackboard, and below it a low bench to aid the smaller scholars in writing on the board. Though less rustic than its predecessors, the school was still drab, as noted by a visitor in the 1890s:

The walls of the room were adorned with geometrically figured paper that inclined to brownness and melancholy in its general tone. In places it had started to crack off, and in one or two spots was stained by leaks from the roof. The woodwork of the walls and doors was painted yellow and stained to represent polished wood. The desks and benches were painted green — all except the tops of the desks, which were white. These soft pine desk-tops offered facilities for hand carving and original decoration, which had inspired the pupils to do a good deal of work on their once fair surface with their jackknives and pencils. It was on the boys' side that the desks were most energetically cut up, the girls' genius running more, apparently, to mild penciling.[2]

As America moved into the twentieth century, her schools improved into the large public systems our children enjoy today. Yet in little New England towns like Parsonsfield the death knell of the one-room schoolhouse has sounded only within the last twenty years, and in hundreds of rural towns many schoolhouses still stand, some now homes or used for storage while others are vacant. These last face an uncertain future that no longer needs their kind.

6 Town Animal Pounds

In early colonial days, each New England village was grouped around a central green, or "common," and there was little problem with grazing animals. Each morning, the livestock would be let out of their pens onto the common, where they spent the day.

As the population grew, and farms sprang up farther away from the common, problems developed. The livestock was let loose each day to graze wherever it wished, and often it wished to be in another farmer's crops. By the early 1700s the courts were clogged with innumerable animal damage suits and countersuits.

To relieve the problem, towns began constructing municipal corrals of wood or stone, the town pounds. Any pig, goose, sow, sheep, goat, or horse caught straying was brought to the pound and held until a fine was paid. The pound was usually located just outside the village, close enough for convenience, but far enough away to keep the animals within from being a nuisance.

One of the earliest stone pounds was built in Durham, New Hampshire, in 1705, seventy years after the town's founding, and in appearance it is similar to most pounds. A rectangle 25 by 40 feet, it has chest-high granite walls. The stones here were cut to fit, but many other pounds simply piled odd-sized stones into a wall. A town's prosperity had a direct bearing on the size and quality of its pound. Some had low walls thrown together haphazardly; others, like the giant pound that still stands in Richmond, Rhode Island, were giant fortifications over eight feet high. The gates ranged from hinged doors to a few boards held up

The Auburn, N.H., town pound. Built in 1843 for the local farmers, it is now surrounded by forest.

by a pole wedged against them. The pounds were usually square or rectangular, but sometimes the towns ordered them to be built in other shapes. The Jefferson, Maine, and Leverett, Massachusetts, pounds are circular, and the Chepachet, Rhode Island, pound is trapezoidal, to fit between two roads near their junction. A few, like the old pound in Foster Center, Rhode Island, had brooks running through for watering the animals. Usually a townsman built the pound after a vote at the town meeting sanctioned its construction.

March 3, 1806, Whitingham, Vermont. Voted to build a Pound of Stone in the following dimensions: 30 feet Squair Within the Walls, the Walls to be six feet high four feet thick at the bottom two feet thick on the top frame together with a Stone Post to Hang the Door or gate on with a hole drilled in the Said Post for the Hinges to be set in, Said Pound to be Completed by the first Day of July next, Said Walls to be Handsomely faced on the inside and Decently faced on the outside to the acceptance of the Select Men.[1]

The bill for this pound came to $34.98.

The specifications for a pound built in 1671 at Scituate, Massachusetts, were much simpler: the town required it to be "horse high, bull strong, and hog tight."

Few old Yankees aspired to the position of poundkeeper, the elected custodian of the menagerie. It was a job involving much more than simply foddering the animals and collecting fines. No matter the number of animals impounded, it was up to the poundkeeper to hold down the lid on these colonial versions of Noah's Ark. On demand, he had to wrestle stray hogs, run down loose horses, and escape roving bulls. Usually the poundkeeper was also liable for expenses in feeding the animal.

Built in 1846, the 8-foot-thick walls of the Richmond, R.I., pound make it one of the most impressive pounds yet standing. Its present use as a pigpen makes it a bit sloppier than others remaining, but its interior is a much closer approximation of how the pounds looked when in use.

In many towns, a poundkeeper was obtained by making that position the first apprenticeship post of aspiring politicians. A few towns followed the practice of appointing as poundkeeper the most recently married young man as of that year's town meeting.

For their troubles, the poundkeepers received a set percentage of the fines collected. In cases where the animal's owner could not be found, the animal was sold at auction after attempts were made to locate him. In the more populated areas, this was done by advertising in the newspaper.

COW & CALF IN POUND

Put in Pound by a Field Driver, on the 30th of July last, a small Red Stear Calf — also, on the 24th of Sept, last, a Dark Brown Cow, line back, with a bell on her neck; the owners are requested to prove property, pay all charges and take them away, as expenses are multiplying fast, and the Pound Keeper is determined to dispose of the Cow in two weeks in order to enable him to pay her bills.

Dexter Brewer, Pound Keeper

Westbrook [Maine] Dec 11th, 1833.[2]

In the days of Yankee ingenuity, the pounds sometimes created as much trouble as they were designed to alleviate. On moonless nights irate farmers reclaimed their animals without bothering to square accounts with the poundkeeper. Often the poundkeeper himself was not above drumming up extra business. There were cases where, even before the farmer discovered his gates open and his livestock loose, the poundkeeper had already herded the "strays" into the pound. While the farmer fumed, the poundkeeper sat back to await his fee.

By the late 1800s the pounds, once common to every New England town, fell into disuse as better communication between farmers made them obsolete. Some had their walls vandalized for other uses, others were leveled into obscure heaps of rubble by years of harsh New England weather; but many still remain, off in the corners of little sleepy towns, as mementos of an agrarian age.

7 The Village Mill

An old gristmill. Here no dam was used and the force of the water running under the wheel turned the machinery. In the distance is a windmill, once a common sight all along the New England shore.

On the self-sufficient farms of early New England, only two needs regularly carried the farmer beyond the confines of his stone fences: to pray with his neighbors in church, and to have his corn ground at the mill.

The first gristmills appeared soon after the founding of Plymouth, and during the seventeenth and eighteenth centuries they could be found in every settlement. Gristmills, and the sawmills that later shared the falls with them, were as characteristic of the old New England towns as the town halls and white clapboard churches. "There is probably no country in the world where millstreams are so numerous and universally dispersed, or gristmills and sawmills so universally erected as in New England," observed Timothy Dwight in 1796.[1]

The mills ground Indian corn, or maize. Hardier and keeping better than grains, it was the staple nourishment for New Englanders throughout the colonial period.

For fresher meal, the farmers only ground a week's worth at a time, and the visit to the mill was as familiar to them as our weekly trip to the supermarket is to us. The farmers loitered and gossiped as they awaited their meal, making the mill the colonial town's social center.

Holding court in their midst stood the miller, the self-proclaimed expert in all matters legal, political, and matrimonial. The miller's mechanical knowledge and business proficiency made him the most respected man in the village — unless, that is, he was addicted to a common miller's affliction: the inability to take only that portion of the ground meal legally his due.

Respectful or not, the old Yankees were quick to complain if things were not to their liking. In the winter of 1652 the New Haven, Connecticut, court records reported:

Sundry of the Town complained that they cannot get their corn ground at the mill, but that it must lie there so long as their families suffer for want of it, or they must go so often for it, as some said it stood them in more carrying and fetching that the corn is worth; which is conceived to come partly by the mill's going so slowly, and partly by the miller's not grinding sometimes in the night when he has much work there; wherefore the Town desired that the committee before named take some course that this grievance may be removed.[2]

If the miller had not inherited the business, he most probably built the mill himself. As a young apprentice, he worked at a mill long enough to understand its machinery and management before striking out for the frontier for a town in need of a mill. There he built his own mill from the ground up. Except for the grindstones (the best of which came from the South, or France), and a few iron strappings, everything — framing, timber, gearing, and waterwheel — was constructed of local materials.

The miller did not work unaided, for his prospective customers knew that the mill would mean they no longer had to grind their corn between rocks, Indian fashion, and willingly pitched in to help.

While the farmers had cleared their land along the ridgelines, the mills were built in the valleys and hillside ravines. If the distance between the mill and the old village were too great, expansion around the mill sometimes doomed the uphill farming area.

In east-central New Hampshire, on U.S. Route 4, the traveler turns from the wide plain of the slowly meandering Smith River and ascends a ravine cut into the foothills of Mount Cardigan to reach the small community of East Grafton. First comes the small town hall, then houses and an old general store. Ascending farther, one sees the church and a few more homes. Lastly, before the road becomes graveled and uninhabited, one finds the old mill. Once the farmers in the hills beyond descended the mountain to have their corn ground, but slowly the population shifted downhill past the mill into the valley where the railroad could supply its needs. Today the hills are covered with regrowth and the old mill, once the first magnet for downhill movement, stands empty and useless.

In other cases, a group of houses clustered around a mill in some little hollow never grew beyond its original size. In the eastern foothills of Connecticut's Litchfield Hills lies such a hamlet. In the town of Bakersville, the 20-foot-wide Nepaug River cuts through Maple Hollow, one bank edged by flat farmland, the other rising directly up a steep wooded hill. Hanging on the hillside, high enough to escape centuries of floodwaters, stands Stedman's Mill. Its tall fieldstone foundation has

Cutaway sketch of a gristmill. The corn is poured into a hopper to be fed between the grindstones. The bottom stone is stationary; only the top stone is turned by the waterwheel. Once ground, the flour is funneled into bags in the basement.

A gristmill built directly over a stream, a hazardous design because of the threat of floods. Nevertheless, a few have survived to the present.

*Stedman's Mill on the
Nepaug River in Bakersville.*

protected it from the river's caprices, and its location in a small forgotten hollow has protected it from the crush of progress.

The many New England streams were not the sole sources of power
for the village gristmills. Along the seashore two other types of mills
were used. One was the tidal mill, which was basically similar to the
inland mills at the falls. Instead of the running stream, however, it
relied on high tide to fill a small enclosed pool or inlet. When the tide
began to fall, the gates that let the seawater in were closed and the
high-tide-level water in the enclosed pool was run through a sluiceway
to turn a wheel before falling into the now-low-tide ocean. Some tidal
mills were equipped with double sets of gears to enable the mill to work
by letting the high-tide ocean water run into the low-tide pond.

But the tidal mills could be used only when there was a difference in water level between the pool and the ocean. Many seashore towns without large streams used windmills instead. They were built on hills and bluffs where the constant sea breezes could turn the sails. To accommodate the shifting winds, the windmills themselves could turn to constantly face the wind. Many of these windmills still survive, especially on Cape Cod.

Except for the windmills, most gristmills differed only in exterior covering — either wood, brick, or stone. The mills usually stood two stories high with an attic, with a door opening off each floor and plenty of windows for ventilation. The highest door had a hoist above it for lifting the meal sacks onto the farm wagons. Inside, the top floor was for storage, and on the first floor were found the grindstones. In the basement stood the great wooden shafts and gears that turned the grindstone.

Some millers had tried using iron gearing, but they found that the iron teeth wore down from abrasion while the more elastic wooden teeth nestled better as time went on. But while wood wore best, it also caught on fire from friction. It was a foolhardy miller who did not daily baste every shaft and gear wheel with a thick animal grease. If the grease were too thin in one spot, friction might start the wood smoldering, which would then ignite the supposedly "protective" grease nearby.

To the farmer, bringing in his corn to fill his meal barrel for another week, the mill's weathered exterior and its yellow-dusted interior, all atremble from the rumble of the great wooden machinery, meant continued sustenance for himself and his family. For the miller and his hands, however, each creak and groan, each sight and sound, even to the shade of the meal dust covering the floor, was either a danger signal or a reassurance of the mill's health. Millers had to be constantly alert for dangers. A breakdown in machinery could send the four-foot disk of granite that was the grindstone on a lethal path. The grindstones' faces had to be periodically roughened with a pick, necessitating the dangerous task of hoisting and turning the stone. Clothing caught in the unprotected gearing meant loss of a limb at best. Though the meal was ground coarse, so it would taste and rise better, unavoidably some corn was ground into fine powder. Without proper ventilation the dust would build up to hang in the air within the mill. Any small spark would ignite the dust, blowing the mill and everyone in it sky high. The waterwheel added further dangers. Its slow, stately turnings denied the remorselessness of its movements. Many a miller was crushed because he slipped while clearing debris from the moving wheel.

Besides being a menace to the miller, the waterwheel restricted the mill's operating season, for it was the one part of the mill's mechanism completely exposed to the elements. Winter ice froze it motionless. A strong mortared foundation and a favorable location could protect the mill from all but the worst floods, but the waterwheel lay dead center in the path of rampaging waters.

A photo, ca. 1890, of the now-vanished Hunt's Mill in Rumford, R.I., built in the 1690s. Notice the shedlike structure to protect the waterwheel.

A family outing at an old mill in North Adams. The dam is timber laid in a latticework.

Kingsley's Mill in East Clarendon, Vt. It expanded to compete with grain brought in from the Midwest, but finally went out of business in the early 1930's. It has remained intact thanks to a high foundation that protects it from floodwaters.

Despite its drawbacks, the waterwheel remained unchanged until efforts were made to improve mill design after the Revolutionary war. At this time Benjamin Franklin and others endeavored to spread knowledge about advanced mill design and generally improve the new nation's industries. One major step was the sponsoring of a book by Oliver Evans, a journeyman millwright, called *The Young Millwright and Miller's Guide.* First published in 1795, with George Washington and Thomas Jefferson topping the list of original subscribers, the book told how to build, operate, and improve a mill. For the first time Evans made public the knowledge that had previously taken years of apprenticeship to learn. For almost a hundred years thereafter, *The Young Millwright* was reprinted, revised, and amalgamated into later editions.

One of the improvements of this era quickly accepted by the New England millers was the "tub wheel," which did much to lick the ice problem. In the mill's basement, or an enclosed area alongside, was built a barrel, or "tub," with a simple turbine wheel within. Piped-in water shot onto one side of the wheel, turning it. This rudimentary turbine was quite inefficient compared to the waterwheel:

These wheels [the tub wheel] cannot be recommended, in consequence of the water not acting to advantage on them, even when constructed in the best possible manner. If the head be low, [the height of water between the top of the dam and the opening where the water shoots out to hit the wheel] it is difficult to get a sufficient quantity of water to act on them, so as to drive them with sufficient power. . . . The tub wheel should not be used where water fails in dry weather; it is only suited to the streams where the water runs to waste the whole year; otherwise they are useless in the season when they are most needed.[3]

Nevertheless, their simplicity appealed to the miller. Instead of the need to convert the ten rpm of the waterwheel to the hundred rpm of the grindstone by gearing, the shaft turning the grindstone could be extended straight down through the floor to become the shaft holding the tub wheel. Construction and maintenance were simplified, to the delight of the miller, and no matter how much water was wasted in comparison to an outside waterwheel, the tub wheel, turning in the basement of the mill, was thus protected from the ravages of the New England weather.

During the first half of the nineteenth century, a great number of millers converted their operations to tub wheels. This is one of the reasons the traveler sees so few waterwheels alongside the New England mills that survive today.

The death knell of the village mills came in the mid-1800s with the introduction of fast railway transportation and the evolution of the tub wheel into the powerful turbine. Now volume production and cheap railroad distribution were driving the village mills into bankruptcy.

Some village mills were themselves able to grow. In East Clarendon, Vermont, as the wide Mill River flows down a gorge out of the Green Mountains, it passes the old Kingsley Mill. Expanded from a small gristmill, this great old wooden structure supplied the needs of the people of Vermont at the turn of the century. Finally, in the 1930s, it too was undercut by midwestern competition and went out of business.

Today the old mill is probably the most commercialized relic of New England's history. Gift shops, candle shops, anything-you-want-to-buy shops, and restaurants inhabit many an old mill and many a new imitation. Those that stand unused are found in isolated areas bypassed by tourists. Though not as pristine as the "restored" mills, they conjure up more feeling for a bygone era than those where the sound of a gurgling stream is muffled by the crunch of automobile tires on Ye Olde Mille's graveled parking lot.

8 The Sawmills and the Lumber Industry

Of all New England's village mills, sawmills have best weathered the centuries' changing economies. Their simple construction facilitated the addition of improvements over the years. Today, though unable to compete with the great industrial lumber mills, they still hold their own cutting firewood and supplying small woodworking shops in Vermont, New Hampshire, and Maine, where good timber is still locally available.

The first New England sawmill appeared in 1623 at York, Maine, then called Agamenticus. The York sawmill did not supply local needs; rather, it provided lumber for shipment to a tree-starved England. This sawmill worked almost the same as the technique used in cutting wood by hand, when no sawmill was available. Colonial hand-sawing was done with "sawpits." The log was stuck out over a pit dug deep enough for a man to stand below the log. This "pit man" gave the downstroke to the upstroke man standing on or astride the log. The saw used was a primitive version of the modern two-man saw. Of poor-grade metal, a square frame often braced the thin blade to keep it from twisting and breaking.

It was this square frame with a six-foot sawblade tensioned within that became the heart of the early "up and down" sawmills. The frame was held vertically in a slotted track and was pushed up and down about twice a second by a system of gearing driven by a waterwheel. While this may seem quite slow in comparison to today's high-rpm circular saws, in the days when all moving parts were wood against wood and animal fat the only lubricant, this was fast enough for the wooden parts to heat from friction, ignite the grease, and burn down the whole sawmill.

Color illustration 6

Along the New England shoreline, windmills also ground grain. This one, on a hilltop in Jamestown, R.I., dates back to 1787.

Color illustration 7

A deserted sawmill on the Mad River in Warren, Vt. Standing a safe distance from the falls, it has been able to survive the river's caprices.

Color illustration 8

The Old Tannery Building, Bakersville, Conn. Three stories high, the first story is obscured by brush in this picture.

Color illustration 9

This view of the Connecticut River Valley drew many visitors to the porch of the old Mount Holyoke House.

Color illustration 10

*The Clarendon Springs
Mineral Hotel, built in 1834.
Though a new roof has been
lately added, it has been a
long time since guests came
to sleep here.*

The sawing frame and cutting bed of an up-and-down sawmill in Ledyard, Conn.

The sawmill itself was simply a long narrow shed, wide enough to cover the machinery and long enough for an uncut log to be laid at one end and a cut log to lie at the other after it passed through the saw at the center.

As no clamping device existed to hold the half-cut log from falling over, it did not pass completely through the blade, leaving a six-inch length uncut at the end. An intrepid millhand "rode" this butt piece to guide the log through the blade. After all the cuts were made, the log was taken from the frame and this butt was hewn off.

The sawmill's power source was not the usual large waterwheel. Its slow, stately, powerful turns required complex gearing to bring

"Riding the butt" at a colonial sawmill on the New Hampshire seacoast.

it up to the 120 strokes per minute needed for the blade. Instead a special wheel, a "flutter wheel," was devised. Proportioned like a rolling pin, its 2½-foot diameter assured a lively speed, while its width, 7 to 8 feet, provided sufficient power to move the blade through the wood. The quick flapping noise produced by the wheel resembled the sound of a fluttering bird, hence its name.

Around 1850, the heavy, wobbly, dangerous, but much faster circular saw began phasing out the up-and-down sawmills. With a circular saw a mill could cut in a day what it took an up-and-down sawmill a week to do.

The early circular saws used weight and speed rather than sharpness to cut the logs. Constantly out of true, they could be relied on to chew out an undulating half-inch width of wood with each cut. Knots and hard spots, or sometimes a premeditated nail (placed by someone with a grudge against the sawmiller), which simply broke the up-and-down blade, tore the circular blade from its pin, and sent it on a fatal arc through the mill. Even in its proper place the whirring blade took its toll of the careless. The sawmiller missing only fingers was counted among the lucky.

Soon after the spread of the circular saws in the 1850s, the turbine began phasing out the flutter wheel. Conversion was easy, as both required a dam providing about a six-foot head of water.

These old milldams did more than simply provide a power source. They gave the miller a storage place for his logs. If possible, trees were felled upstream and floated down to the millpond to avoid being laboriously dragged overland by oxen. A wooden ramp led from the pond to the mill. An agile millhand would skip out across the floating logs, hook his mark, then "haul it up the brow" onto the sawing bed with a winch.

Although the turbine could operate in icy weather, the sawmills still operated only in warm seasons since the miller knew of no way to cut frozen logs. Only when steam power came into use in the larger sawmills in the late nineteenth century did mills operate year round. Pipes laid at the bottom of the millpond kept the water bubbling with escaping steam that thawed the logs.

Though sawing became a year-round operation, the winters were still the time of felling trees, as the hard-packed snow made dragging the oak and spruce giants much easier. This was as true for the local sawmills as for the great lumber industry that had grown up in the great North Woods since the first 1623 sawmill.

When great stands of timber edged the New England shoreline, lumber towns could be found only a few miles from colonial cities. In East Haddam, Connecticut, at the complex of cellar holes once known as Millington Green, lumber was cut to supply shipbuilders along the Connecticut River. With the last stand of timber gone, Millington Green fell into limbo and decay until now only rubble remains.

By 1800 the lumber companies had cut all the way to the uninhabited regions of northern Vermont, New Hampshire, and Maine. Here the great spruce still grew to enormous size as they awaited the woodsman's ax.

Until the 1860s, wood felled was used for lumber only. In 1863 the lumber market expanded when a technique was developed in Maine to make paper from ground-up logs (before, all paper had been primarily of rags). Now the lumber cutters searched not only for good wood for boards, but also for good stands of trees for pulpwood as well.

Unlike the smaller-scale lumbering operations in southern New England during the colonial period, when permanent communities were established to cut the wood and drag it to nearby mills, the great demand for wood in the nineteenth century created a need for nomadic encampments, set up for a winter's cutting, then abandoned when spring came.

In the late fall, a couple of "timber hunters" set out into the northern wilds to scout for likely stands of evergreens. They then returned downriver to report their findings and the logging company then either bought or leased for cutting the desired land. With the paperwork completed, the scouts returned to the backwoods and built the house, stables, and roads needed by the logging crew.

For the winter the crew's home was a long, low cabin, with a sloping roof only a few feet from the ground at its eaves.

A door and a window vis-a-vis at the ends, and a square hole in the roof afford exit and entrance for smoke, air, light, and the body corporate. Moss packed tightly between the logs, and a layer of hemlock boughs upon the long split shingles that tile the roof, together with the huge drifts of snow that the first winter-storm piles above, insure a warmth within and a protection from the biting cold. . . . Within, the center of the apartment is appropriated for the camp-fire, while

The sawmill at Sage's Ravine, Salisbury, Conn. Here a large waterwheel was used and the power transferred by belts missing when this picture was drawn.

Hauling logs up "the brow" in an 1877 sawmill.

next to the walls, on every side, hemlock boughs are spread upon the earth for beds, or rude berths, arranged in tiers, furnish ample accommodations for the sleepers.[1]

Not all the loggers fit the Paul Bunyan image, as seen by this 1889 account of New England's "legendary woodsmen":

They are thinly clad, heavy clothes being an impediment to their work. Contrary to one's ideas of a woodsman, they do not appear robust; many of them are pale, hollow-cheeked, and with sunken chests. Cases of consumption, we are told, often develop among them. The spicy mountain air cannot negative hot soda bread, greasy doughnuts, and the perennial bean thrust into exhausted stomachs. Not seldom a poor fellow is brought in from the woods with a gash in his foot and is condemned to "sit round" till it heals.[2]

These men spent the winter felling the trees, removing the bark, and dragging them by horse or oxen to the bank of a nearby river. There the logs awaited being "driven to the booms" on the spring freshets. All the work was dangerous, from chopping trees with snow-laden branches poised to fall from above, to piling great logs on the riverbank where any slight miscalculation meant rolling logs and crushed bodies. The woodsmen could do little for the victim of such calamities.

A couple of barrels, strapped together, was his coffin, and his own clothes his winding sheet. Placing these into the hastily dug grave, they trampled down the earth and left him, without prayer or funeral service. A half-suppressed sigh or unbidden tear, hastily brushed aside, were the only tributes to his memory.[3]

For the river drivers, the men who for weeks on end coddled the logs down the river to the sawmills come spring breakup, life was even more perilous. Persons hunting in the North Woods can still find the solitary memorials where a crushed river driver was pulled from the river: the man's boots nailed to a tree above an otherwise unmarked grave.

The river drives lasted well into the second decade of the twentieth century. Great drives came down the Penobscot in Maine to Bangor, and down the Connecticut River all the way from the Canadian border to the sawmills in Holyoke, Massachusetts.

Around the turn of the century, however, the logging contractors began replacing both the horses that dragged the logs at the winter camps, and the river drives themselves, with steam-powered movers. The first and most famous of these was the Lombard log hauler, a truly spectacular affair consisting of a small railway locomotive on caterpillar treads.

In the growing mechanization of the northern New England timber drives, the lumber companies began laying out logging railways to carry

timber to the river for the drive or all the way to the mill. In the more inaccessible regions, once track was laid and the trains had served their purpose, it was cheaper to abandon them than carry them out.

Probably the most fascinating group of logging remains are clustered around the Maine Forestry Service Camp at Eagle Lake on the Allagash Wilderness Waterway. Here at this remote site, 13 miles by canoe from the nearest road, one finds the old tramway that carried logs, rafted across nearby Chamberlain Lake, down a slope to Eagle Lake in preparation for the drive to Bangor. Nearby one also finds the terminus of the Eagle Lake and West Branch Rail Road. Between 1927 and 1933 pulpwood logs were carried out of the backwoods on a 16-mile route to be dumped at Eagle Lake. Today the old tracks still make their rusty way through the woods and over Chamberlain Lake on a high trestle. The most spectacular sight, however, is that of the two old steam locomotives that once pulled the logs over the route. These grand old engines, one over ninety tons, stand forgotten here as the woods they once cleared now grow back to hide them.

Farther downriver, at Churchill Depot, are other remains: two gas-powered Lombard haulers, later modernizations of the original steam Lombards.

Railway logging operations also took place in New Hampshire's White Mountains, but unlike northern Maine the mills were built

Winter quarters of a logging crew in 1856.

Winslow Homer's Lumbering in Winter.

Remains of a water-powered sawmill in Boxford, Mass. The belts and wheels connected the turbine below with the cutting blade above.

close by. Once a network of tracks ran through the forest's Pemigewasset Wilderness Area. Hikers today can follow trails laid out on the old roadbeds, and pass the last of the old trestles across the mountain streams. Farther downriver, at Lincoln, New Hampshire, stands the Franconia Paper Company, the terminus of the old logging roads. Here some of the old rolling stock remains and more is on exhibit at Clarks Trading Post in nearby North Woodstock. The Franconia mill itself is on the verge of following the logging railway into extinction. Located in the heart of the White Mountain National Forest, the paper mill has been unable to afford the pollution control devices required today and, in the last decade, has alternated between closure and attempts to reopen.

Just the other side of the mountains, in nearby Crawford Notch, stood another mill town that thrived on the trees of the Pemigewasset Wilderness. This was Livermore, once home to two hundred people, but since 1951 officially disincorporated as a town and today all but overgrown. In the last quarter of the nineteenth century, the Grafton Lumber Company built the town, its sawmills, and the miles of track into the forest. By the turn of the century the hamlet boasted a boardinghouse, two sawmills, stores, company offices, and workers' row houses, all perched along the steep ravine of the Sawyer River.

In the 1920s successive tragedies struck Livermore to cripple its one-business economy. A 1920 fire swept through the sawmill, destroying it and almost devastating the rest of the town. Seven years later, floods washed away most of the logging railway. Unable to replace the track, the company closed the sawmills in 1928. Livermore's inhabitants quickly left to find work elsewhere, leaving the town to disappear into the great forest around it.

Livermore, N.H., in the 1890s. Today only the forest remains.

9 The Village Tannery

In a 1629 report to the colonial governor, the citizens of Salem, Massachusetts, described their apparel as "sutes, dublett and hose, of leather . . . and . . . breeches of leather drawers to serve to wear with both their other [cloth] sutes."[1] Besides clothes, colonial leather served also in the making of shoes, carriages, harnesses, ships' rigging, and any other place where a strong flexible material was needed.

This early reliance on leather forced the colonies to place strict controls on the quality, export, and pricing of leather. They appointed inspectors to examine the leather produced by local tanners and affix passed hides with an official seal. Heavy fines threatened tanners who sold hides without the "sealer's" mark. In the winter of 1642–43 the New Haven Court reported that

*the Town was acquainted that the sealers for leather & shoemakers
had been with the Gouvernor to let him understand that there is several
hides tanned by Jeremiah Osborne which the sealers cannot seal,
it is so bad, and by means of his ill tanning of the hides formerly the
Town hath suffered exceedingly, and the shoemakers are discouraged in
their trade; upon which grounds there was some debate aboute putting
Jeremiah Osborne down from taning any more hides to sell, and of
getting another tanner.*[2]

The everyday dependence on leather lasted far into the nineteenth century, virtually demanding that, like the gristmill, there be a tannery in every community.

TANNER & CURRIER

The process of tanning leather, converting "green" hides from slaughtered animals both wild and domestic into finished leather ready to be worked by artisans, was a mechanically simple but dirty, lengthy process.

First the hides, bought by the tanner or given to him for processing by the farmers, were washed for one full day. The earliest method was to submerge the hide with rocks in a nearby stream. After most of the filth had been washed away, the next step was removing the hair. The hide was laid in a square wood-lined vat, about five feet on a side, dug into the ground. Crushed lime dissolved in water, called "milk of lime," went in over the hides. It took from four months to a year for the lime to loosen the hairs.

Tanning in 1836. At right, the tanner scrapes the hides. In the background, the hides in the tanpits are stirred and turned. At left, the finished hides are worked.

Before removing the hairs, however, the hides, stiff from the action of the lime, had to be softened. The tanner immersed the hides in another vat filled with "bate," a softening solution of water, salt, and bird dung. After this soaking the hides were washed again and brought to the "beam house." Here the tanner laid the hides across a rounded plank, or "beam," and slowly rubbed off the hairs. This was a strenuous process, and at the end of a day's work an exhausted tanner had only a dozen cleaned hides for his labor.

Finally the hides were ready to be tanned. The tanner again immersed the hides in a vat, this time filled with a solution of tannic acid, which came from the crushed inner bark of trees, the "tanbark." Another year passed before the hides were finally removed and given a final cleaning before being sold to the local artisans or returned to the farmers who had brought them to the tanner years earlier.

The necessary use of lime and guano, compounded by the piling up of the offal scraped from the hides into "tanhills," as these rotting masses were called, did not make the idea of a tannery next door very popular. Only the dire necessity of leather forced the reluctant towns-people to allow tanneries to be constructed nearby. In 1641 the Boston town fathers gave two men permission "to sink a pit to water their leather," but with the proviso "and if it be found an annoyance to the town, then they are to fill it up again."[3]

In the period between the first colonial tanneries and the mid-1800s, tanneries showed little basic change. This description of a tannery in Quincy, Massachusetts, might have been recorded at any time during that period:

The earlier tanneries were strange, primitive establishments. The vats were oblong boxes sunk in the ground close to the edge of the town brook at the point where it crossed the main street. They were without either cover or outlets. The beam-house was an open shed, within which old, worn out horses circulated round while the bark was crushed at the rate of half a cord or so a day by alternate wooden and stone wheels, moving in a circular trough fifteen feet in diameter.[4]

The art of tanning had remained unchanged for centuries simply because there was little in the process that lent itself to mechanization. The slowness of the tanning itself did little to encourage speedier methods in the steps requiring human labor.

Had the tanner wished, he might have adopted water-powered machinery to crush the bark, but for the most part he stayed with the old horse-powered tanbark mill. This was a circular stone trough within which heavy stone wheels rolled along the groove, powered by animals attached to the wheels' axle. Lengths of bark were laid in the trough and a tap given to the yoked animals to get them started. Then,

the tanner's son . . . walked behind the horse, rake in hand, drawing upon or from the bed the crushed pieces, to be again and again crushed

by the stone in its weary round. One cord per day was thus macerated,
at the cost of many tears shed by the unfortunate child.[5]

In the mid-1600s, when New England had only a few dozen tanneries in the towns surrounding Boston, sumac bark was used for tanning. Later, as the frontier moved farther west, the new tanneries that arose along its edge used the larger and more numerous hemlock. The tanner's constant need of trees for bark gave him an important place in rolling back the wilderness. As he felled the trees, he gave the community an ever increasing acreage of cleared, arable land that could quickly be turned into new farms.

At first the tanner was welcome to chop and debark trees at his pleasure. As the towns grew, however, they passed laws to make the tanner first clear the forests close to the village to facilitate the steady expansion of the town. As usual, New Haven's Jeremiah Osborne got into trouble over this matter in 1654.

Jeremiah Osborne was complained of for felling about thirty trees
in the [town] ox-pasture in a disorderly way; he said it was to get bark
for his trade, and desires the Towne to consider [i.e., excuse] it,
and his men falled more than he did intend, and some of them was in
Mr Atwaters lott, which [he] had liberty for, and some without
the two mile.[6]

Osborne not only cut trees outside the town limit but also those standing on the town commons. By 1687 the scarcity of trees near the towns forced the Connecticut General Court to order

that if any taner or taners in this Colony shall fall . . . wood in the
comons, for barke, within the towne bounds, without lycense first
obtained from the town, [they] shall forfeit five shillings for every
tree they . . . cutt down, the one halfe to the complayner, the other to
the use of the poore of the towne. . . .[7]

Soon many New England tanners gave up cutting their own bark and depended on shipments from the forests of Maine.

By the beginning of the 1800s speedier, but costlier tanning methods were adopted by some tanneries. While the primitive village establishments carried on in the old way, others grew into factories. In the greater Boston area, the descendants of the original half-dozen Puritan tanneries grew into the nation's leading shoe manufacturers during the nineteenth century.

Another offshoot of nineteenth-century expansion today stands empty in Bakersville, a quiet town in northwestern Connecticut. Known locally as the Old Tannery Building, it is a three-story, red wood structure built around 1850. The tannery and the town itself were founded by a tanner and shoemaker named Scott Baker, who came from Bridgeport, farther south in the state. His sons and grandson carried on the busi-

An English tanbark crusher in 1751. Virtually the same scene could be viewed at a colonial American tannery. In the background stand drying racks, a tanner scraping hides, and fowl being raised for their dung.

ness, expanding it into a thriving industry. Farmers from miles around sold their hides to the Bakers, who turned them into shoes and boots. The tannery was the little town's lifeblood, and even the local dances were held on its upper floor.

As time passed, the Baker tannery, like so many small businesses, was pushed out by larger competition, and Scott Baker's grandson turned to manufacturing wooden shingles. Later the building became a condensed milk factory. Today it is vacant, the old vats that stood across the street are no more, and Bakersville is just a little farming town without industry.

Most of the old tanbark mills now lie lost and forgotten. Once abandoned, their low circle of stones quickly disappeared beneath a few years' overgrowth. In Totoket, Connecticut, what may have been a tanbark mill shows its stones to the light of day. Standing in the yard of a colonial homestead, this circle is overgrown only by flowers, as its present owners have made a small garden within its ring.

Mineral Springs and 10 Mountaintop Resorts

With the close of hostilities with England after the War of 1812, American businessmen were left to develop industry and trade unencumbered by the Crown or the threat of war. It was the new nation's first era of real prosperity. The frontier had been pushed west, the land was settled, all was at peace, and for the first time there was a sizable group of Americans who could afford extravagances.

One of their first steps was to escape from their cities and southern plantations during the hot summers. The antebellum southern gentry came north to escape the damp heat and mosquitoes. The northern city-dwellers, like the Bostonians, journeyed inland from cities that dumped their sewage into nearby mud flats to await disposal by the tides. The goal of many of these people was the latest European rage: the spas, or mineral springs.

Over the ages, men have attributed healing powers to ground seepage suddenly forced from the earth by underlying layers of impervious rock. In most cases this underground water dissolved minerals in the porous layers of rock and carried them with it as the water appeared on the surface. Some carried away sulfur; some, metallic ores like iron; others, soft limestone, and still others, alkaline salts.

The procedure was to bathe in or drink the water or both, depending on the water's properties.

> *. . . they drink*
> *The waters so sparkling and clear;*
> *Though the flavor is none of the best,*
> *And the odor exceedingly queer;*
> *But the fluid is mingled, you know*
> *With wholesome medicinal things,*
> *So they drink, and they drink, and they drink —*
> *And that's what they do at the Springs![1]*

Thus a Vermont poet wrote about the nineteenth-century spas.

The exploitation of the mineral springs in America was not solely a nineteenth-century development. At Stafford Springs, Connecticut, long before the coming of white men, Indians were taking the water of an iron spring that was later a colonial iron ore site and a post-Revolutionary mineral spa.

Today Saratoga, New York, is the name most associated with northern mineral resorts, but in the nineteenth century "water takers" thought of many New England resorts as well.

Vermont had the greatest density of the nineteenth-century spas. At one time no corner of the state, from Brattleboro on the Connecticut River near the Massachusetts line to Alburg on Lake Champlain at the Canadian border, was without a mineral spring house.

Some of the hotels were simple affairs, converted taverns and inns blessed with a nearby spring, while others were great resorts with walks, gardens, and every conceivable amenity.

One of the grander remnants of New England's spa era stands a few miles southwest of Rutland, the Clarendon Mineral Spring House. According to *The Geology of Vermont,*

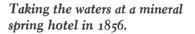

Taking the waters at a mineral spring hotel in 1856.

Tradition informs us that their medicinal virtues were first discovered in 1776 by one Asa Smith, who resided in the eastern part of the township. He is reported to have "dreamed" of a spring in the western part of the town, and full of faith started through the wilderness, and over the high hills that separated the two portions of the town, in search of the spring that should restore him to health. Arriving at the spot, he recognized it as the one he had seen in his dreams, and accordingly at once drank the water, and bound clay saturated with it on his swollen and inflamed limbs.[2]

Cured, Smith returned home to tell of the miracle. Local people, seeing more the money than the miracle, quickly built a small hotel on the site. The spring, the first to become a Vermont spa, grew steadily in reputation. By 1834 a great three-story brick edifice, surrounded on three sides by great porches and columns in a style familiar to its southern boarders, replaced the original hotel.

An 1855 edition of *Mineral and Thermal Springs of the United States and Canada* gave this account of Clarendon's waters:

The Clarendon waters enjoy a reputation in cutaneous diseases, chronic bronchitis, anascara, and especially in irritable bladder. The quantity drank in the twenty-four hours varies from five to twenty half pint tumblersfull. At first they excite a warmth and aching on the surface, sometimes added with a slight nausea. These sensations disappear when their diuretic action begins. This occurs in about six hours after drinking them.[3]

The Clarendon Springs Hotel and its grounds, as seen in an 1853 painting by James Hope.

While the gaseous Clarendon waters were drunk, other springs, like those in Brattleboro, called for extended periods of cold bathing. Needless to say, the less painful the cure, the more fashionable the spa.

The Civil War had a crippling effect on the Clarendon Spa, as the postbellum Southerners had neither the money nor the inclination to disport themselves in "Yankeeland." Despite the loss of its southern clientele, the mineral spring craze lasted throughout the century.

Many other smaller hotels arose for a new post–Civil War class of "water takers," people of modest means who came more for the cure than the social season. The Caledonia Mineral Spring Hotel was one such example. A two-story red brick house, converted from a wayside inn, it stands today in the small hamlet of Wheelock, Vermont. Behind

PROSPECT HOUSE, MT. HOLYOKE.—Built in 1851.

PROSPECT HOUSE IN 1861 AND 1888.
The Finest Cultivated View in New England.

Two miles from Mt. Tom station on the Conn. R. R. R., three miles from Northampton, and three miles from Hadley on the Central Massachusetts. Is situated on the most commanding spot on the range, and is fitted up expressly for the Views, with good Telescopes and every appliance to get it in the best form. The beautiful view, pure air and clear spring water make it a desirable place to spend an hour, a day, or a week. Connected by telegraph and telephone, via Holyoke. P. O. Address,

J. W. FRENCH, MT. HOLYOKE, NORTHAMPTON, MASS.

the now-empty building was the spring, a sulfur swamp first considered a public nuisance by the townspeople. During the 1860s it became the town's livelihood as people arrived to take its waters.

While incredible claims were usually made for the mineral springs' curative effects, there was some truth to their powers. In an age where baths were infrequent, a balanced diet and vitamins unknown, and most patent medicines mere "snake oils," the mineral-rich waters did provide some aid. Anemics who drank iron-rich water were simply taking the Geritol of their time. Today, sulfur, which was then bathed in, forms the base of many patent medicines for minor skin problems. For our indigestion we need only reach into the medicine cabinet for an Alka-Seltzer, while our ancestors took a much longer journey to the waters of a carbonated spring.

The downfall of the mineral springs came around the turn of the century, and the overblown claims of the spa owners were its death knell. As the muckrakers of the late 1800s exposed the meat and patent medicine industries to the public eye and the government acted to curb their abuses, the mineral spas were also discredited.

Some spas survived through their reputation as grand hotels rather than as curehouses, as was the case at Poland Springs, Maine, until 1975. In that year the great Victorian Poland Spring House burned to the ground, a fate that overtook many of the old wooden resort hotels.

Another mineral spring hotel, the Mount Equinox House in Manchester Center, Vermont, sits at this time, empty of guests, awaiting reopening. Farther north, the empty Clarendon Springs Hotel stands amid a small park of stately trees. Once the moneyed families of America strolled, gossiped, intrigued, and courted here,

> *Now they stroll in the beautiful walks,*
> *Or loll in the shade of the trees;*
> *Where many a whisper is heard*
> *That never is told by the breeze;*
> *And hands are commingled with hands,*
> *Regardless of conjugal rings;*
> *And they flirt, and they flirt, and they flirt, —*[4]

And that's what they did at the springs.

Nineteenth-century Americans not only took to the water, they also took to the hilltops.

In 1821 some enterprising men from Northampton and Hadley, Massachusetts, climbed to the summit of nearby Mount Holyoke to build a log cabin. This "mountain house" provided shelter for those who, since 1676, had climbed the mountain to enjoy the view.

The view enjoyed from the top of the mountain, the height of which is 830 feet from the river at its base, is considered the richest in

Color illustration 11
preceding page

The hearthface of the Mount Riga Furnace, built around 1810, high in the hills near the Connecticut–Massachusetts–New York border. The "1845" chiseled into the stone at left is when the furnace was last overhauled. Two years later it was abandoned.

Color illustration 12

Beckley's Furnace in East Canaan, Conn. One of the last to be in operation in New England, it produced high-grade iron until 1923.

Color illustration 13 opposite

The Crown Mill, North Uxbridge, Mass., built in 1825. Once the Crown and its sister mill, the Eagle (hidden by trees on the left), helped make New England the great textile center of America. In 1975, soon after this photograph was taken, a fire swept through the mills, leaving them a rubbled shell.

Color illustration 14

A millworkers' church, Wauregan, Conn., no longer used now that the mill has closed and its workers dispersed.

Color illustration 15

Millworkers' house, Carolina, R.I. Factory-owned, it has been vacant since the mill closed around World War I.

An illustration ca. 1870 of the
original and "improved" cars
on the Mount Holyoke
railway.

New England; and notwithstanding the laboriousness of the ascent,
the traveler will find himself amply repaired for all his pains, on
arrival at the summit.

Thus read an 1824 brochure published by the Mount Holyoke entrepreneurs.[5] While the gradual slope of most mountains put the valley
below at some distance from the summit, the precipitous drop of
Mount Holyoke's northwest face literally laid the Connecticut River
Valley below the climber's feet. Over the years it was to be called the
most cultivated view in America.

    While the steep face of the mountain improved the view, it also
made the ascent a formidable undertaking.

Whoever has weak nerves, a delicate constitution, or is subject to
giddiness, I would particularly recommend to abstain from visiting the
summit of Mount Holyoke. Not only is a person obliged at certain
places to take giant steps from tree to branch, and from branch to
tree, but to tread on stones without any solid foundation whatever!
These, very unceremoniously, slip away under the weight; and if
particular attention be not paid, the visitor is apt to take a leap down
the precipice in company with the fragments of rock,[6]

reported a traveler in the 1830s. Despite the dangers, six to eight
thousand travelers, among them Charles Dickens, were making the
few-hour ascent each year.

    In 1851 the little summit house was expanded into a hotel.

Here individuals or parties can obtain refreshments at short notice,
and on reasonable terms. There are one or two sleeping apartments

The Mount Holyoke House, ca. 1890. The long shed down the slope is the "improved" railway.

where those who are desirous to witness the setting and rising of the sun may pass the night. A dense fog, resembling the ocean, sometimes rests upon the valley below, and shuts out the sun while it shines in all its glory upon the hills around the observer on the mountain. . . . On the top of the building is fixed a large telescope for use of visitors, and below is a circumvolving machine, in which the more juvenile portion of them appear to take sensible delight in riding.[7]

The builder of this new hotel, The Prospect House, with its observatory and merry-go-round, was John W. French, who for the next forty years made Mount Holyoke internationally known.

After finishing his hotel, French attacked the problem of making the ascent of the mountain easier. Wagons were used on the lower half of the slope but visitors still scrambled the last 365 feet over a steep field of broken rock. In 1854 French built a mountain railway, in actuality a primitive cable car. The car itself was the backseats of two sleighs, connected to face each other. It ran up a 600-foot stairway with rails laid on each side. A horse on the summit provided the power that drew the car up on a rope. The stairs were both for those dubious of French's creation and for times when rains shrank the rope and the car could not make it all the way to the bottom.

While easier on the muscles of the visitors, it still did not completely eliminate the emotional strains of the ascent:

Everybody who rode it considered it a very serious matter, and the outcome extremely doubtful, but for a person with steady nerves, the experience was a delightful one. . . . The climax came when the car rolled up the steep ledge not far from the summit. In a moment the height seemed almost dizzy and the view immensely broadened, and if not too frightened at the thought of what might happen if the rope broke, this moment was wonderfully exhilarating.[8]

In 1867 French rebuilt the railway, protecting it from the elements and installing steam power.

The Mount Holyoke house was by no means the only mountain house and mountain railway in New England. Throughout the region, from Mount Tom across the river from Mount Holyoke, to Mount Washington at the top of the White Mountains, there were hotels and railways. Today only a few remain, almost all vanished through the same cause: fire. At Mount Monadnock, where Emerson and Thoreau once wandered, Acadia National Park, Mount Wachusett, Mount Tom, Nonotuck Mountain, Mount Mansfield, and Mount Moosilauke, one can still find the cellar holes and burnt remains of once-fashionable mountain houses. Only on Mount Washington does the railway, built in 1869, still puff up the side of the mountain to the summit. Here, though it no longer takes lodgers, the old Summit House, built in 1915 to replace the original 1853 structure, still stands at the top of New England.

The Mount Holyoke Prospect House met its end during the hurricane of 1938. Severely damaged, it never reopened and was given to the state as a park. Today picnickers can drive up the old carriage road and its new extension to park at the summit. The old hotel is closed to lodgers and only open the few times a year that there is water for its toilets. The rest of the year visitors can only walk its verandah for the view that has entranced the eye since 1676 — a broad valley, sided by gently lifting hills; farms and forests combined into a soft patchwork of greens and browns; Northampton with all its factories and schools; little Hadley, a few paralleling streets of colonial homes; and the Connecticut River, meandering out of the distant haze to flow past the very foot of the mountain.

Many other peaks have a higher altitude and offer wilder and more unmixed natural scenery — but no other blends in its wide prospect so much that is rich in soil and cultivation . . . mingled with so much that is wildly majestic and inspiring. . . . Nowhere else are the dwellings of man so beautifully and harmoniously blended with the works of the creator.[9]

11 Mining

The story of New England mining is, for the most part, the history of small deposits worked not for their quality or size but for their accessibility to the first settlers. At different times the New England soil has yielded up such materials as iron, copper, lead, gold, silver, emery, asbestos, and coal to the picks and black powder of its miners.

In every case the discovery of greater deposits elsewhere lowered prices below that at which the New England deposit could be worked profitably. Though the mine then closed, a raising of the ore's selling price from increased demand or wartime necessity reopened it until prices dropped and it was again abandoned.

New England's first mines were worked by the Indians, who dug out red ocher and graphite for body paint. In 1633 two scouts from Plymouth met Indians in the area around Sturbridge, Massachusetts, whose faces had been blackened with graphite. Learning the location of their mine, the scouts returned to Plymouth to report their find. In 1638 the white men arrived to work the site, which was worked off and on until 1900. Today the old mine is a complex of tunnel mouths and deep vertical cuts. The machinery of past centuries is gone and only a sign on a dirt road south of Sturbridge identifies the site.

Another important colonial mine lies on a hillside in Granby, Connecticut, where a copper deposit was found on town land at the start of the 1700s. A company of people formed to work the bed, under the agreement they pay 3⅓ shillings to Yale College and 6⅔ shillings to "the able schoolmaster of Simsbury" for every ton of ore raised, a reflection of colonial enthusiasm for support of local education.[1]

Problems began as soon as the first ore was raised, for no one knew how to smelt out the copper. In these times the only "learned" people in the area were the clergy, so the company gave their ore to three local ministers to smelt. Unfortunately the churchmen were not as learned as they claimed to be and the company soon sued for the return of their ore.

Extremely strict British laws forbidding the smelting of ore in the colonies might have had some effect on the perseverance of these reverend gentlemen. The Coppermine (as the area was then called) Company next tried doing things legally and sent their ore to England for smelting. After two ships were lost at sea this solution was also abandoned. Next German coppersmiths were smuggled in to set up a clandestine works a few miles from the mine. In 1725 the British got wind of the operation and attached the works. After this the mine was operated on and off as different speculators tried their hand, only to go away poorer than before.

In 1739 the people connected with the mine again fell afoul of the Crown, this time for minting "Granby coppers." This was a grave infringement on the monopoly of the Royal Mint and the local blacksmith who minted these coins was quickly stopped. Although no more were struck, the coins, one side showing a stag and the motto "Value me as you will," the other side showing three sledgehammers surmounted by crowns and the motto "I am good copper," circulated throughout the colonies for many years thereafter.

In 1773, the Colony of Connecticut bought the mine, not for its copper but to use as a prison. The mine could not have been very valuable by then, since it cost the state a total of $375 to purchase and fortify. The prisoners lived down in the tunnels, fettered with chains and manacles. The place was named Newgate in honor of the worst of the English prisons. During the Revolution, Newgate became the home of many British sympathizers. Two such unfortunates related how they were

Higley's Granby Coppers. The design represents three blacksmith's hammers surmounted by crowns.

first conducted through the apartments of the guards, then through a trapdoor downstairs into another. . . . In the corner of this outer room . . . opened another large trapdoor, covered with bars and bolts of iron, which, was hoisted up by two guards by means of a tackle . . . and opened the jaws and mouth of what they called Hell into which they descended by means of a ladder. . . . Finding it not possible to evade this hard cruel fate they bade adieu to the world and descended the ladder about thirty-eight feet more, when they came to what was called the landing, then marching shelf by shelf till descending about thirty or forty feet more till they came to a platform of boards laid under foot, with a few more put overhead to carry off the water which keeps continually dropping. Here . . . they . . . found the inhabitants of this woeful mansion who were exceedingly anxious to know what was going on above.[2]

Newgate Copper Mine and Prison in 1838.

In 1793, while prisoners languished in Newgate, farmers in Strafford, Vermont, were investigating strange explosions and soil blackening on a nearby hillside. Clearing away the topsoil, they found a deposit of copper and iron pyrites, crystals of sulfur in combination with the metals. At first the farmers rejoiced at the iron deposit in their backyards. When the Franconia Iron Furnace opened about twenty years later, the Strafford farmers sent a load of ore to Franconia for smelting. Unfortunately, the sulfur acted to block the melting of the ore and instead froze everything in the furnace into a solid block. After it cooled the furnace had to be dismantled stone by stone, the block removed, then the stones reassembled before it could be put back to work. Needless to say, this was the last Strafford ore accepted at any ironworks.

This drastic demonstration of the ore's content put the Strafford people on the right track and in 1809 they formed the Vermont Mineral Company. They dug out the pyrites to assist the natural process that originally attracted them to the site: i.e., the combination of the ore with water to form a weak sulfuric acid that heats the ore and breaks it into a blackish material called sulfate of iron. It was better known as "copperas," and was popular as a black dye and disinfectant.

In the early 1800s the farmers worked the mine for copperas, but around the middle of the century they had gone deep enough to discover a great copper ore deposit.

At the same time, a similar find eight miles to the north was also made. This was the discovery of copper ore at Vershire, Vermont, in 1854. At first the ore was sent to Massachusetts and New Jersey to be smelted. This was an economic handicap, as only one-tenth of the ore was copper. What the Vershire mine needed was its own smelter, which it got in 1868 after the old company officials were replaced in 1865 during a clandestine meeting of the stockholders. The new president was now Smith Ely, a retired furniture tycoon from New Jersey.

When the smelter went into operation, the Vershire mine became the greatest producer of copper in America until the discovery of larger deposits in the Great Lakes region. Where a few farmers had leached the soil for copperas in their spare time, over 850 laborers, many from Cornwall and Ireland, now worked the mine and the smelters.

This glory lasted only until the early 1880s. New copper deposits discovered out west were cutting the price of copper and the Vershire mine could no longer clear a profit. Late in June 1883, the Vershire miners were notified that unless they took a cut in pay, the mine would be closed. The miners rose in revolt, taking over the town. After they had held the town for a week, the Vermont National Guard was called up. Marching on the town, the guardsmen were besieged not by bullets but by tales of hardship from the miners and their families. The sympathetic guardsmen quickly distributed their rations to the strikers and left. This show of nonviolence quickly catapulted the miners into the national spotlight.

Public sympathy and some tinned meat, however, did little to solve the mine's finances. Most of the miners soon left, and those who stayed collected little more than a fifth of their due when the mine was sold at public auction in 1888. The winning bid for the mine, for which Smith Ely had once been offered a million dollars, was $36,000.

After this, the Vershire mine, like the earlier Newgate mine, passed from speculator to speculator. There was ore still to be found but it was too expensive to mine.

Finally, in 1905 a heavy tax assessment on the abandoned homes and mine buildings forced the owner to level the community. Where there was once a great smelter, company buildings, over fifty homes, two churches, and a store, only one house remains. All the rest is desolate rubble. No trees or vegetation has closed the wound that was the Vershire Copper Mine; the sulfur dioxide released in the smelting process has poisoned the soil to leave a brick-strewn desert for years to come.

This was not the final chapter of Vermont copper. World War II created a need for copper, reopening the old Strafford mine, which had operated intermittently until 1930. After the war production continued with marginal profits until a decrease in the copper content of the ore raised smelting costs and the old mine again closed. Since February 1958 the mine and its building have stood silent, awaiting another demand for Vermont copper.

While the Strafford mine and its buildings stand almost intact, this

The Strafford Copperas Works in 1844. The ore was dug out at a and piled at c, where rainwater leached through it to form the black tarnish called copperas, later sold for inks, dyes, and disinfectants.

is the exception for New England mines. Most reward the visitor with a view of rubble, open pits, and tunnel mouths.

In what was Davis, Massachusetts, high in the hills above the Mohawk Trail, only a little schoolhouse on a dirt road marks the site of the mining village. Here, in 1882, Herbert J. Davis opened a mine to extract pyrites. The operation was quite small, employing only eighty men, but the high grade of the ore made the mine profitable. Few of the miners were New Englanders; rather, Davis brought in experienced men from Ireland, Italy, Austria, and Cornwall, England. The works lasted until 1910. When it closed, the foreign miners, with no ties to the area, left to find work in other mines. The deserted village soon crumbled under the harsh New England weather and today only 150-odd cellar holes, the little school, an old dam, and the shaft mouth mark the site.

Farther south in the Berkshires, another old mining town is more inhabited. This is Chester, once the largest producer of emery in America. Unlike in Davis, the people of Chester stayed when the mines closed. But the town's opulent old homes, standing side by side next to empty and boarded-up buildings, tell us that Chester's days of glory have passed.

Today many mineral deposits still lie untouched in New England's bedrock, waiting to be mined. They lie there like a dirty penny in a gutter, hardly worth the effort to pick it out.

The Iron Industry 12

During the Ice Age, the great glaciers that pushed across New England gouged out innumerable depressions in the earth. As the ice retreated meltwater collected in these depressions to form thousands of lakelets, ponds, and bogs. Over the ages, many disappeared as new streambeds sprang up, but others, especially in the flatter regions of New England — such as the North Woods of Maine, Rhode Island, and southeastern Massachusetts — still cover the countryside.

As the rainwater collected, it brought with it traces of iron washed from the soil. Certain microorganisms common to these bogs absorbed the iron to form little armor shells. After the organisms died, their carapaces sunk to the bottom, covering it with a crude iron deposit.

The colonial settlers, constantly needing firearms, cooking utensils, nails, and hardware (like hinges and door latches), quickly set up little ironworks wherever such ore was found. Without microscopes, they had no idea what caused these deposits, but they knew that "the period of growth of these deposits is supposed to be about twenty-five years; and it is found in various depths of water from two to twenty feet. A man accustomed to the employment being in a small boat, with an instrument similar to oyster tongs, can raise from its watery bed about half a ton of ore a day."[1]

Once the ore was collected it was brought to the village forge. This was scarcely more than a common blacksmith forge. Bellows, driven by hand or waterwheel, blew air into a crucible filled with charcoal, lime, and the iron ore. The burning charcoal, livened by the constant blast of

air, melted the ore. The lime acted as a flux as it rose to the top of the molten mass, taking most of the impurities with it. Once this "dross" was skimmed off, the layer below was more or less pure iron.

The ironmaker could now do one of two things. He could pour the molten iron into sand molds to make "hollow ware," as cooking utensils were then called, or perhaps rectangular plates, called fire backs, that were mounted in fireplaces to hold the fire's heat. These cast iron items were able to take great heat without melting and were quite hard, but they were full of impurities and therefore brittle. If struck or dropped onto a hard surface they quickly shattered.

The ironmaker could also make wrought iron. Here he cast the molten iron into bars, or, as they were later called, pigs. These he reheated and pounded with a hammer to flatten and drive out more of the impurities. After repeated heating and hammering the iron became tough and shatter resistant, but it could easily be bent from either pressure or heat. While today we use wrought iron for fences, in colonial times it was made into nails.

There is one more variety of iron that combines the hardness of cast iron with the resistance to shattering of wrought iron. This is steel, made by constant pounding to remove impurities and controlled cooling to leave it hard but not brittle. This is an exacting process and the early ironmakers had neither the ability nor the high-grade ore needed to make it.

Today all of the local forges are long vanished. The only remains are the little damsites and spillways that powered the waterwheels. Many of these sites are covered with the remains of later industries, but in Middleton, Massachusetts, a beautiful little stone-walled spillway still stands at the outlet of a small pond. Here, from about 1700 until the 1790s, a forge made iron products for the town out of the ore dredged from the bottom of the pond.

Not all colonial ironmaking was a local venture. The early Massachusetts government quickly recognized the need for good iron and supported an attempt to make it in quantity. This was Hammersmith, an ironworks in what is today Saugus, ten miles north of Boston. Bog iron had been discovered in the area soon after settlers arrived in 1629. John Winthrop, Jr., son of the governor and developer of the Sturbridge Lead Mine, obtained royal permission to erect the works and he brought experienced ironworkers from England to run it in 1643. After a few false starts, the governor was able to write his son, who had by now moved on to new things, "The iron work goeth on with more hope. It yields now about 7 tons per week."[2]

These seven tons were not ladled out crucible by crucible from small forges, but poured in great quantities from America's first successful blast furnace. This type of furnace, developed in Europe, was the last great refinement in ironmaking before the Bessemer process revolutionized the industry in the latter half of the nineteenth century. The blast furnace was a large, cube-shaped edifice of stone, about 25 feet on a side. Within, a brick-lined chamber opened to the sky at the furnacetop and to a hearth face at the base of one of its sides. Beside the furnace, two water-powered bellows pumped air into the interior chamber.

First the empty furnace was gradually heated by throwing in burning charcoal over a stretch of about ten days.

When the whole internal furnace has acquired a strong, white heat, the bellows are put in motion, and the ore, charcoal, and shells [seashells for lime], being duly proportioned, are thrown in at the top by small quantities every hour. The ore descending to the hottest part of the furnace, at length gradually melting, drops down, through the fuel into the receiver, where at an aperture left for the purpose, the scoria floating on the surface of the metal, resembling lava from a volcano, is occasionally removed by a long iron hook. A sufficient

Opposite: A typical colonial iron blast furnace. Above: The workmen pour lime, iron ore, and charcoal into the furnace. At left: The bellows and waterwheel. Counterweights keep the bellows in an open position. A shaft turned by the waterwheel has cams that catch the edge of the bellows, closing them and forcing air into the furnace. When the cams release the bellows, the counterweight automatically expands the bellows. At the hearthface: An ironworker pokes a hole into the clay seal to let the molten iron run out onto the mold, where other workers stand with shovels of sand to pour over the cooling iron. The workers wear leather aprons and thick-soled boots for protection from the molten metal.

quantity of pure iron being collected in the receiver, the action of the bellows is discontinued for the space of about twenty minutes for the purpose of casting. The fluid metal is dipped out at the aperture with iron ladles well covered with a composition of clay . . . and with them is poured into the several molds prepared for the purpose, and is thus formed into the various utensils and machinery.[3]

This continued for about five months before the inner lining of the furnace crumbled from the heat and had to be rebuilt.

Nearby, finery forges similar to the small local forges converted the cast iron bars into wrought iron by continued heating and hammering. Here a giant water-driven hammer called a triphammer pounded the metal. This was a great iron sledge swung on an oaken beam. Water-powered gearing raised the head a few feet above the anvil before it dropped to strike the heated metal bar held in place by a workman. Constant heating and pounding slowly drove out the impurities until the bar was but a fraction of its original size.

The Hammersmith venture operated for only a few decades until poor production and financial problems arising from lawsuits over water rights shut it down. "Instead of drawing out bars of iron for the country's use, there were hammered out nothing but contentions and lawsuits," observed one writer in 1677 as the Hammersmith Works were slipping into bankruptcy.[4] Today Hammersmith is a National Historic Site and has been restored to its probable appearance of 1650.

As the Hammersmith Works were closing, others were firing up their blast furnaces wherever bog ore was located. The largest concentration of these colonial ironworks was in southeastern Massachusetts.

Around 1751, in Kingston, Massachusetts, near Plymouth, one Joseph Holmes went fishing in Jones River Pond. Like most unlucky fisherman, he quickly snagged the bottom. Yanking the hook out he found, instead of the proverbial boot, a large chunk of bog ore at the end of his line. By the Revolutionary War the site of Holmes's fishing trip was supplying cannon shot for colonial troops.

Though the furnace could produce shot, its ore was not pure enough to be cast into cannons, which must be able to withstand the heating and pressure of firing. Iron such as this was to come from furnaces and forges 140 miles west of the Kingston furnace. This was the iron industry that grew up around a deposit of ore discovered in Salisbury, Connecticut.

In 1731 two men, John Pell and Ezekiel Ashley, laid hold of a tract of land in northwestern Connecticut that they knew to hold an iron deposit. At that time the area was uninhabited and called simply "Town M." on state maps. When they began mining the ore a year later it proved to be incredibly free from impurities. As most ironmaking costs involved the removal of these impurities, the mine attracted a slew of little forges that sprang up along nearby streams where water-power could pump bellows and raise triphammers.

Among those attracted to the Salisbury Iron District, as the area grew to be called, was an outspoken freethinker whose main defense from public censure was his readiness to fight anyone who disagreed with him. This was Ethan Allen, later the leader of the Green Mountain Boys who captured Fort Ticonderoga. In 1762, at the age of twenty-four, Allen bought into a partnership bent on converting one of the small forges into a great blast furnace. Three years later Allen sold his interest, but by this time the little forge in the town of Lakeville had become Connecticut's first blast furnace. It produced excellent pig iron that was then sold to the small forges to be recast or hammered into pots, kettles, nails, tools, and other retail products.

The brawling Allen, who settled his differences in taverns or on the public highway, epitomized the early ironworkers. Theirs was a hard, dangerous profession where a slip meant maiming or death. There was no protection from the flames and poisonous gases that belched from the furnacetop for the men who poured the ore, lime, and charcoal into the molten mass below. The ironmaster himself periodically hung over the furnacetop as he poked the burning mass with a measured pole to determine the height of the charge. Down below the men pouring the metal had only leather aprons for protection from the white-hot metal that came out at their feet. At the refining forges there was also the problem of gradual deafness from the noise of the great trip-hammers.

"The workmen are thought to be very chargeable and froward," complained a letter describing a new forge set up in New Haven contemporary with the Hammersmith Works.[5] At Hammersmith itself the English ironworkers had quickly alienated themselves from their Puritan neighbors by refusing to stop work on Sundays and by drinking an inordinate amount of rum no matter what day of the week.

Things were no different at the Lakeville Furnace, and when the Revolutionary War turned it into the Continental army's source for cannons, the ironworks' 59 laborers were given whatever they needed "to enable them to better carry on the Furnace and continue the blast," by a 1777 order of Connecticut's war office, the Council of Safety.[6] Among these "necessities" were pork, blankets, exemptions from conscription, and a good deal of rum. In turn the Salisbury Furnace turned out cannons and soldiers' cookpots.

As the tide of battle turned to the side of Washington's army, the need for more cannons dropped off; the colonists now used captured British guns. Soon the furnace was no longer needed in the fight for independence, and within a few decades it had fallen to ruin. Today only an old cannonball cast in the Lakeville Furnace stands in the town near the site of the old ironworks.

With the War of 1812, the Salisbury Iron District again rose to prominence, this time by means of a blast furnace located in the high plateau of Mount Riga, far above Salisbury. The Mount Riga Furnace first went into blast in 1810. Unlike the area's other furnaces and forges,

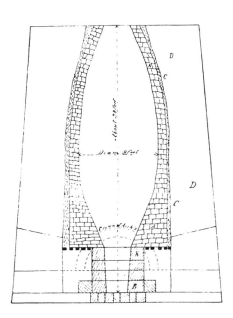

Cross section of Ethan Allen's furnace at Lakeville, Connecticut's first blast furnace. A: the fire-brick lining; B: the hearthstone where the molten iron collects; C: a separating insulator of sand or loose stone between the inner lining and D: the permanent outside walls of the furnace.

which lay in the region's valleys, the Mount Riga Furnace was built a thousand feet higher than the Salisbury mines. Ore was first carried to the furnace in saddlebags, and later by wagon, up a steep, winding trail. Despite this, the Mount Riga Furnace had an ideal site. Built at the outlet to a large lake, it could depend on steady waterpower without the hazard of flooding that threatened the ironworks in the narrow valleys. The high plateau itself was a primeval wilderness that promised a seemingly inexhaustible supply of timber for charcoal.

When hostilities reopened with England in 1812, America's new navy began ordering its anchors from the Mount Riga Furnace. Naval officers arrived with great fanfare to inspect the newly forged anchors before accepting them for use on the *Constitution, Constellation,* and other men-of-war. The whole town, by then numbering over one hundred households, would turn out for the proving ceremony. The anchor was hoisted high in the air to the peak of a great wooden tripod, then dropped to smash against a granite block below. If the anchor bounced off intact, the navy inspectors accepted it, the Mount Riga Furnace was still in the black, and the townspeople celebrated with general festivities.

These Mount Riga townspeople — charcoal burners, furnacemen, smiths, and others — were a more international lot than their counterparts in the valleys. The spectacular growth of the works taxed the local supply of qualified workers and forced the owners to look overseas. Soon old Yankees were working alongside experienced men from Switzerland, Russia, and Lithuania, as well as Hessians and French soldiers from both sides of the Revolutionary War.

Like the Lakeville Furnace before it, the Mount Riga Furnace fell into hard times once the War of 1812 drew to a close. With no dependable navy contracts, it fell back into competition with new furnaces springing up around the iron deposits that were found all along the Appalachian Mountain Range. Even worse, the high plateau was running out of timber, and the charcoal burners had to drive their slant-sided wagons down into the valleys below to find fuel for the furnace.

The end finally came in 1847. A breakdown in the bellows allowed the charge in the furnace to cool, and before anything could be done, it had cooled into one solid mass, called a "salamander." This catastrophe occurred all too often in ironmaking. Sometimes the aggravated ironmaster brought in a small cannon and tried to smash the furnace by firing into the hearth face at point-blank range. But the Mount Riga Furnace just didn't have the money to shut down operation, remove the salamander, and start up again. Instead they gave up and left the old furnace to the elements. Today it still stands in the wilderness of the Mount Riga plateau. The little boom town that once surrounded it is reduced to a few cabins, and the only other remnant of its anchormaking days stands in front of the Salisbury Town Hall in the valley far below: the old triphammer that long ago pounded hot iron into great anchors.

By the time the Mount Riga Furnace had cooled for the last time, there were over thirty blast furnaces streaming molten iron into the

The Mount Riga Furnace, high in the wilderness plateau above Salisbury.

sands of New England's pouring rooms. Many operated sporadically, depending on local prices, demands, and ironmaking ability.

In 1805 investors from Boston and Salem began the New Hampshire Iron Foundry in Franconia, New Hampshire, a few miles north of the famous Old Man of the Mountains in Franconia Notch. It smelted a rich vein of ore discovered that same year on a mountainside just three miles from Franconia Village. The strike assayed out as the richest in iron of any bed then known. Unlike the lowland bog ore sites, this was a wall of iron ore running deep into the hillside.

The company hired ten men at $15 a month to blast out the ore and cart it downhill to a blast furnace built by the New Hampshire Iron

Foundry in 1811. Year after year the men worked the wall of ore until, by 1849, the mountainside had a vertical slice cut out of it measuring 660 feet long, 144 feet deep, and about 4 feet wide.

By 1817 the works had grown into "a blast furnace, with a reservoir of water near the top as a precaution against fire, an air furnace, a steel furnace, a pounding machine to separate the ore from the cinders, a forge with four fires and two hammers, a turning table, and a trip-hammer shop. . . ."[7]

Production and profits grew steadily to their peak around 1840. Besides the usual pig iron, the Franconia works also produced finished items — nails, horseshoes, kettles, axes, tools, and the once-famous Franconia Stove, a box-shaped wood stove highly regarded by its owners. At its high point, the works employed fifty men to serve year round and another fifty for the sixteen to twenty-six weeks that the big furnace was actually in blast.

Generally, the autumn and winter months are chosen to put the furnace in blast, the workmen then being obtained at lower wages [as there was no competition for farm labor this time of year] and the outdoor workmen being called in. It has been ascertained, also, that a larger quantity of iron is reduced, in a given time, in the winter months, which is supposed to be dependent on the more condensed and drier state of the atmosphere, by which the nature of the blast is modified; while the draught of the furnace is also affected by the heated gases and the surrounding air.[8]

So wrote the New Hampshire state geologist in 1844 after a visit to the ironworks.

In spite of its high-grade ore and its quality products, the Franconia Furnace, nestled high in the White Mountains and cut off from the main transportation routes, simply could not compete with more accessible furnaces. By 1855 the Franconia labor force had shrunk to thirty men, and ten years later the works closed for good. An 1884 fire gutted the old buildings, leaving only the old blast furnace standing, as it does today, solitary and monolithic beside the Gale River.

The most northerly of all the New England ironworks lay in the foothills of Mount Katahdin, Maine's highest mountain. This works began in 1843 after a great ore deposit was discovered there.

The ore is obtained from the side of a mountain, about a mile from the works. It is of the bog variety, lies on the surface, about an average of four feet thick, and after the scurf of earth and recent vegitation are removed, is blasted and broken into coarse lumps. The ore is full of roots, trunks, and branches of trees, which have been turned into iron, under the long continuing effects of the mineral waters of the mountain percolating among them.[9]

Color illustration 16

The Gilbert Clock Company's steam boilers.

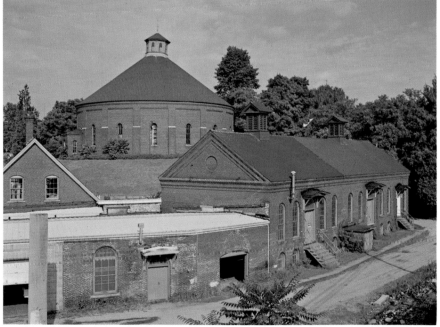

Color illustration 17

The Concord, N.H., gasholder house, built 1888. The white gauge in the center window indicates the height of the gas in the tank within.

Color illustration 18

The Hesper *(left) and the* Luther Little, *derelicts of New England's great schooner fleet.*

Color illustration 19

Looking down the interior of the Charlestown Navy Yard ropewalk, built between 1832 and 1837. At left is the machinery for twisting separate strands of rope into a thick cable.

Color illustration 20
following page

The railroad station at Maplewood, N.H. A spur line once passed through here to bring vacationers to this town nestled in the White Mountains. Today the old right-of-way has disappeared and the station stands in dense woods.

Katahdin Iron Works.

No. 1. Iron Mountain, and Mine.
2. Cupola Blast Furnace.
3. Charcoal Depot and Tramway-bridge.
4. Eight 2 story Charcoal Kilns and Reservoirs, (Brick, and Iron Bound.)
5. Forest of Hard-wood.

No. 6. Pig-Iron Foundry.
7. Blacksmith Shop and Mill.
8. Stove-casting Foundry.
9. Saw Mill.
10. Water Power.

No. 11. Hotel.
12. Barn, with stalls for 75 Horses.
13. Chapel.
14. Double Store and Offices.
15. Puddling-works.

No. 16. Dwelling Houses.
17. Pleasant River.
18. Road to Bangor.
19. Roasted Ore.
20. Superintendent's House.

The Katahdin Iron Works in 1863, from a promotional booklet issued by speculators. They bought the works upon the death of the previous owner, David Pingree of Salem, Mass., in the hopes of a profitable resale.

The ironworks ran continuously from 1843 until 1856, producing pigs of iron that were dragged out of the Maine wilderness on sleds during the long winters. After 1856 it worked intermittently, due to better-situated competition. A number of fires also hampered production, but

Works at Kent Furnace, Conn., as seen in 1872. Note the tophouse and chimneys over the furnace itself, which still stands.

East Canaan's Beckley Furnace (left) and Furnace No. 3 (right) in 1899, which both operated until 1923; the Beckley Furnace still stands.

the old furnace hung on until 1890 before finally going under. Today the state maintains the ruins as a park.

As many of the New England ironworks lost ground at midcentury, the blast furnaces in the region around Salisbury were still going strong.

With the Civil War, Salisbury Iron again turned to the making of cannon. The cessation of hostilities, however, forced Salisbury to other products. As the iron was so free of impurities, it was highly prized for making railway car wheels and axles, which, like the cannons before them, had to stand up under terrific strain.

The appearance of the blast furnaces themselves also began changing around this time. The interior chambers were redesigned to circulate the heat better and to prevent the occurrence of "salamanders." Wooden pistons replaced the old leather bellows. The furnaces themselves were built higher and "top houses" came into existence. These were structures that sat atop the furnace to protect the material as it was thrown into the blast. Previously, ironmakers had kept the furnacetop open from fear of fire, but now they optimistically built chimneys, small preparatory furnaces, and wooden sheds atop the furnace. Despite assurances by the builders to the contrary, the belching flames often went up the wrong flue, set the top house afire, and quickly burned down the whole ironworks.

But as this went on, a greater threat than fire was taking shape to destroy the whole New England iron industry. In 1865, Alexander

Richmond Furnace, Massachusetts's last furnace, a few years before its end in 1923. Note the large tophouse.

Looking up the interior of the Richmond Furnace. Near the top, some of the old firebricks still remain.

Holley, a Salisbury-born engineer, set up America's first Bessemer steel-processing plant at Troy, New York. The plant utilized the discovery, made a few years earlier in England by Henry Bessemer, that by blowing a massive amount of air into even the poorest iron ore as it lay molten in a furnace, an extremely pure grade of steel could be made. Suddenly the value of iron ore changed from its pureness to how cheaply it could be delivered to the ironworks.

As Holley built other Bessemer plants in Illinois and Pennsylvania, Salisbury iron went into eclipse. The development of massive low-grade iron deposits along the Great Lakes in the 1870s further doomed the Salisbury deposits and the New England works. Soon the gradual exhaustion of nearby trees was sending up the price of charcoal for the Salisbury furnaces while the midwestern Bessemer plants were lowering their prices as they improved their methods. By the turn of the century only three furnaces in New England were still functioning. These were the Richmond (Massachusetts) Iron Works and the Canaan No. 3 and Beckley furnaces just over the state line in East Canaan, Connecticut. All three specialized in railway products and were able to hold on by completely rebuilding their works around the turn of the century with every known improvement. But in 1923, the plummeting price of Pittsburgh steel and the skyrocketing price of charcoal had their effect. These last three furnaces were abandoned and the New England blast furnaces were no more.

Today the roar of the furnace, the pounding of machinery, and the industrial smog lies to the west in the Pennsylvania steel towns. The Salisbury Iron Region, Franconia, and Katahdin are all quiet rural delights, with only the monolithic furnace stacks to tell that once these were centers of industry.

The epitaph to their work and the salvation of their scenic beauty can be said to be the answer given by Alexander Holley when asked why he bypassed his hometown as a site for a Bessemer steel mill — "Because I like Salisbury!" he said.

13 The Kilns

High on a grassy plateau in western Connecticut the night stars shine clear and bright above the village of Ellsworth. This town of cultivated fields and dignified old farmhouses lies far from the pall of urban and industrial haze; but once, long ago, its air was filled with a choking blue smoke and the sounds of falling trees. The iron furnaces in the Housatonic Valley below demanded great quantities of charcoal and Ellsworth was one place that supplied it.

Charcoal burners came to Ellsworth to cut down her trees, heap them in dirt-covered mounds, and set them afire to smolder into charcoal. Each iron furnace consumed one thousand acres of forest each year, and it took about twenty-five years for the trees to grow back. The land needed to make charcoal was therefore tremendous and created a nomadic clan of people who followed the forests as they worked their calling.

A rude, rough, hardy set of men they are, dwelling deep in the forests, knowing little and caring still less about the wants and usages of conventional life; bound together by a community of interests, having laws and regulations of their own, which are troubled by no legal technicalities, though marked by a rude sense of justice, and enforced with a promptitude which might put many of our learned advocates to the blush. Sometimes they spend weeks and weeks alone in the woods, with their pits, sheltering themselves from the storms and night air in the little, miserable burrows made of sticks and turf, which they

A charcoal burner sleeping by his kiln. He often spent a week keeping a constant vigil to insure that the mound only smoldered and did not break into open flame.

dignify with the name of "houses," but which look more like the den of some mammoth rabbit than anything else, seeing no one but the solitary hunter, or the wife or child who comes, at regular intervals, with a supply of food.[1]

In the winter, when the sap was low, the charcoal burners cut their wood, preferably the slower-burning hardwoods like beech and oak, which was laid to season until the arrival of milder weather. Come late spring, the charcoal burner stacked the wood into mounds about twenty-five feet across. The mounds, also called pits, kilns, or hearths, were carefully covered with a mixture of sod, dirt, and leaves. The charcoal burner climbed the pile and dumped live coals down inside, igniting the wood.

For the next two weeks he lived by the mound, carefully adjusting the burn by opening and closing holes in the covering. This kept the mound smoldering, but prevented it from breaking out into open flame. Finally he removed the covering and raked out the charcoal to let it cool before bagging it for shipment.

In the nineteenth century, charcoal burners' settlements could be found in many New England backwoods, but as coal grew in popularity as a heating fuel, they slowly disappeared. The woods returned, and only the circular trenches that kept rainwater from the mounds remain as a memento of the old camps.

In a few places the charcoal industry was more settled and large kilns were built. These stone domes took the place of the dirt covering used by the itinerant burners. Near Lisbon, New Hampshire, are the remains of an old kiln built in the 1860s that once used the scrap lumber from local sawmills to make charcoal for the Franconia Iron Furnace just over the mountain.

Scenes in a charcoal burners'
camp in 1873.

In Leverett, Massachusetts, and Union, Connecticut, two old charcoal works can still be seen with their scrapwood piles, their kilns, and their columns of blue smoke rising above the trees. Other kilns were used to make bricks, pottery, cement, and limestone.

Lime burning, like charcoal burning, was another solitary profession. Since ancient times men have heaped wood and limestone, the

hardened remains of ancient seashells, together to burn into a fine powdery residue called lime, highly prized as fertilizer and building mortar.

A brick charcoal kiln in North Leverett that still operates.

In the 1850s Nathaniel Hawthorne visited the limestone beds near Adams, Massachusetts, and described a lime kiln there as

a rude, round towerlike structure about twenty feet high, heavily built of rough stones, with a hillock of earth heaped about the larger part of its circumference; so that blocks and fragments of marble might be drawn by cart-loads, and thrown in at the top. There was an opening at the bottom of the tower, like an ovenmouth, but large enough to admit a man in a stooping posture, and provided with a massive iron door. With the smoke and jets of flame issuing from the chinks and crevices of this door, which seemed to give admittance into the hillside, it resembled nothing so much as the private entrance to the infernal regions.[2]

The "blocks and fragments of marble" were limestone chunks dug from one of the many widely scattered limestone beds found folded into the New England bedrock.

Working a lime kiln.

The lime burner first built a vaulted roof of limestone blocks within the kiln and piled atop it a mixture of limestone and wood or charcoal. It was then lit, and soon,

all these innumerable blocks and fragments of marble were red-hot and vividly on fire, sending up great spouts of blue flame, which quivered aloft and danced madly, as within a magic circle, and sank and rose again, with continual and multitudinous activity.[3]

For the next week the lime burner tended his kiln, ever watchful of the fire's progress:

At frequent intervals he flung back the clashing weight of the iron door, and, turning his face from the insufferable glare, thrust in huge logs of oak, or stirred the immense brands with a log pole. Within the furnace were seen the curling and riotous flames, and the burning marble, almost molten with the intensity of heat.[4]

The lime burner's constant vigilance prevented the fire from dying out as well as from completely burning the limestone blocks, or from getting too hot and melting the limestone into slag rather than the fine powder desired by farmers and builders.

Interior of a lime kiln. Note the arch of limestone blocks that creates a free space for the fire below.

After the mixture burned itself out, it was packed into casks for shipment. It had to be moved fast because the lime quickly absorbed moisture to form into clumps or, even worse, heat from a chemical reaction with the water and catch fire. In more remote areas, as the Adams, Massachusetts, of Hawthorne's day, production was restricted to that which could be immediately used locally. Here many farmers had their own kilns where once a year they burned enough lime for fertilizing their fields.

Limestone discovered nearer cities and transportation routes fared better, such as the beds in Limerock, Rhode Island, and along Maine's Penobscot Bay. The Limerock production could be quickly casked and sent still warm to nearby Providence. In Maine the kilns stood at the ocean's shore and the lime was loaded aboard coastal schooners, called limers, for fast runs to Boston and other New England ports. Sailing aboard a limer was a heart-in-mouth profession, for there was constant danger of seawater igniting the cargo.

The production of lime as described by Hawthorne was tedious and could not keep up with the needs of the many new industrial cities

A turn-of-the-century lime kiln at Rockport, Me. Lime chunks were thrown in at the top, passed through the hearth at the center, and emerged as powder at the base. They were then loaded aboard ship for quick delivery along the coast.

A perpetual kiln that stood in Charlestown, R.I. The lime-stone blocks were broken up, at left, and hauled up on wheelbarrows to be dumped in at the top. Later the lime-stone powder that sifted to the bottom was put in casks ready for shipment.

growing up in America during the nineteenth century. As the railroads began connecting the cities with the lime regions of the Appalachians, the lime burners suddenly found themselves with a new market for all the lime they could produce. To meet these demands, the perpetual kiln was developed. Rather than burning just one charge at a time, the perpetual kiln could burn continuously, with lime being raked out the oven mouth at the base while fresh charges were being poured in at the top.

Today, although limestone is still mined in New England, new processes have long since outmoded the old kilns. Like the abandoned kilns to be found in Hawthorne's day,

long deserted, with weeds growing in the vacant round of the interior, which is open to the sky, and grass and wildflowers rooting themselves into the chinks of the stone, [they] look already like relics of antiquity, and may be yet overspread with the lichens of centuries to come.[5]

The Textile Industry 14

On December 2, 1789, a twenty-one-year-old immigrant named Samuel Slater wrote to the wealthy Providence merchant Moses Brown:

Sir: A few days ago I was informed that you wanted a manager of cotton spinning, in which business I flatter myself that I can give the greatest satisfaction in making machinery, making as good yarn, either for stocking or twist, as any that is made in England. . . . If you are not provided for, [I] should be glad to serve you.[1]

Slater had lately escaped England with intimate knowledge of the first mechanical cotton spinning machine, knowledge that by British law was not to have left the country. Moses Brown, meanwhile, had been looking for a means to expand the small household cotton manufacture in Providence that wove southern and West Indian cotton into cloth for sale to its growers. The result of this letter was the first successful cotton mill in America, and the beginning of our industrial age.

When the Slater Mill began producing cotton thread in 1791, other Providence merchants began journeying up to Pawtucket to examine the new mill. Employing nine children to watch over the "spinning jennys," the Slater Mill produced cotton yarn, which was then distributed to the local population for weaving. The Providence men marveled at the simplicity of the machinery and made plans to build cotton mills of their own.

Since transportation was still quite limited, these men chose nearby sites. The earliest mills were along the Blackstone River, which flowed out of Massachusetts to meet Narragansett Bay at Providence. The merchants hired Slater, or one of a group trained by Slater, to build their mills. By 1810 there were over a hundred cotton mills in New England. The Blackstone was now lined with a succession of mills and mill dwellings, and on its tributaries every little falls with enough power to turn the wheel likewise held a mill.

At first only cotton yarn was made, but within a few years power looms were introduced, and the mills began producing bed ticking, shirting cloth, sheets, and coverlets.

The first mills were two- or three-story wooden structures resembling slightly oversized gristmills. Yet their modest size belied the great transformation they brought about in New England's economy and social structure. In 1790, as Slater was building his mill, 85 out of every hundred New Englanders lived on a small farm. As the mills grew in number they drew on these farmers for labor, and by 1820 only 72 out of every hundred now worked on the farms and 21 worked in the mills.

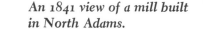

An 1841 view of a mill built in North Adams.

The Providence millowners adopted the labor system Slater brought over from England in dealing with their workers. Whole families were employed in the mill. Men and women attended the looms while their children stood by the yarn-spinning machines tying broken strands.

At first the work was pleasant, especially in comparison to the drudgery of the farm. An experienced loomgirl spent only a small percentage of the working day actually attending the looms, "the remainder she will spend according to her taste; either in solitary thought, in chatting with her associates, or in sitting down by her looms with a book, or with knitting or needle-work in her hands."[2]

Payment was in scrip redeemable only at the mill-owned store, and lodging came as part of the wage.

The mills' need of waterpower for their machinery required that the millworkers' houses be built in the river valleys, inland from the coastal cities and usually some miles distant from the hilltop-hugging farming towns. "In the most desolate and rocky situation, avoided by all human beings since the settling of the Pilgrims as the image of loneliness and barrenness, amid rocks and stumps and blasted trees, there is a waterfall. . . . Here factories are erected in this barren waste, and suddenly a large population is gathered," wrote one person describing the manufacturing towns springing up in New England.[3]

In 1825, Roger Rogerson, a Boston merchant, hired a journeyman millwright to construct a mill on the Mumford River, a tributary of the Blackstone. Near the granite, three-story mill, Rogerson built a handsome complex of little brick houses for his workers. A church was also constructed at Rogerson's expense, which he dedicated "to Christian worship without regard to sect."[4] This little village had, according to those who visited it, "more of the quality of perfection than almost any other manufacturing village in New England."[5] For Rogerson and other millowners of his era, the life of his workers was as important as the profits he reaped from them, and in his enlightened thinking the very idea of wringing the last penny from them was an abominable notion.

Rogersonville, as it was called, prospered in its early years, and in 1829 a second mill was built just across the river from the first. On March 12, 1830, Rogerson's venture was incorporated into the Proprietors of the Crown and Eagle Mills. Rogerson had flamboyantly styled his first mill The Crown, and the second The Eagle, after England and her new offspring.

As Rogerson and others were creating their little industrial Edens around Providence, mills of a different pattern were springing up around Boston. Francis Cabot Lowell, like the Providence merchants, had been finding that there was more money to be made in the textile industry than in his earlier shipping ventures. Unlike the individually built mills erected at small falls around Providence, Lowell's plan was to build a huge complex of mills at one large waterpower site, with the costs shared by a group of investors rather than met by one individual. Lowell's greatest creation was the city named after him. He chose a sleepy little farming town on the Merrimack River, north of Boston. There he built mills that not only spun and wove the cotton, but also printed and worked it into finished products. Twenty years after the

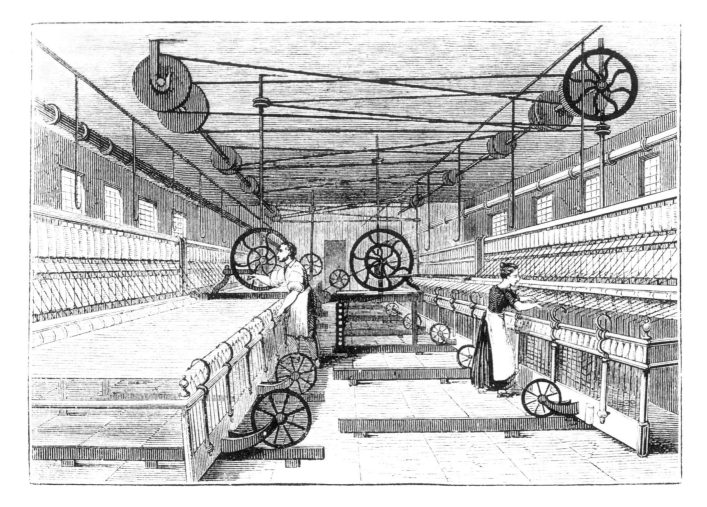

Interior of a textile mill's spinning room in 1843.

mills opened in 1822, Lowell was the second largest city in New England with 20,000 inhabitants.

To save the cost of building homes for its workers, the Lowell System hired young girls who came off the farms to live in privately owned boardinghouses. As in the early mills around Providence, the life of the "factory operatives," as the girls were called, was at first good. On a visit to Lowell in 1842, Charles Dickens declared,

[F]rom *all the crowd that I saw in the different factories that day, I cannot recall or separate one young face that gave me a painful impression; not one young girl whom, assuming it to be a matter of necessity that she should gain her daily bread by the labor of her hands, I would have removed from these works if I had had the power.*[6]

Soon after Dickens's visit this idyllic scene began to change in both the Slater and Lowell mills. The influx of Irish immigrants during the 1840s created a pool of unemployed willing to work for whatever wages were offered. Concurrently, the financial chaos that followed President Andrew Jackson's closing of the National Bank was bringing bankruptcy to many of the old millowners. In Rogersonville, the Crown and Eagle Mills passed, on December 5, 1840, into the hands of creditors, and the village's population of 400, of which 120 males and 80 females worked in the mills, no longer lived beneath Rogerson's benevolent despotism. The millowners were now absentee landlords, shareholders in a company bent on profit only, with no thought to the well-being of their workers.

Wages slumped as working hours grew. No more towns like Rogersonville were built; instead, shanty dwellings went up for the workers, dirty crowded houses with no yards and only the bare necessities.

Even in the Lowell System towns, which paid cash rather than scrip, efforts were made to keep the workman's money flowing back into the mill. One 1843 poster read:

*Notice. Those employed at these mills and works will take notice
that a store is kept for their accommodation, where they can purchase
the best goods at fair prices, and it is expected that all will draw
their goods from said store. Those who do not are informed that there
are plenty of others who would be glad to take their place at less wages.*[7]

No longer did the factory girls leave the farm of their own accord. Instead, they were tricked by promises of incredibly high wages to climb aboard

*a long, low, black wagon, termed a "slaver," [which makes circuits]
in Vermont and New Hampshire, with a commander who is paid $1
a head for all he brings to the market and more in proportion to the
distance — if he brings them from a distance they cannot easily get back.*[8]

While the cotton mills were growing up around Providence and the Merrimack River Valley, the woolen mills, the second half of the New England textile industry, were coming into existence in more widespread locations throughout New England. Unlike the cotton industry, which began officially with the construction of Slater's Mill, the woolen industry evolved from the spinning wheel of the colonial hearthside. As early as 1656, the General Court of the Massachusetts Bay Colony proclaimed, "All hands, not necessarily employed on other occasions, as women, girls & boys, are enjoyed to spin according to their skills and ability."[9] The sheep raised in colonial times discouraged woolen manufacture, as their shearings were coarse and short. It was not until 1802, when David Humphreys imported long-haired merino sheep to supply his mill in Derby, Connecticut, that New England had a workable wool. Soon woolen mills began dotting the landscape. Where the cotton mills were located in the country surrounding the seaports in order to obtain raw cotton from the South, the woolen mills sprang up inland in the hills where the sheep were raised.

On New Hampshire's Contoocook River, in the township of Hillsborough, one George Little set up a small mill in 1806. His enterprise

Rogersonville, now North Uxbridge, ca. 1830. The Crown and Eagle Mills stand at left.

Boilerhouse and rear of the Eagle Mill.

grew and by 1865 the site held a giant three-story wooden knitting mill. As described earlier in the case of so many other farming towns, the original Hillsborough high in the hills became Hillsborough Center, and the mill community went from Hillsborough Bridge to simply Hillsboro. As the woolen mills caused population shifts within the farming towns, objections were heard. "Many an old parish is weakened rather than strengthened by the growing up of a manufacturing village at the distance of some three or four miles from the old place of worship," complained the American Home Mission Society in 1849.[10] If one "observes how constantly new [manufacturing] villages are created in these eastern states . . . it cannot but occur that the men who own and control the capital by which these villages are called into existence, are the depositaries of a power which affect, widely and permanently, their fellow men," said the society in calling for a benevolent attitude from the millowners. But the age of Big Business was now beginning, and the Golden Age, where labor and owner lived in concert, had passed.

By 1850 the turbine began to be installed in mills, allowing a greater amount of machinery to be run from one waterpower site. The steam engine had also come into use, but it was still twice as expensive to run as a turbine. But by 1870 it was sufficiently perfected that forty percent of all power to the New England mills came from steam. In what is now North Uxbridge, Massachusetts, the Crown and Eagle Mills added a boiler house in 1874. Up in Hillsboro, steam was added in 1888.

With the perfection of steam, the mills no longer had to depend on falling water to drive their spindles and looms. They quickly expanded to dwarf the pre-1850 mill buildings in both size and number. By 1880, seventy-five percent of America's cotton goods were coming out of New England. The steam engines and the coal they used caused other problems, however.

The mills became dependent on the railroads to deliver their coal. Thus the remote towns bypassed by the railroad declined, while those on the tracks grew to large industrial cities.

To work the expanding mills and to keep a steady surplus of workers, the millowners brought in wave after wave of immigrants to replace the old Yankees who had gone elsewhere for employment or who had graduated to the management and had moved from the workers' shanties to individual homes on Overseers' Row. By 1902, worker turnover in a "good mill in New England" was estimated at five percent per week.[11] In that year an English visitor reported,

There are towns in Massachusetts whose cotton mills thirty or forty years ago were filled with American-born workpeople of a very good class, earning wages higher than are paid even today. As wages gradually fell by successive "cuts" . . . these towns were swept by waves of foreign invasion. Weavers from England and Scotland first drove out the Americans, only to be driven out in their turn by an army of Irish.

The original building, built in 1865, of a Hillsboro, N.H., woolen mill.

The Irish began after a while to be troublesome, and crowds of French Canadians were summoned from over the border to take their places. Even the docile "Kanucks" have now given way in some places before the invasion of Portuguese, Greek, and Syrian immigrants, and the mill superintendents are wondering what will come next. I have seen some mills' notices printed in four languages and orders given by gestures or through interpreters.[12]

The introduction of steam power, besides stimulating the growth of New England's textile industry, also portended its downfall. The South, previously hampered by the lack of large waterfalls, also began building mills; by 1905 it had surpassed New England in cotton production. Though it was not until 1914 that New England reached its greatest number of mills, it was by then producing only half the nation's cotton goods.

Fluctuating prices and a shaky economy in the early 1920s brought on a crash in 1923. All over New England cotton mills closed down, some never to reopen. One was the old Crown and Eagle Mills. On the first of July that year, the mill stopped operating, the business dissolved, and the once-classic community of workers' homes was sold off to the laborers.

The woolen mills were able to hold out a little longer. Their production had peaked in 1919 and they were just beginning to feel the pinch. For them the problem was not the South, but foreign imports,

new synthetics, their own overproduction, and the hard times that came with the Great Depression.

World War II buoyed production to some degree, but afterward the woolen mills began falling as silent as the cotton mills. Up in Hillsboro the old wooden mill let its 260 workers go in March 1952. From the 1939 figures of 281,000 textile workers in New England, the figures in 1964 read only 99,000.

While many of the old mills are now silent, others were able to attract new industries, especially electronics and plastics firms. When the little mill in Wauregan, Connecticut, not far from the Rhode Island border, closed in 1958, attempts were immediately made to find new users. The floor space was divided up and rented to whoever would pay

Textile mill in Woonsocket with a conglomerate of additions, each styled according to the taste of the day.

Looking in the front door of a millworkers' duplex on the grounds of the deserted mill complex in Carolina, R.I.

for it. In 1961 the building had fifteen tenants who, among other things, made electrical equipment, sewed shirts, sold mill remnants, assembled fishing rods, molded nylon parts, recapped tires, and graded eggs. Today the old building still buzzes with life, but the sluicegate house no longer regulates the water to the turbines, and uphill in the village the old Congregational church, once the house of worship for the mill's Yankee foremen and management, is silent and empty.

Older and less conveniently located mills fared worse. In the southwestern corner of Rhode Island a group of small towns show possibly the worst effects of the mill closings. In towns like Shannock, Carolina, Woodville, Potter Hill, and Hope Valley stand long-silent mills, their For Sale signs as crumbling and faded as the mills themselves.

In Potter Hill one can stand on a bluff and look down on a hundred years of mill design. Near the falls is a classic mill of the first decades of the 1800s, a small square building built in 1812 resembling a large gristmill. Stretching along the riverbank behind it are a succession of wooden and stone additions that slowly rise in height and stature to the design common to the large mills of the turn of the century. As in so many mill towns, one can even find a few deserted workers' homes in Potter Hill.

A dozen miles away in Carolina, the desolation is even larger. This hamlet, whose cotton mill began operating in 1841, was built on the Slater System, with everything owned by the mill. Once the mill closed, the workers, unfettered by real estate holdings, left for better pastures. Outside the mill complex new homes have sprung up, but surrounding the falls still stand the original complex of mill buildings, warehouse and store, overseers' houses, boardinghouses, and a little row of laborers' duplexes.

Long ago the noise of the mill machinery filled the air of the village with a muffled humming sound, a soft and dreamy clatter. Today all is silent and empty as the mill, the homes, and other buildings slowly crumble into the Rhode Island scrub.

Manufacturing 15

Textile manufacturing was not the only industry to rise out of the industrial revolution as it swept across New England in the early nineteenth century. In many places small manufacturing towns appeared, some individually, others in groups, to produce quite sophisticated products. While these manufacturing towns can be found throughout New England, a great number of them are located in the western half of Connecticut. Here can still be found the clock, silver, brass, copper, hat, and tool industries that grew from post-Revolutionary roots, roots that by the Civil War had made New England the manufacturing center of America.

The story of Yankee craftsmanship began on the isolated hill farms. There, generation after generation of New Englanders lived self-sufficiently, making most of whatever they needed themselves. As transportation routes improved, the farmers were able to market not their produce, which would probably spoil on the long trip, but rather their hearthside products. Suddenly the straw bonnets, boots, wooden chairs, buttons, palm leaf hats, barrels, brooms, and farm tools previously fashioned for home use could be carted to the cities to be sold at a profit.

Often the arrival of one skilled craftsman would turn the whole town toward that specialized manufacture. For instance, in 1780 Zabok Benedict opened a hat shop in Danbury, Connecticut. Soon his three-man shop spread until the little town was one giant hat factory. As these specialized areas grew, new customers for the increased production had to be found. Thus began the Yankee pedlars. A young man would

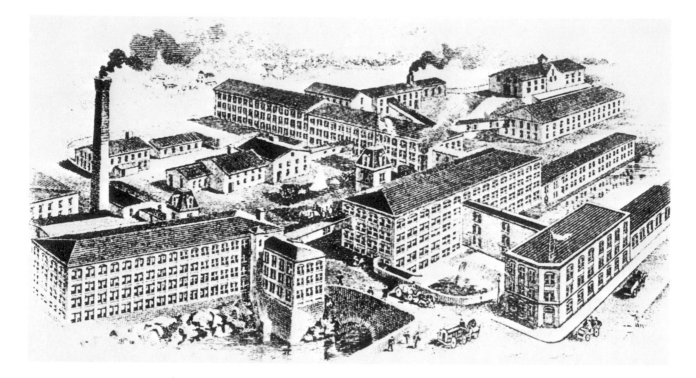

The Gilbert Clock Company in 1903.

load up the town's production on a wagon and wander from town to town selling and bartering his merchandise until his wagon was empty. He usually then sold the horse and wagon as well before returning home to start again.

The next stage in New England's industrial growth was the change-over from hearthside to factory production. Once again the effects of hill farm life aided the effort. While the adult farmers had slipped into the drudgery of the hill life, their children were still enjoying challenges as they learned the resourcefulness and versatility that by adulthood could become boring repetition. Those who escaped the farms with their enthusiasm intact carried with them the germs of innovative genius that ushered New England into the mechanical age. Accustomed to getting by with what was available, they adapted the rude mill machinery to new uses; as workers, their versatile skills made up for the shortcomings of the original equipment as they turned out quality products, and through their mechanical knowledge they improved upon the crude machinery until it was transformed into instruments of mass production.

It was this self-reliant attitude of the New England people that gave America so many of its industries. But today technical craftsmanship is not limited to New England — or even to America, for that matter. New England industry, the sole producer of many sophisticated items in the nineteenth century, must today compete in a market against more modern factories closer to raw materials and power sources. No longer will a modest waterfall supply enough energy to keep factory machinery

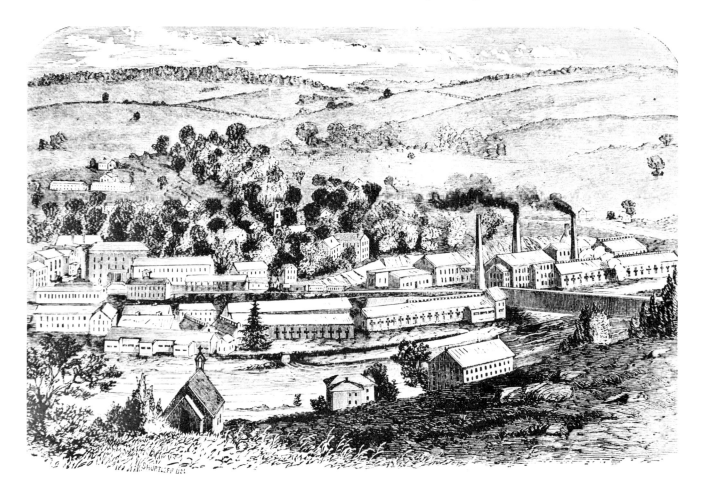

turning. In many cases the machinery itself, while constantly upgraded, has changed little since the nineteenth century. Many of these old New England industries now operate on a thin profit margin, and any large incident such as a fire or flood, which a hundred years ago served as an opportunity to rebuild with better and newer equipment, is too much for the company's shaky finances and forces it under.

Two such old factories, the Gilbert Clock Company in Winsted and the Collins Ax Company in Collinsville, lie in the watershed of Connecticut's Farmington River, where so many industries first grew, attracted by the many falls and fast-running streams. But on August 19, 1955, a great flood hit the area and destroyed many of the old factories both physically and financially.

In 1771, the little town of Winchester, Connecticut, high in the Litchfield Hills, was officially incorporated. Like so many other hill towns, it was soon abandoned by progress when the newly completed Greenwoods Turnpike bypassed it to snake up a nearby valley in 1799.

Sometime in between these dates, one Abraham Filley, who worked in a gristmill in the turnpike valley, whittled himself a clock. By 1803 the waterwheel that turned the grindstones where Filley worked was also powering primitive clockmaking equipment. Within three years,

Collinsville and the Collins Ax Company in 1872. A one-business town, it, like so many other New England factory and mill towns, operated much the same as a feudal barony.

the gristmill was entirely devoted to the manufacture of clocks, and these wooden timepieces were being carted over the turnpike to be sold throughout the eastern seaboard.

The enterprise grew as more and more farmers left the high farms in Winchester and Barkhamsted, the towns on both sides of the little valley settlement, to make clocks. As the settlement grew it took its name from both parent towns to become Winsted.

The Winsted works was not the only clockmaker in Connecticut. There had been many local clockmakers and some, such as Eli Terry at Terryville, Seth Thomas at Thomaston, and others at Bristol, had adapted machinery to the production of clockworks.

Not all the designs of wooden clocks were entirely successful, as this advertisement in an Easton, Pennsylvania, newspaper of 1831 relates:

NOTICE

Whereas Henry Lewis, a Yankee Wooden Clock Pedler, some time in December, 1831, sold . . . a number of Wooden Clocks which he guaranteed as patent and to keep good time — and took in payment thereof our notes of hand [promissory notes]. . . . Now this is to give notice to all persons not to buy said notes, as we are determined not to pay them unless compelled by law — the said Clocks not performing in the manner warranted.

Robert Newel
Abraham Levering
John Merwine
Sarah Sox

Mount Pocono, Dece. 15th, 1831.[1]

It apparently was not a Winsted clock, for the clockworks prospered and expanded throughout the nineteenth century. The first simple clock-making equipment — water-powered punches that shaped the clock's few metal pieces — slowly gave way to a completely mechanized factory by 1872.

A year earlier the original works had burned down and the company's president, William L. Gilbert, determined to build a modern factory in its place. Gilbert, who had taken command in 1845 — and for whom the company was then named — was himself an eccentric sort. When awakened one night with news that the factory was ablaze, he calmly said, "Well, I don't know that I can help it," and went back to sleep.[2] A thrifty old Yankee, he was always pinching pennies. One story goes that an employee once told him, "If I had your money, I certainly wouldn't live like you do. I would get some enjoyment out of life," only to have Gilbert tell him, "Do you know what would happen if you had my money? I'd have it back again in two years."[3]

Though Gilbert was always interested in profits, he did not want to gain at the expense of his workers. Like so many of the industrial barons of nineteenth-century New England, Gilbert was a benevolent despot. He financed schools, old people's homes, and recreation areas, improved Winsted's streets, and built homes that his laborers could purchase on long-term agreements. After he died in 1890, the Gilbert Company weathered the changing economy of the first half of the twentieth century, but it was slowly being pushed out by other American companies as well as Swiss, German, and Japanese imports.

Around 1950 the Gilbert Company tried diversifying into business machines. But before it could recoup its expenditures in tooling up, the August 1955 flood buried the factory in mud and debris.

While it quickly rebuilt on the million dollars' worth of ruins, the company was too shaky to last. In 1970, the factory that stood on the site of the old gristmill where Abraham Filley whittled his first clock closed its doors for good.

A dozen miles from Winsted, the waters that flow past the empty buildings of the Gilbert Company make their way through the power canals and over the dams that once powered another old New England factory. Here, in the classic company town of Collinsville, Connecticut, an old blacksmith shop–gristmill–sawmill was converted in 1826 to the world's first ax factory. Previously, all axes had been hammered out by local blacksmiths at a rate of one per day, but two young brothers, Samuel and David Collins, aged twenty-four and twenty-two respectively, thought they could do better. Instead of one man working the ax from start to finish, the Collins brothers divided the production into four phases: cutting the metal into its basic shape, hammering it into a hard temper, sharpening its edge on great grindstones, and finally polishing the finished ax. By 1828 the Collins Company was putting out eight axes a day for every man employed. In 1831 Samuel Collins wrote of his axes, "Having taken unbounded care to make a superior quality of work, without reference to cost, the demand increased rapidly."[4] In the 1860s 1,500 tools were leaving the plant each day.

Under the Collinses' guidance, the factory and the town around it grew steadily. The company built homes and stores, and converted one of its buildings into a church–dance hall–theater–library for its workers. According to Samuel Collins, "It has been said that our manufacturing villages have a demoralizing tendency. I wish to show there can be an exception. I would rather not make one cent than to have men go away from here worse than they came."[5]

Collins kept a rapport with his workers; in hard times he gave them a straight-from-the-shoulder explanation of finances and in turn listened to their side. This penchant for listening to others was what really sent the Collins Company into the forefront of edge tool manufacture. In 1850, a Cuban importer of Collins axes decided to write the home company to ask if they would make a machete of his design that would cut sugar cane. The Collins Company quickly filled the order and many other requests for specially designed knives began arriving. Soon the Collins forges were turning out a variety of machetes, one just right for

A Collins Company steam triphammer in 1872. It replaced the old water-powered triphammers.

A row of grinding wheels for sharpening the Collins tools. While the barriers provided protection from flying chips, there was no shield from the dust that hung in the air to debilitate many workers with the commonly fatal ailment called "grinder's lung."

The Collins Company buildings today.

sugar cane, another for banana harvesting, and so on into 150 different designs. In South America a "Collins" became the staple tool for every agricultural activity, not to mention the basic armament of many a Latin American revolution.

While Samuel Collins listened to his workers and customers on business matters, there was one subject he closed his ears to — alcohol. One of Collins's first acts in developing the settlement that grew into Collinsville was to buy out every place in town that sold liquor, one drugstore and two taverns. At one point he went so far as to pay a "bad influence" to sign a promise that he would leave the town and never come within ten miles of it again.

Yet for all its success, the town and its factory could not stand up to the massive industrial plants that were its competitors in the twentieth century. The eighteen acres of buildings and yards survived until 1966, when the factory closed down.

The Collins Ax Company flourished in a time when waterpower lifted the old triphammers, and raw materials came in by saddlebag and wagon from the Salisbury Iron District to the west. Its name still lives, but it appears on the tools of competitors who bought out the old name of this modest factory on the banks of the Farmington River.

16 The Gasholder Houses

At a few sites scattered across New England — in Concord, New Hampshire; Boston and Attleboro, Massachusetts — stands an all-but-forgotten remnant of the Gay Nineties Gaslight Era, the gasholder house: a circular brick building a few stories high, with a peaked roof topped by a cupola and weathervane.

Looking to all the world like huge, bricked-in merry-go-rounds, the gasholder houses protected the early versions of the battleship-gray gas storage tanks that today rise many stories above our cities' industrial sections. Between the 1870s and 1920s, gasholder houses could be found in most New England cities. They were built from an unlikely blend of economy, technological ignorance, aesthetics, and deceptive packaging.

The gaslight of the last century was not the natural gas in use today, but rather the highly toxic vapors liberated from heating coal in a closed space. Although knowledge of coal gas goes back to the ancient Chinese, it was not until 1802, when inventor James Watt used it to power his steam engine, that its practical aspects were recognized. Within the next decade, the production of "gaslight" became a thriving business, and in 1822 Boston became the second city in the United States (after Baltimore) to have a gasworks.

With the rise of industrialism in the last half of the nineteenth century, the gasworks began expanding production. Like the nuclear plants of today, this new source of power had problems. The greatest was storage. There were times of the day when little gas was used and

other "peak periods" when all over the city householders were turning on their lamps and lighting their stoves. At night the streetlights came on, adding to the daily fluctuation of gas consumption.

Rather than attempting to match production of gas with the hour-by-hour demand, the gas companies built tanks to store the gas produced during slack hours for use during times of heavy demand. These storage tanks had to be collapsible to push the gas out through the mains to the users' lamps. When constructed, they resembled great iron pots hung upside-down in a deep pool of water. One pipe fed the gas just produced into a tank and a second carried it from the tank to the street mains. The giant, riveted tank rose and fell on pulleys as the gas was

Making coal gas in 1862. The coal is cooked in ovens, at right; the liberated gas is collected above in pipes that feed the gas to the gasholder tanks.

The Lowell Gas Light Company in 1884, a typical gas-making plant of its time. The problem of increased need was solved by constructing additional gasholder houses to compensate for the greater fluctuation in use.

pumped in or piped out while the pool of water beneath kept a perfect seal around the base.

Though simple in principle, the gasholders were anything but that in operation. The summer sun on the dark iron tank heated the gas within to many times its normal volume, cutting the tank's storage capacity. The winter weather froze the water seal, piled heavy snow on the delicately balanced tank, and clogged the movement of the pulleys and counterweights. The tank itself sprung leaks between its riveted cast iron plates whenever temperatures became extreme. This leaked gas sometimes ignited, touching off the whole gasholder tank and laying waste to the surrounding neighborhood.

Fear of the gasworks was quite widespread, and in 1866 the Boston city physician replied to a city hearing on gas plants:

With regard to your question, whether I would be willing to occupy a house in the immediate vicinity of such works, I must unhesitatingly reply in the negative. I would on no consideration voluntarily subject myself or my family to the chance of inhaling or being annoyed by the smell of this gas.[1]

Other Boston opponents to the expansion of the gasworks also claimed that

*the Gas House corrupts the air; it emits a smell that has a tendency
to suffocate invalids; the Gas deposits a powerful oil which penetrates
the soil; and the overflow enters the drains, to the annoyance of
the neighborhood.*[2]

To alleviate fears and to remedy the problems inherent in the tanks, the gas companies surrounded the tank with a building, a gasholder house, to protect the tank from the elements.

The walls of the building supported the tank as it rose and fell each day. Despite all efforts, the tank still leaked a bit, so a cupola was built at the top to provide an exit for the fumes. At the gasholder house's small, porchlike entranceway was located the machinery that regulated the gas flow in and out of the tank. For measuring the volume of gas within, pulleys attached to the top of the tank ran an indicator along a giant yardstick on the wall. In Concord, New Hampshire, this measuring scale can be seen on the gasholder house's outer wall.

In addition to supplying protection from the elements, the gasholder houses served a psychological end as well. Like the strange shapes of today's nuclear power plants, the naked holding tanks of the early gasworks, with their skeletons of girders, were a new and uncomfortable sight to people, adding just one more reason to dislike them. A rounded brick building, on the other hand, was something more familiar, especially when windows were added to give it a look of human habitation.

The most impressive gasholder house still standing is in Concord, New Hampshire, on the grounds of the city's gasworks. The Concord gasholder house, like the hundreds of others across the countryside at the turn of the century, became outmoded in the 1920s. By this time engineers had licked the problems of faulty seals, ice on the balance pulleys, and all the gas tank hazards. Now, instead of a number of gasholder houses, they could build one gigantic boilerplate tank to meet the twentieth century's growing need for energy — a growth that can be easily seen at the Concord gasworks, where the quaint old gasholder house is toylike compared to the great steel plate and girder gas tank that shades it.

17 The Coastal Schooners

The history of New England sailing ships and the sea is long and varied. There were the Nantucket and New Bedford whalers, the Salem China trade, clipper ships rounding the Horn, Revolutionary War privateers, and more. Today the ships that served these trades have almost all vanished, and only a few survivors are preserved in the maritime museums. Yet there is one chapter in New England's age of sail that has been for the most part forgotten — the heyday of the coastal schooners around the turn of the century, the last era of sail before engine-powered ships relegated sailing ships to their present status of pleasure craft.

The story of the schooner began in 1745, when a New England shipbuilder got the idea of adding a second mast to a sloop, a one-masted ship similar to our common sailboats. When the ship was launched, the momentum gained in sliding down the waves carried her far out into the harbor. This prompted a bystander to exclaim, "See how she schoons!" an old New England word meaning to skim like a flat rock skipped across the water. The ship's owner, hearing this, decreed with typical brevity, "A schooner let her be."

The first two-masted schooners were built for fishing, but for the next hundred years they acquired a reputation along the Atlantic coast as excellent trading vessels as well. From the 1750s to the 1850s, however, they were overshadowed by another type of sailing ship, the square-rigger. On this ship square sails were hung from horizontal yards attached to the masts. This was the classic seagoing design used on whalers, clippers, merchantmen, men-of-war, and on almost all great sailing ships. Its popularity came from its ability to carry the maximum amount of sail, giving it the great speed needed in long ocean voyages. The one problem with the square-riggers was the great number of men needed to climb the mast, walk out on the yards, and haul and furl the sails, but as long as there was no competition, large crews of fifty or more men were simply an expected part of expenses.

In the mid-1800s this domination of the seas was challenged by the new oceangoing steamships. The deciding factor against the square-riggers was found to be the great cost of maintaining their crews. Steamships used costly fuel, but it did not equal the payroll of fifty men. One by one the square-riggers disappeared; rich shipowners converted their fleets to steam while their poorer cousins simply ran their ships till they rotted or foundered. The shipmasters knew, however, that if they could only reduce the need for such a large crew, they could successfully compete with steam. To do this they returned to the design of the schooner. Since the schooners' mainsails were not hung off fixed horizontal yards but run up the masts from the deck, all that was necessary were a few strong backs on deck. From a gang of over fifty sailors scrambling over a square-rigger, only a dozen men were needed on the same ship converted to schooner sails. Also gained in the transition was the ability to get under way quickly. It took a square-rigger crew a half day to unfurl sails while the same-sized schooner had its sails hoisted in half an hour.

Maneuverability was a third gain. While the square-rigged ships needed to be driven by winds from the rear, the schooners could tack like a sailboat, choosing a course independent of the prevailing wind.

Winter at Sea — Taking in Sail off the Coast, by Winslow Homer, 1869. A crew of a dozen or more men is needed to change the sails.

A two-masted schooner at the mouth of the Park River in Hartford. With a ship of this design, a crew of only two or three can hoist and lower sails with pulleys from the deck.

This flexibility was a great advantage in coastal trade. Schooners could zip into a harbor, unload, and be gone again in no time. By the 1850s, when steam began edging out square-riggers, the schooner had become a common sight in American seaports.

The first four-masted schooner appeared in 1880. By then the schooners rivaled the great clipper ships in size. For the most part the schooners stayed close to America's coastal waters on short, few-day hauls, although they also ventured through the Caribbean to South America or across the open Atlantic to Europe if that was where a profit was to be found.

At the turn of the century, New England shipyards were turning out hundreds of schooners with five, six, and even seven masts.

One of the old schooner shipyards still remains. This is the now-silent Percy and Small Yard in Bath, Maine. Once the whole New England coast was covered with these yards wherever there were quiet water and good timber. Unlike the great shipyards of today, the old ones were modest affairs, with about three or four barn-sized buildings for storage and rigging. The actual work of building the ship was done on the ways, where shipwrights used hand tools to chop and carve the ship from the keel up out of raw lumber.

The greatest of all the schooners was launched at the Percy and Small Yard in 1909. This was the six-masted *Wyoming*, 330 feet long, the largest wooden ship to that date. Despite its size it needed only a fourteen-man crew.

Yet there are few people who know the history of this great ship. Unlike the romantic whalers, clippers bound for China, or fast trans-atlantic packets, the *Wyoming* was simply a giant freight hauler. She carried two hundred railroad cars' worth of coal on each week-long voyage from Chesapeake Bay to New England until she went down in a storm in 1924. Other schooners carried such varied cargo as sugar, guano, coconuts, ice, casks of lime, lengths of timber, or giant granite blocks — in short, whatever was in bulk and near the sea.

While the clippers had been built well ballasted and with a deep keel to take the waves and strong winds of the open seas, the coastal schooners had no ballast and a flat, relatively shallow bottom to be able to work in small harbors. Sometimes, when there was no wharf available, the schooners sailed up onto the beach at high tide and unloaded their cargo when the receding tide left them high and dry.

To compensate for the lack of a deep hold, the schooners had a wide beam. While this design was ideally suited for small harbor work, it tended to make the ship a wallowing bathtub in the high seas. To counteract this, the schooner shipwrights curved the lines of the ship to carry the bow and stern farther above the water than amidships.

Probably the highest bow of all the schooners was that of the *Cora F. Cressey*, a five-master built in 1902 at the Percy and Small Yard. She was 273 feet long with a 45-foot beam and a draft of only 30 feet. It was said that, even fully loaded, her bow stood 40 feet above the water and that no storm wave ever broke over it. Like the *Wyoming*, the *Cressey* was built to carry coal on the Chesapeake Bay–New England run.

While her bow might tower over the waves, the schooner's midships usually rose only a few inches above the level of the sea, as it was common practice to load every last ounce of cargo possible without sinking her. At sea, every little wave washed across the decks. This overloading, besides being a safety hazard in storms, put a terrific strain on the ship's hull. With these problems constantly at hand, the schooner captains were a quite conservative lot when it came to facing bad weather, and at the first sign of a storm they quickly made for the nearest harbor. Many a schooner was lost by foundering because she was caught by a storm too far out to make it to a safe anchorage.

In 1924 the *Cressey*'s high bow apparently saved her from such a fate when she was able to ride out a gale that sent two companion ships to the bottom. From then on, the *Cressey* was known as the Queen of the Atlantic Seaboard.

The feel of one of these old schooners in motion comes across well in this account of sailing on the 180-foot *James E. Newson* into Edgartown Harbor on Martha's Vineyard:

"Queen of the Atlantic Seaboard" was the name given to the Cora F. Cressey because of her high bow.

Then, with the ship racing along a good nine knots, the order was given to come about. No sluggishness now! She came up and fell off almost with the quickness of a large yacht.

On this course nearly six points from the wind, the NEWSON picked up speed until she was making better than 11 knots, and the sensation experienced while at the wheel, or standing about amidship, was one never to be forgotten. It was not the push of steam nor yet the pull of a fast sloop — it was both, and more. To me it seemed as though we had become part of some tremendous and irresistible force which nothing could stay. The hurtling of the water along the sides and hum of wind in the rigging blended into one great roar as we swept down past the buoy and hauled up past Cross Rip L.V. [lightship]. We bore on for Edgartown with diminished speed but with windage to spare, for the captain's calculations had worked out perfectly, and about 5 o'clock he ordered sail off, shot the ship into the wind, and let go the anchor just off the bell buoy at Edgartown. It was all done as smoothly and as quickly as it could be done in a 60-footer.[1]

A view of the action on the deck of the Cora F. Cressey. *Today the ship is a lobster storage pound on the coast of Maine.*

Yet this idyllic picture was not the norm. For one, it was almost always impossible to stand amidships, as the deck was piled high with cargo. When lumber was carried, the ship was loaded until it literally foundered with only the buoyancy of the cargo keeping her from sinking. One sailor told of shipping out "with a deckload so high that the man at the wheel had to stand on the wheelbox in order to see the end of the bowsprit."[2] Once in port and unloaded, the ship would be pumped out, ready for another run.

Pumping seems to have been the major occupation of the schooners' crews. The overload literally split the ship at its seams and separated the relatively short boards used in building the hull. Every captain had his own remedy for leaks, some quite peculiar. "I have seen the old skippers take a bucketful of dried out horse manure, or fine sawdust, tie it to a pole, and push it under the bottom, where it would be sucked in some of the leaks," wrote one observer.[3]

These captains were themselves quite rugged individualists, many starting as deckhands in childhood and working their way up. On the smaller, two- and three-masted schooners, the captain was often the owner, relying on shipping brokers in different ports to line up his cargoes. The bigger ships were usually part of large shipping fleets that transacted all their own arrangements.

At their peak at the turn of the century, life was good on both large and small schooners. The ships were never more than a few days from port, and there was neither the monotony of longer voyages nor the problem of keeping fresh food. Like the logging camps, the reputation of a schooner hung on the quality of its cook. Tales are told of a Martinique cook whose ship hit a storm off Cape Hatteras: "For several days the steward stood in the galley with water half way up to his knees, boiling coffee in a pot that was wired to the stove, and he apologized each day to the captain for not giving him his 'regular roast.'" Not long afterward the good man reacted to a disparaging remark about his cooking by attempting to behead the offender. At the next port the berserk cook was delivered to the authorities and a new one hired. The new cook proved so poor that the captain finally decided, "The next time he would hold on to the good cook, even if he were a murderer, as he preferred to be chopped to pieces to being slowly starved to death."[4]

Short voyages also allowed the skipper's wife and family to live aboard. Ofttimes the crew of a small schooner were a half dozen of the captain's sons, cousins, or other assorted relatives. This became more and more common in the 1920s and 1930s, when competition from steam began edging out the coastal schooner trade. As in the case of the square-riggers, the cost of the crew was forcing the schooners into bankruptcy, so the use of unpaid relatives was the only solution.

While the slow decline of the schooners began only a few years after their high point at the turn of the century, they experienced a brief resurgence when World War I created a great need for any type of seagoing transport. The old schooners found themselves back making a profit and schooner shipyards resumed production.

Two such ships were built at the yards in the now-quiet village of Somerset, Massachusetts, a town that shows only a few stone wharves and sea captains' mansions to remind visitors of its important link with the sea. These ships were the *Luther Little* and the *Hesper*, built in 1917 and 1918 respectively. Both four-masters were over 200 feet long and spent the postwar era running the Atlantic coast of both American continents, and even a few trips to Europe, with cargoes of lumber, guano, and coal. But they sailed with ever-decreasing profit, as seagoing tugs came into prominence and many an old schooner was stripped of her masts to become a barge, towed in line with others behind the tug.

By the 1920s the schooners were in such poor condition, physically and financially, that every year about ten percent of the remaining schooners was lost at sea or, for the lucky, grounded out in some harbor. It was by then generally assumed that every surviving schooner had gone down and been subsequently raised at least once.

Planking the hull of a schooner at a New England boatyard.

With such staggering mortality figures, insurance companies under-writing the voyages either stopped writing policies or did so at astro-nomical rates. The shipowners were forced to sail without insurance and soon the only cargo offered them was the virtually unsinkable lumber.

Marine law inhibited owners from converting their coastal schooners to diesel or steam. While making no rules about the size of crews (which by now were pitifully low), marine law required that any engine-powered (as opposed to sail-powered) boat have three licensed mates, two licensed engineers, and at least two men forward. A crew this size was much too great to allow the schooner a fair profit from the type of hauling it carried on.

During the 1920s and 1930s, schooner after schooner was simply laid up in some harbor and abandoned. In 1927 the *Cora F. Cressey*, the Queen of the Atlantic Seaboard, was reported by the Coast Guard to be "derelict and a menace to navigation" as she sat at anchor at

Searsport, Maine.[5] Ransacked, stripped of her sails, her hold half filled with water, and listing badly, her end looked near. Yet she was reprieved. A group of Boston businessmen towed her to their city, fixed her up, and opened her up at one of the city's docks as the Showboat, a floating restaurant and dance hall. In 1938 the Showboat closed and the *Cora F. Cressey* made her last trip Down East to Maine, where she has since spent the passing years as a lobster storage pound.

Other schooners were not abandoned by their skippers but lost in sheriffs' auctions to pay back debts. In June 1932 the *Hesper* and *Luther Little* were acquired in this way by Frank W. Winter of Auburn, Maine. It was Winter's plan to build a railroad from the seacoast at Wiscasset, Maine, north to Quebec, with the schooners serving as an extension of this route to Boston. The schooners were towed to Wiscasset for repairs and docked at the wharves of a narrow-gauge logging railway that was to be the first part of the Wiscasset to Quebec line. Before Winter could complete his plan, the country's deepening depression forced him to give it up, and the schooners were abandoned to the worms.

Today the *Luther Little* still carries her masts and much of her rigging. The *Hesper*, grounded out beside her, though mastless, still shows the ornately painted designs of her bowsprit. They stand in the harbor like two great dark titans, surrounded by little white lobster boats and pleasure craft. They dwarf the modern ships that now fill the harbor, giving observers a feeling for the grand scale upon which New England once carried out her romance with the sea.

The **Luther Little**, *aground at Wiscasset. Much of her masts and rigging still remains, though she has greatly deteriorated since she was laid up in 1932.*

18 The Ropewalks

Through the ages, sailors and fishermen have relied on good strong ropes for their livelihoods. Without them, from thin fishing line to heavy mooring hawsers, man's travel on the sea would be quite limited.

Today we take for granted the large rope companies whose machines twist out rope for a multitude of uses. Not so long ago, however, good rope, rope that a sailor could bank his life on, was not so easy to come by. Then all rope was twisted by hand from flax and hemp fibers, and its strength depended entirely on the ropemaker's ability to keep the rope taut and the fibers well twisted as he worked it.

To do this the ropemaker used the ropewalk. This was a long plot of ground with a device similar to a carnival wheel of fortune at one end. The fibers were first attached to points on the wheel, and as an apprentice spun the wheel, twisting the fibers together, the ropemaker would slowly back away from the wheel, laying in more fibers as he went. The ultimate length of the cord made in this way depended on how far the ropemaker could "walk." After one light cord had been walked out, it would then be retwisted with others to be "laid" into a rope. In the old ropemakers' terminology, a few fibers made a yarn, several yarns made a strand, three strands made a rope, and three ropes a cable. In this manner rope could be made in one whole, strong length, with no weak spots from braiding shorter lengths together.

The first ropewalks were simply open fields, but later they were covered by long narrow sheds for protection from the elements. In the

1850s Henry Wadsworth Longfellow wrote of the great ropewalks:

> *In that building long and low,*
> *With its windows all a-row,*
>   *Like the port-holes of a hulk,*
> *Human spiders spin and spin,*
> *Backwards down their threads so thin*
>   *Dropping, each a hempen bulk.*
> *At the end, an open door;*
> *Squares of sunshine on the floor*
>   *Light the long and dusty lane . . .*
>   *In that building long and low;*
> *While the wheel goes round and round,*
> *With a drowsy, dreamy sound,*
>   *And the spinners backward go.*
> — *"The Ropewalk"*

Rope spinning. The spinner at left is covered with hemp fibers. He lays these into the strand being twisted by an apprentice turning the hooks on the wheel at right.

In the colonial days in New England, the settlers had no ropemakers and suffered for their lack. "For though our bays and creeks are full of bass and other fish, yet for want of fit and strong seines, ropes and other netting, they, for the most part, break through and carry all away before them,"[1] they complained in a letter to England, for though rope-twisting was mechanically simple, it required a skilled artisan.

It was not until 1642 that America had its first ropemaker. This was John Harrison, who brought his wife and eleven children from Salisbury, England, to Boston on the promise that he should have sole colonial monopoly of the industry.

Near the present site of Boston's South Station, Harrison began America's ropemaking industry by spinning the rigging for the colonies' first ship. His ropewalk was 10 feet, 10 inches wide, and a few hundred feet long. It was open to the weather, and only wooden posts set at intervals, off which the ropes were suspended during their spinning, defined its limits. Later he built a shed over the walk.

After Harrison's death, the monopoly expired and the long, low, narrow sheds that marked the ropemakers' trade began to characterize the waterfront of every major colonial seaport.

Boston, the hub of New England shipping, had the most colonial ropewalks. By the Revolutionary War, the ropemakers of Boston outnumbered the workers in any of the city's other mechanized trades. It was there also that the actions of a few now-forgotten ropemakers precipitated events that as much shaped the course of America's history as all the ropes that enabled colonial America to grow and profit from the seas.

According to later attempts at reconstructing the story, it all began on March 2, 1770, at the 774-foot ropewalk of Boston's John Gray, not far from the site of John Harrison's first primitive "ropefield." Around noon that day, Patrick Walker, a British ropemaker impressed

Individual strands being twisted, or "laid," into a thicker rope.

into King George's army, entered Gray's ropewalk and inquired about a part-time job. History is at odds as to who replied but all agree upon the response. The poor Lobsterback was told by a hostile ropemaker that the only job he was fit for was cleaning the outhouse. Words soon developed into fists and the British soldier Patrick Walker took the worst of it. Beaten and bruised, he fled to his barracks for reinforcements. When Walker returned with friends, they too were bloodied by the ropemakers.

Over the next few days, the British soldiers returned in larger and larger groups to the ropewalks, seeking revenge for previous defeats, each time to be beaten back by a growing population of ropemakers and other Bostonians.

On March 5, 1770, both sides, the British soldiers and the Boston citizenry, met one last time in a fatal encounter that was the flint striking steel of our country's birth: the Boston Massacre. When the smoke cleared, three colonists were dead from British muskets, two more lay dying, and the American colonists had a rallying cry against British rule.

After the Revolution, a series of disastrous fires, fueled by the piled hemp and tar (for coating the finished rope), swept the Boston ropewalks. As the land had become quite valuable with the steady growth of the city, the city fathers induced the ropemakers to move

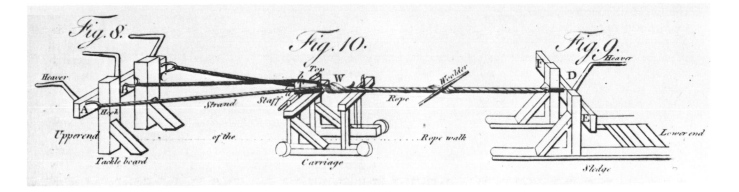

elsewhere by giving them land by the Common. Here too, however, more fires destroyed the walks. Finally the city fathers, fearful that the next conflagration might engulf the city, bought the land back from the ropemakers in the 1820s. The ropemakers' land was turned into a part of the Public Garden and the ropemakers moved out to set up their walks in the cities surrounding Boston.

One of these was the Plymouth Cordage Company's ropewalk in Plymouth, Massachusetts. Begun in 1824, it achieved a length of 1,000 feet by the time it was dismantled in 1947. Today a 250-foot segment of the old ropewalk is on display at the Mystic Seaport Museum in Connecticut.

The grandest of America's ropewalks now stands vacant at the U.S. Navy Yard in Charlestown, Massachusetts. It made, until around 1970, all the rigging, rope, and cordage for the navy. The two-story granite structure was begun in 1832 and finished five years later. Measuring 1,350 feet, it is 100 feet longer than the distance from the ground to the top floor of the Empire State Building.

By the 1850s it employed 55 ropemakers, who turned out 400 pounds of rope per day. On the top floor men spun the hemp into yarn. The light twine was then taken to the main floor, where it was laid and relaid into thick cables. To do this the ropes were laid out down the length of the ropewalk. At one end they were securely anchored to a "sledge." At the other, a "tackle board" held and twisted the individual ropes. As the rope was twisted the ropemaker moved up the ropewalk, forcing the rope to combine into a cable by means of a grooved cone called a "top." Though the navy yard ropewalk was modernized over the years, its equipment still follows this basic technique established hundreds of years ago.

Not all ropewalks made rope, however. In 1824, Captain Lester Crandall, a noted fisherman of the village of Ashaway, Rhode Island, decided that the best way to get good fishing line was to make it himself. He beat a path along the banks of the Ashaway River, set a spinning wheel at one end, and began making the best line around.

Apparently the good captain did little fishing thereafter, for today the Ashaway Line and Twine Manufacturing Company still carries on

A diagrammatic view of the preceding illustration. The carriage at center moves to the left as men stationed at the cranks, or "heavers," provide the necessary twist to keep the rope together.

The great U.S. Navy ropewalk at Charlestown in 1852.

The unused ropewalk of the still-operating Ashaway Line and Twine Company.

his work. Although the modern factory uses methods that have long outmoded the ropewalk, one still stands alongside the main building. A two-story wooden structure 725 feet in length, it is representative of the many that once dotted the eastern seaboard.

Not far from the well-maintained shell of the Ashaway ropewalk stands the remains of the Yawgog Line and Twine Company's ropewalk in Rockville, Rhode Island. Stretching 600 feet into the Rhode Island scrub behind a fieldstone factory built in 1851, it is slowly crumbling from the weight of neglect. Waterpower from a nearby pond once drove spinning wheels and carriages that shuttled up and down to replace the backward-walking ropemakers to make rope less vital than that made for ships' riggings.

Here was made the once-well-known "apple cord." This sturdy twine hung in bobbins in every general store in America and was used to tie bundles. It got the name apple cord because the thrifty Yankee farmers found it just right for stringing their apple crop up in the attic rafters, to store it protected from nibbling mice.

But be it rope, fishing line, or cable, they were once all made

> *In that building long and low;*
> *While the wheel goes round and round,*
> *With a drowsy, dreamy sound*
> *And the spinners backward go.*[2]

19 The Railroads

The railroads mark the final chapter in this story of New England's
many relics. While they did much to bring about the decline of New
England farming, the disappearance of local mills and industries, the
rise of New England as a textile power, and other events of the previous
chapters, the railroads too must be added to our list.

Unlike the canals and turnpikes, which developed out of earlier
overland and water routes, the railroads appeared suddenly on the New
England scene in the 1830s and quickly spread across the countryside.

One day a town would be peacefully sleeping in rural isolation;
the next a construction gang would pass through laying track, and
suddenly everything that had come before would be irreversibly changed
with the arrival of the first train:

*The citizens of this village, as well as the horses, cattle, etc., were
nearly frightened out of their propriety on Wednesday afternoon last
about five o'clock by such a horrible scream as was never heard to
issue from any other than a metallic throat. Animals of every description
went careening around the fields, snuffing at the air in their terror,
and bipeds of every size, condition and color set off at a full run for
the railroad depot. In a few moments the cause of the commotion
appeared in the shape of a locomotive, puffing its steam and screaming
with its so-called whistle at a terrible rate,*

reported a Stamford, Connecticut, newspaper on the arrival of the
town's first train in the fall of 1849.[1]

QUINCY RAIL-WAY

Railway Wheels

Lith. of Pendleton. *Pub. by A.J. Allan N.º 72 State street*

The first time this event occurred in New England was in 1834, when rail travel commenced between Boston and Newton, a few miles west. Even this cannot be called the earliest "rail road" in New England. On Boston's Beacon Hill a tramway had been built in 1796 to lower dirt-filled cars by ropes down the slope to provide fill for the nearby "back bay." In Quincy, Massachusetts, a railroad had been opened on October 7, 1826, to carry granite block from a quarry to tidewater docks two miles distant. From there the cargo was shipped to Charlestown to build the Bunker Hill Monument. The Quincy Granite Railway, while having cars for the granite and rails to move them on, still relied on horses for motive power.

America's first real railroad as defined by the modern conception of the term, was not in New England but in the South. This was the Baltimore and Ohio Railroad, which had steam engines pulling cars along 12 miles of track in 1830. It was the success of the B&O venture that fired New Englanders to build their own lines.

The first three of these lines radiated from Boston. The Boston–Newton tracks were the first section of a 44-mile line west to Worcester to compete with Providence for the trade along the Blackstone Canal. A second line went north along the Middlesex Canal to the great textile city of Lowell. This 25¾-mile railway cemented the shaky bond between Boston and Lowell that the old canal had begun. The third line cut southwest 41 miles to Providence in the hope that Boston could profit from the many textile mills being built there. All three of these lines opened their full lengths by the summer of 1835.

The men behind these ventures were prominent Bostonians who saw the commercial possibilities of the new railroads: men like George

The Quincy Granite Railway. Its success in 1826 spurred further interest in railroads and created the soon-discarded assumption that horses would provide the main locomotive power.

The crossing of the tracks of the Boston to Worcester Railroad and the Boston to Providence Railroad in Boston's Back Bay in 1841. Note the different passenger car designs of the two railroads.

W. Whistler, an engineer trained at West Point, and the father of the famous artist; Loammi Baldwin, Middlesex Canal builder turned railroad enthusiast; Josiah Quincy, Jr., one of a long line of patriots, presidents, and public servants. Men like these realized that Boston must have railroads or forever remain a small, local port.

Yet with all their expertise, even these men had no idea how radically different the railroads would be from all earlier means of transportation. At first it was assumed that, like the Quincy Granite Railway, horses would provide the motive power. Cars running on the tracks would be privately owned, as in the case of the canals and turnpikes. In accord with this belief, the State of Massachusetts granted charters to early railroads under the agreement that "all persons paying the Toll . . . may, with suitable and proper carriages, use and travel upon the said Rail Road."[2] Even the most learned railroad treatise of the day declared, "Nothing can do more harm to the adoption of railroads than the promulgation of such NONSENSE as that we shall see locomotive engines travelling at the rate of twelve miles an hour."[3]

As the first locomotives chugged down the tracks radiating from Boston in 1835, the naïveté of these early conceptions was quickly recognized.

On May 27, 1835, James F. Baldwin, the younger brother of Loammi Baldwin, wrote in his diary of the first round trip on the Boston and Lowell Railroad.

We left Lowell 24 minutes past seven and got to Boston in 1¾ hours — We rallied the Directors and a few stockholders etc. — to the number of 24 and started for Lowell at nine minutes past 12 — and arrived at Merrimack town in 1 hour and 17 minutes . . . all were

A decorative cut showing the first train on the Boston to Lowell Railroad in 1835. Each passenger car is three stage-coach bodies hooked together. Note the ornate station at right.

pleased with the travelling and the Engine worked well and the country people were out on the bridges and banks and the Track laborers swung their hats with huzzars.[4]

The train had sped along the track at almost fifteen miles an hour. By the fall passengers were charged $1.00 for the one-way trip.

The tracks used were not the familiar T-shaped rails used today, but simply flat strips of wrought iron laid over wood. Often the weight of a passing train pulled these strips loose, bending them upward into the floor of the passenger car overhead. These "snake heads," as they were called, were a constant threat in early railroad travel.

Another threat was the engine itself. The pioneer designs resembled a boiler on a flatcar. They lacked lights, cowcatcher, and cab, and quite often safety valves for escaping steam. The constant emphasis on speed that characterized the early railroads sometimes resulted in an exploded boiler and a maimed cargo. Until the 1860s, most locomotives burned wood rather than coal. The smoke from these engines carried sparks and bits of flaming wood off to ignite the surrounding country-side as well as the train itself.

The early passenger cars were carriage bodies set on railway wheels and linked together with chains. Within, passengers were heated from stoves that usually overturned in any mishap to end most wrecks with total destruction by fire.

Topping this list of early railroad dangers was the practice of running trains in both directions on the same set of tracks. Special sidings were set up for one train to pull off onto as it awaited the passing of the oncoming train. Often, however, a mixup in schedule or an impatient engineer resulted in a head-on collision.

An 1857 cartoon depicting a traveler's "bad luck" in missing his train. Accidents like this were common, as many railroads ran trains in both directions on a single line of track.

Unlucky Dog.

Traveler.—JUST MY LUCK, ALWAYS TOO LATE! IF I HADN'T STOPPED TO SPEAK TO SMITH, I SHOULD HAVE BEEN JUST IN TIME!

Charles Dickens, in his tour of America, rode the Boston and Lowell in 1842 and wrote of it in his *American Notes*:

The train calls at stations in the woods, where the wild impossibility of anybody having the smallest reason to get out, is only equalled by the apparently desperate hopelessness of there being anybody to get in. It rushes across the turnpike road, where there is no gate, no policeman, no signal: nothing but a rough wooden arch, on which is painted "WHEN THE BELL RINGS, LOOK OUT FOR THE LOCOMOTIVE." *On it whirls headlong, dives through the woods again, emerges in the light, clatters over frail arches, rumbles upon the heavy ground, shoots beneath a wooden bridge which intercepts the light for a second like a wink, suddenly awakens all the slumbering echoes in the main street of a large town, and dashes on haphazard, pell-mell, neck-or-nothing, down the middle of the road. There — with mechanics working at their trades, and people leaning from their doors and windows, and boys flying kites and playing marbles, and men smoking, and women talking, and children crawling, and pigs burrowing, and unaccustomed horses plunging and rearing, close to the very rails — there — on, on, on — tears the mad dragon of an engine with its train of cars; scattering in all directions a shower of burning sparks from its wood fire; screeching, hissing, yelling, panting; until at last the thirsty monster stops beneath a covered way to drink, the people cluster round, and you have time to breathe again.*[5]

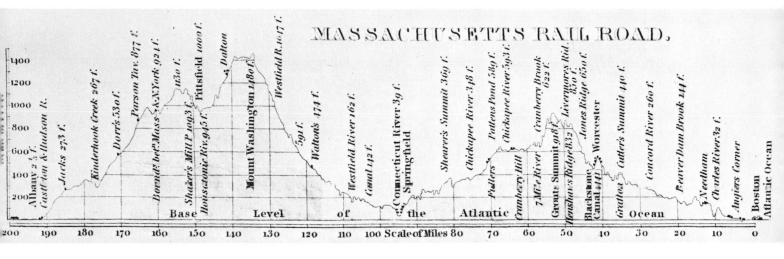

By the time Dickens was taking his ride, there were about 500 miles of track in New England; by 1851 this had increased to 2,845 miles, divided up among 61 different railroad lines.

Like the turnpikes before them, these individual lines formed links between nearby cities, and to travel any distance meant riding a number of lines. When a person traveled north from Boston into New Hampshire, he first took the Boston and Lowell, then the Lowell and Nashua, and finally the Concord Railroad. As time passed, these many small companies were, by hook or by crook, consolidated into larger trans–New England railroad systems. While the intercity lines had a great effect on the economies of the towns they reached, it was the "thru lines," especially those headed west, that affected New England as a whole.

The first of these lines was the Boston and Albany. In its original form it was three railway lines. From east to west the traveler took the Boston and Worcester to Worcester, then traveled almost the rest of Massachusetts on the Western Railroad before finishing off a short stretch of Massachusetts and entering New York State to end up just across the Hudson River from Albany on the Albany and West Stockbridge Railroad. When the complete line opened in December 1841, it became the first rail link to the eastern end of the Erie Canal. In doing so, it allowed Boston to replace New York as the Atlantic port for all trade on the canal, since traffic chose the new railroad over the old route by boat 150 miles down the Hudson River to New York City. For once in its long competition with New York, Boston became, at least for a short while, "the best market in America for the produce of the West, and the great center and depot of American manufactures."[6]

The view held by those at the western end of the Boston to Albany railroad link was a bit more droll, as they declared, "Boston may now double her importation of wooden nutmegs and basswood cucumber seeds and all the other knick-knacks that render life agreeable.

A profile of the first railroad from Boston to Albany. While the gradient is somewhat exaggerated, 200 miles to 1,500 feet, it was still no mean accomplishment for the engines of the day to pull a loaded train over the top of this route.

The Titan *and her crew: an 1867 locomotive on the Boston and Albany Railroad.*

Bring them on gentlemen, bring them on. Here is a westerly world now, open to Yankees, which all your ingenuity and industry cannot fill."[7]

By 1850 two other routes had opened New England to the west. They left Boston heading northwest, cut up through New Hampshire and Vermont on separate routes before merging near Lake Champlain and connecting with routes to Canada and the Great Lakes. They opened the Lake Champlain area and made Boston the winter port of lower Canada when the St. Lawrence River was icebound.

While these northern routes operated without competition for a great while, the Boston and Albany Railroad did not fare as well. New York City, seeing trade turn toward Boston, finished its own rail link with the Erie Canal in the 1850s. Traffic turned south down the Hudson Valley and Boston's dream of being the main port for the northern part of North America once again vanished.

Boston still kept increasing its links with the western lands, and in 1875, after twenty-five years of work, a tunnel was completed through the Hoosac Range of western Massachusetts to create the Hub's best

route west. It was a monumental effort, and when finished the 25,000-foot tunnel of the Fitchburg Railroad had cost over twenty million dollars.

The opening of these links to the West was, as described earlier, extremely detrimental to the local economies of many a New England village. As the railroad passed through the many self-contained economic systems, it flooded them with outside products that quickly undercut small, local manufacture.

The turnpike and canal companies were also quickly bankrupted. They could in no way compete with the railroad's ability to speed goods from place to place. The straight-lined canals became the road-beds for the new railroads while the many turnpikes fell into disrepair and returned by law to free-access public roads.

Also hard hit were the farmers. Strangely enough, it was often this group who had originally advocated railroads in their locales. "The farmers of central Vermont are wakening up to their true interest. The new railroad passing by them will add fifty to one hundred per cent . . . to the . . . value of labor to all those within twenty miles of its reach," reported the *Montpelier Farmer's Monthly* in 1848.[8] This was the case while the New England railroads were not yet linked with the West, but as soon as western grain began finding its way into New England in the 1850s, the farmers found themselves worse off than before. In 1867, a description of the New England railroads reported that of the 600,000 barrels of flour per year that left Albany to be shipped down the Western Railroad into Massachusetts, "40 per cent. is sold along the line, in what was once an agricultural region."[9]

While the railroads ultimately brought nothing but trouble for the New England farmers, they were a mixed blessing for the towns.

Railroad map of New England in 1900, showing the Fitchburg Railroad's Hoosac Tunnel route.

In manufacturing towns where goods were made to be sold in other regions, as Gilbert's clocks, or the Collinses' axes, the railroads brought the blessing of cheaper and faster distribution. In other towns, however, where manufacturing was sold only locally, as in the case of the Franconia iron furnace, the railroad brought large-scale competition, which the local manufactures quickly succumbed to.

Despite the ultimate benefit or harm of the railroad on the towns it passed, most people were originally opposed to having the railroad go through their towns. Dickens, in his journey up the Boston and Lowell, noted that the train kept stopping at stations far removed from towns. This was because the towns along the B&L's route steadfastly refused permission for the tracks to be laid near their villages. Once the line opened, however, these little towns realized the industrial possibilities of having a nearby railroad and soon the town centers migrated toward the outlying stations.

In the previously inaccessible regions of New England, the coming of the railroad allowed local manufacture to turn to the production of items previously too bulky for overland transport. Many upland towns turned to manufacturing products out of their most plentiful raw material, wood. As the Western Railroad wound its way up through the Westfield River Valley up across the top of the Berkshires and down into the Hudson River Valley, it created a whole string of industries based on the local wood: papermaking in Pittsfield, Russell, and Bancroft; lumber, tanbark, and charcoal in Becket. Other industries encouraged by the line were the emery mines in Chester and the ironworks in Richmond. Today papermaking continues, but many of the other industries are abandoned or have waned.

Farther east on the Boston and Albany route lies the industrial city of Worcester, which grew from a sleepy town to a great industrial center by virtue of the railroad passing through it. Before the railroad, the nearby town of Sutton, up in the hills, was a greater manufacturing center due to its terrain and consequently greater number of waterfalls, but the railroad bypassed Sutton and took a lowland route through the area. Sutton was left without an easy outlet for its goods while Worcester could ship as much as it could make. Today Worcester has a population of over 175,000; Sutton has gone from an 1839 population of 2,457 to a 1970 population of 4,590.

The gap between railroad and nonrailroad manufacturing towns continued to widen in the 1870s and 1880s, as the factories and mills turned from waterpower to coal-fed steam engines. Sutton might have had more waterpower sites than Worcester, but Worcester could build as many factories as it wished, confident that the railroads would bring in the coal to power them.

Up in the remote river valleys the factory towns realized that they too needed railway links if they were to survive. In 1849 Winsted, Connecticut, completed a railroad to the seaports along Long Island Sound, allowing speedy distribution of, among other products, the

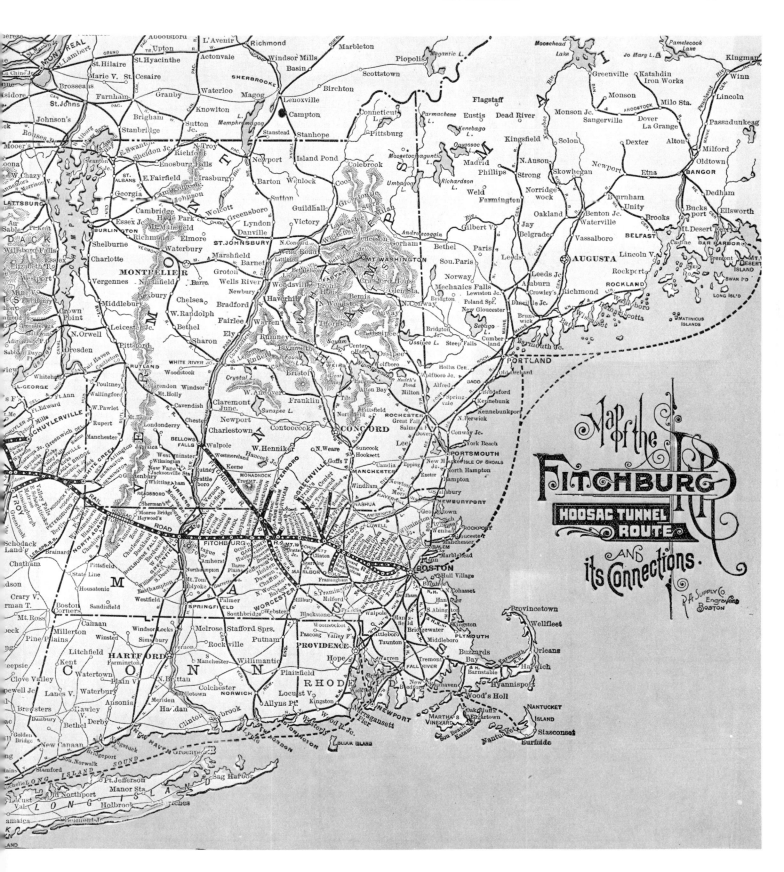

Gilbert Company's clocks. One year later the Collins Ax Company added a branch line from its factory to the main line of the New Haven and Northampton Railroad being built over the old Farmington Canal.

Though the railroad did much to force the abandonment of much New England farmland, some farmers were able to make a profit from the railroad. They turned from raising grains to livestock, which could be shipped to the cities for slaughter. This lasted only a few decades, as the expansion of the railroads into the Great Plains after the Civil War brought western beef to undercut the market. The farmers next turned to dairy products, with more success, and each morning the old "milk trains" stopped at every depot to pick up milk, butter, and cheese to be sold still fresh to urban populations later that morning.

Sometimes hill communities bypassed by the railroads built lines of their own. One such branch line was opened to connect Litchfield, Connecticut, with the through line in the valley to the south. The tracks ran a twisting 32 miles along the banks of the Shepaug River on a roadbed that included one 495-foot tunnel and 193 curves. The Shepaug, Litchfield, and Northern, as the line was called, not only carried produce to metropolitan New York, but brought summer visitors back to Litchfield, further bolstering the old hill town's economy. Like so many of the shorter New England railroads, the SL&N was financed by the people it served, but was ultimately absorbed into one of the larger railroad systems, in this case, the New Haven system in 1898. As the small lines were gradually conglomerated, the New England railroads went from control by local businesses, who profited from their existence, to control by great railroad moguls, who were interested in massive profits and, more often than not, the chance of a dishonest dollar.

By the turn of the century the hundreds of New England railroad companies and the over 7,500 miles of track were controlled by ten systems, and by the 1920s the New Haven and the Boston & Maine systems controlled almost all of New England's railroad lines. For a while it looked as if the B&M would itself be swallowed up by the New Haven until the courts stopped the takeover. The man behind the New Haven's almost complete monopoly of New England railroads was its president, Charles S. Mellen. Becoming head of the company in 1903, and with the backing of names like J. P. Morgan, Mellen began buying up, buying out, and buying control into everything in New England on rails. At the same time he invested great sums into new rolling stock, upgraded trackage, and every modern improvement that he could make on the lines he took over. The New Haven's finances slowly strained to the limit, but Mellen kept pointing to previous purchases that after a few years' deficit turned a profit. Soon, however, the Interstate Commerce Commission began examining the New Haven's financial dealings to find not a small amount of shady practices going on behind the scenes. Mellen left the presidency in 1914, but his legacy lived on.

When the new transportation lines of the twentieth century rose to challenge the railroads, the New Haven could not withstand the

An 1899 railroad map showing the Air Line route traveled by the White Train. Today the section of track between Middletown and Franklin is gone. Another now-abandoned line shown here ran from the intersection east of Danbury up to Litchfield.

onslaught and in 1935 declared bankruptcy. Buses and automobiles were hurting the railroads' short- and medium-distance passenger travel. Trucks were found more suited to the New England industries' emphasis on low volume, high technology products. As roads improved, the milk train gave way to the milk tanker truck up in the hills. Later, pipelines appeared, as did airlines, to challenge the railroads in the long-distance movement of people and supplies.

The railroads' answer to these problems has been bankruptcy, reorganization, and the abandonment of less profitable lines. From a high point of almost 8,000 miles of trackage in New England around 1920, abandonment reduced that number to 5,673 miles by 1968, and every year the number shrinks still lower, despite the reorganization of the New Haven system into the government-run Amtrak system in 1971. Many of the abandoned lines are old branch lines, built by local money to profit local industries. On the old Shepaug, Litchfield, and Northern, the last train ran in 1948, and today the right-of-way is simply a path along the banks of the twisting Shepaug River. The old tunnel is left for the occasional curious hiker to explore, and the produce of the area now goes by truck. In Collinsville, the eight miles of roadbed that connected the ax factory with the main line still makes its cindery way down to the junction, and the great iron railroad bridge across the Farmington River still stands near the factory, but the rails have been removed since the Collins Company closed and the line was abandoned in 1967.

Branch lines were by no means the only trackage abandoned; some were the main lines themselves, through lines that developed out of the connecting intercity lines that became unprofitable when the systems they were consolidated into had paralleling lines. One such route was the Air Line of the New York and New England Railroad. Unlike most other lines between New York and Boston, which followed either the Upper Path or Lower Path of colonial days and the businesses that grew up along them, the New York and New England completed a route in June 1876 that followed an almost straight "air" line between the two

The famous White Train posing for its publicity photo just outside the New York and New England Terminal in Boston. Before South Station was built on this site in 1900 and the tracks rearranged, trains leaving the terminal swung out over Boston Harbor on the trestle shown here before reaching trackage on dry land in South Boston.

cities. It used part of the New Haven system out of New York and through some of Connecticut before entering the NY&NE lines, a consolidation of the Midland, Norfolk County, Southbridge and Blackstone, and Boston, Hartford and Erie railroads. In 1882 the NY&NE itself was swallowed up by the New Haven system and the route became the New Haven Air Line. While the Air Line cut a direct path between Boston and New York, it did so at the expense of curving over and around the many rolling hills of the eastern Connecticut countryside, an area that had previously been serviced by north-south rail lines that followed the river valleys and the factories in them.

In 1884 the New Haven began running passenger expresses along the route, and on March 16, 1891, the most famous of these trains (and possibly the most legendary of all New England trains) went into service. It was a seven-car express "painted white and delicately ornamented and lettered in gold."[10] Inside, it was no less ostentatious:

The parlor cars are furnished with velvet carpets, silk draperies, and white silk curtains; the chairs are upholstered in old gold plush,

and large plate glass mirrors set off the car handsomely. . . . The royal buffet smokers which will be run in addition to the ordinary smoking cars are decorated in the same manner as the parlor cars and contain 20 handsomely upholstered chairs for the accommodation of parlor car passengers. Two card tables with stationary seats and writing desks with all needed stationery for letters or telegrams are also provided.[11]

The Worcester Station as it once looked, one of the many ornate stations in New England's larger cities. Today it is disfigured and crumbling.

A suburban station at the turn of the century in Windsor, Conn.

The same station today. Still basically sound, but lacking porch, doors, or windowpanes, it awaits an uncertain future.

It left Boston at 3 P.M. and rolled across the New England countryside, and just east of Middletown, Connecticut, passed its twin running in the opposite direction. Finally, after a six-hour ride covering 213 miles, it rolled into Grand Central Station at 9 P.M.

It was officially called the New England Limited, and unofficially the White Train, by the railroad. Along the route, however, it had another name. The New Englanders who saw it pass in the early evening felt the hair on the backs of their necks rise as the pale gold train cut through the twilight. They called it the Ghost Train. The Ghost Train lasted only four years and was discontinued and replaced in October 1895, but in that time its strange appearance created a legend familiar to every New England railroad buff to this day.

Like the Ghost Train itself, the line it ran on was also finally discarded. The reason why harkens back to the abandonment of some of the old turnpikes — the line was too hilly and bypassed the cities. Between 1963 and 1969, 112 miles of the Air Line route was abandoned, the stretch between Portland, Connecticut, and Franklin, Massachusetts.

This 1888 station in Stoughton, Mass., will survive. Its beautiful architecture combined with its modest size has guaranteed sufficient enthusiasm and funds to maintain it.

Today the tracks have been taken up, but all along the line great cuts and embankments can be found where the railroad builders tried to tame the rolling New England countryside. The viaducts are especially beautiful, as the great stone arches frame the streams that flow beneath, now unpolluted by the smoke and coal dust that once drifted down from passing trains.

Besides the more than 2,300 miles of abandoned right-of-way in New England, there are many other relics of bygone railroading to be found on the lines still used. These are the depots and village stations where the train no longer stops. In some towns they have found new uses; others simply rot. Even in the cities the once-grand stations have fallen into disrepair. Originally built without regard to cost in the manner of Byzantine buildings, Italian Renaissance palaces, and even English churches, today they look more like the results of a wartime bombing.

Even the condition of the present railroad system in New England leaves much to be desired. Few lines are in good repair, and despite the efforts of Amtrak, the traveler arrives exhausted from crowded cars, long delays, and bumpy roadbeds. An admirable summation of today's railroads was given in the mid-1960s in a newspaper interview with an elderly American Indian on his first trip to the East. After riding the New Haven main line into Connecticut, he was asked what he thought of eastern railroads. The old chief answered, "My ancestors attacked trains like these."

New England Today

The list is ended, at least for now. The hill farms are summer homes, the textile mills make computers and plastic products, suburbs cover the lowland farming regions, and only hikers are seen on the old railroad lines. And in the many forgotten corners are the relics of New England's slow transition from rural Yankeedom to a great northeastern megalopolis.

The future of these relics is uncertain. Some will be preserved and restored by future generations, others will be converted to new uses; but many will simply disappear, destroyed by the harsh climate and the often harsher hand of man. Their slow decline from the weight of successive winters is sometimes cut short as they are bulldozed to make way for the new.

Probably the greatest cause for the widespread disappearance of many of these relics is their original commonness. It is the old adage, Familiarity breeds contempt. The best example is the old railway stations. Once they could be found in every town on the line. The result is that even today it is very hard for a "save our station" committee to convince their fellow townspeople to spend money to save *their* station from the wrecking ball.

So it went for all the others — the canals, mills, mines, schooners, and the rest. They served their purpose and were then discarded. Only after their numbers shrank considerably were efforts begun to preserve some of the remains. This, unfortunately, must always be the case. Human nature dictates that time must distance us from the days of their use, and the uniqueness of a few must arise from the wholesale destruction of the many. Only then will man recognize these relics as a part of his heritage worth preserving and make efforts in their behalf.

Notes

Introduction

1. Captain Edward Johnson, *Wonder-Working Providence of Sion's Savior in New England* (London, 1654), p. 248.
2. Ibid., pp. 246–247.

2 Paths, Post Roads, and Turnpikes

1. Harral Ayres, *The Great Trail of New England* (Boston, 1940), p. 91.
2. *The Journal of Madame Sarah Kemble Knight*, 1704 (New York, 1825).
3. J. L. Ringwalt, *The Development of Transportation Systems in the United States* (Philadelphia, 1888), p. 22.
4. Isabel S. Mitchell, *Roads and Road-Making in Colonial Connecticut* (New Haven, 1933), p. 7.
5. Samuel A. Green, "Old Milestones Leading from Boston," *Massachusetts Historical Society Proceedings* 42 (1908–9):89.
6. *Acts and Laws of the State of Connecticut* (Hartford, 1796), p. 319.
7. George J. Bassett, "The Derby Turnpike," *Papers of the New Haven Colony Historical Society* 10 (1951):105.
8. Timothy Dwight, *Travels in New York and New England* (New York, 1821), Letter 44 in "Journey to Berwick."
9. S. W. Johnson, *Rural Economy* (1806).
10. Frederic J. Wood, *The Turnpikes of New England* (Boston, 1919), p. 402.
11. Dwight, *Travels*, Letter 52 in "Journey to Berwick."
12. Ibid.
13. Wood, *Turnpikes*, p. 361.
14. Ibid.

3 The Canals

1. Robert Fulton, "Mr. Fulton's Communication, December 8, 1807," *The Second Crisis in America, by "A Citizen of Philadelphia"* (New York, 1815), p. 76.
2. Albert Gallatin, *Internal Improvements of the United States* (Washington, 1808).
3. Henry David Thoreau, *A Week on the Concord and Merrimack Rivers* (Boston, Cambridge, 1849).
4. Ibid.
5. Ibid.
6. *Report and Resolution in Favor of a Loan of Credit by the City in Aid of the Canal* (New Haven, 1839), p. 5.
7. *The Northern Traveler* (New York, 1826).
8. *Engineer's Report on the Survey from New Haven City up the Canal to Plainville* . . . (New Haven, 1845), p. 8.
9. Samuel T. Dole, "The Cumberland and Oxford Canal," *Collections and Proceedings of the Maine Historical Society*, 2nd series vol. 9 (1898):271.

4 The Farms on the Hills

1. William Tudor, *Letters on the Eastern States* (New York, 1820), pp. 200–201.
2. Abby M. Hemenway, *Vermont Historical Gazetteer* 3 (Burlington, 1871): 873, 975.
3. James M. Swank, *Statistics of the Iron and Steel Production of the United States* (Washington, 1881), p. 90.
4. *New England Farmer*, n.s. vol. 1 (1867).
5. John Hayward, *A Gazetteer of New Hampshire* (Boston, 1849), p. 22.
6. *Wisconsin Farmer*, 8 (September 1856):397.
7. William H. Dean, "The Decay of New England," *The Nation* 8 (May 27, 1869):410–411.
8. William W. Newton, "The Decline of New England," *The Penn Monthly* (January 1876):59.
9. Rollin L. Harte, "A New England Hill Town," *Atlantic Monthly* 83 (1899): 561–574.
10. Charles C. Nott, "A Good Farm for Nothing," *The Nation* 49 (1889):406.
11. Zephine Humphrey (Mrs. Wallace Fahnestock), "The New Crop," *The Outlook* 134 (July 1923):380–381.
12. See Betty F. Thompson, *The Changing Face of New England* (New York, 1958), and Robert W. Eisenmenger, *The Dynamics of Growth in New England's Economy 1870–1964* (Middletown, Conn., 1967).
13. Clifton Johnson, *A Book of Country Clouds and Sunshine* (Boston, 1896), p. 177.

5 Rural Schools and Churches

1. J. W. Dearborn, *A History of the First Century of the Town of Parsonsfield, Maine* (Portland, 1888), p. 160.
2. Clifton Johnson, *The Country School in New England* (New York, 1893), pp. 59–60.

6 Town Animal Pounds

1. Clark Jillson, *Green Leaves from Whitingham, Vermont* (Worcester, 1894), p. 221.
2. *Portland Eastern Argus*, December 17, 1833.

7 The Village Mill

1. Dwight, *Travels*, Letter 36 in "Journey to Berwick."
2. Franklin B. Dexter, ed., *Ancient Town Records: New Haven 1649–1684*, vol. 1 (New Haven, 1917–19), pp. 159–160.
3. Henry Pallett, *The Miller, Millwright, and Engineer's Guide* (Philadelphia, 1866), p. 231.

8 The Sawmills and the Lumber Industry

1. "Life Among the Loggers," *Harper's New Monthly Magazine* 20 (1859–60):441.
2. Mary F. Butts, "The White Mountains in Winter," *New England Magazine*, n.s. vol. 1, no. 6 (February 1890):602.

9 The Village Tannery

1. Joseph B. Felt, *Annals of Salem* (Salem 1842), 1:49–50.
2. Dexter, *Ancient Town Records*, 1:159.
3. Edward H. Dewson, *The Tanning Industry of the South Shore of Massachusetts* (Boston, 1859), p. 4.
4. Charles Francis Adams, *Three Episodes of Massachusetts History* (Boston, 1892), 2:929.
5. Dewson, *Tanning Industry*, p. 2.
6. Dexter, *Ancient Town Records*, 1:219.
7. James H. Trumbull, ed., *The Public Records of the Colony of Connecticut*, 15 vols. (Hartford, 1850–90), 3:236.

10 Mineral Springs and Mountaintop Resorts

1. John Saxe, "What Do They Do at the Springs?" *Poetical Works of John Godfrey Saxe* (Boston, 1882), p. 49.
2. Albert D. Hager, *Report on the Geology of Vermont* (Claremont, N.H., 1861), pp. 865–866.
3. John Bell, *Mineral and Thermal Springs of the United States and Canada* (1855), p. 144.
4. Saxe, "What Do they Do . . ."
5. *Mount Holyoke*, n.d., n.p., ca. 1824.
6. C. D. Arfwedson, *The United States and Canada in 1832, 1833, and 1834* (London 1834), 1:114–115.
7. John Eden, *The Mount Holyoke Handbook and Tourists' Guide* (Northampton, Mass., 1851), pp. 17–18.
8. Clifton Johnson, *Mt. Holyoke Handbook*, ca. 1890.
9. "Mount Holyoke," publicity brochure, ca. 1870s.

11 Mining

1. Richard H. Phelps, *Newgate of Connecticut* (Hartford, 1876), p. 15.
2. Ibid., p. 38.

12 The Iron Industry

1. James Thatcher, "Observations upon the Natural Production of Iron Ores, with a Description of the Smelting Furnaces, and Some Account of the

Iron Manufacture in the County of Plymouth," *Collections of the Massachusetts Historical Society* 9 (1804):254.

2. Swank, *Statistics of Iron and Steel*, p. 84.
3. Thatcher, "Observations . . . ," pp. 262–263.
4. Swank, p. 84.
5. Ibid., p. 86.
6. *Public Records of the State of Connecticut*, 1:389.
7. Eliphalet and Phineas Merrill, *Gazetteer of New Hampshire* (Exeter, N.H., 1817).
8. Charles T. Jackson, *Final Report on the Geology and Mineralogy of the State of New Hampshire* (Concord, 1844), p. 196.
9. *Katahdin Iron Works* (Boston, 1863), p. 5.

13 The Kilns

1. Martha Russell, "A Glimpse of the Charcoal-Burners," *Knickerbocker Magazine* (November 1852):429–430.
2. Nathaniel Hawthorne, "Ethan Brand," *The Snow Image and Other Twice Told Tales* (Boston, 1852).
3. Ibid.
4. Ibid.
5. Ibid.

14 The Textile Industry

1. Samuel Batchelder, *Introduction and Early Progress of the Cotton Manufactures in the United States* (Boston, 1863), pp. 41–42.
2. T. Throstle, "Factory Life in New England," *Knickerbocker Magazine* 30 (December 1847):517.
3. "Manufacturing Corporations and Villages," *New England Magazine* 7 (1848):241.
4. Henry Chapin, *Address Delivered at the Unitarian Church in Uxbridge, Mass.* (Worcester, 1881), p. 154.
5. William R. Bagnall, "Sketches of Manufacturing Establishments in New York City and the Textile Establishments of the Eastern States," unpublished manuscript at Merrimack Valley Textile Museum, North Andover, Massachusetts, ca. 1885.
6. Charles Dickens, *American Notes for General Circulation* (London, 1842), chap. 4.
7. Joseph Brennan, *Social Conditions in Industrial Rhode Island 1820–1860* (Washington, 1940).
8. J. T. Adams, *New England in the Republic 1776–1830* (Boston, 1926), p. 398.
9. *Wool Technology and the Industrial Revolution* (North Andover, Mass., 1965).
10. "Manufacturing Corporations and Villages," *New England Magazine* 7 (1848):240.
11. T. M. Young, *The American Cotton Industry* (London, 1902), p. 12.
12. Ibid.

15 Manufacturing

1. Alvin F. Harlow, *Steelways of New England* (New York, 1946), p. 12.
2. Stanley Ransom, "History of the William L. Gilbert Clock Corporation, Winsted, Ct." *Lure of the Litchfield Hills* (1972), p. 7.
3. Ibid., p. 6.
4. Collins Company, *A Brief Account of the Development of the Collins Company* (Hartford, 1935), p. 9.
5. Ibid., p. 10.

16 The Gasholder Houses

1. *Report of the Commission in Relation to the Supply of Gas in Boston* (Boston, 1876), p. 367.
2. *Report of a Hearing of the Board of Aldermen in Boston* (Boston, 1874), p. 13.

17 The Coastal Schooners

1. Paul C. Warren, "Coastwise on a 4-Master," *Yachting*, November 1927, pp. 86–88.
2. William Douglas, "Old Coasters," *Yachting*, September 1932, p. 78.
3. Ibid., p. 43.
4. "The Coastal Schooner Is Still a Moneymaker," *The Sun*, October 20, 1912.
5. "Inglorious End for Old Vessel," *Boston Herald*, April 7, 1927.

18 The Ropewalks

1. American Trust Company, "Rope Making," *Manufacture in New England* (Boston, ca. 1915).
2. Ibid.

19 The Railroads

1. Stephen Jenkins, *Old Boston Post Road* (New York, 1913), p. 173.
2. Harlow, *Steelways*, p. 50.
3. N. Wood, *A Practical Treatise on Rail-Roads and Internal Communication in General* (New York, 1832, first Amer. ed.).
4. Edward C. Kirkland, *Men, Cities, and Transportation* (Cambridge, 1948), p. 123.
5. Dickens, *American Notes*, chap. 4.
6. Kirkland, *Men*, p. 125.
7. Harlow, *Steelways*, p. 132.
8. *Farmers' Monthly Visitor*, Montpelier, Vt. 10 (January 31, 1848):9.
9. L. Stebbins, *Eighty Years Progress of the United States* (Hartford, 1867), p. 197.
10. *Boston Herald*, March 17, 1871.
11. Ibid.

Site List By State and Town, with Driving Directions

The sites are listed alphabetically under the appropriate town or location as shown on the road maps published by each state. These are the most detailed maps that are readily available and can be obtained free of charge at each state's many tourist information centers or by mail from their departments of tourism.

For those who wish to do further exploration, more specialized maps are listed in the Bibliography and in the Site List by Subject.

Directions, unless otherwise noted, start from the center of the town under which the site is listed.

Though most of the sites are unused or abandoned, some working, inhabited, or restored sites are listed where they are especially interesting or informative; many inaccessible sites have been deleted from the list.

It should be stressed here that many of these sites are on private property and should be viewed from the public roads only.

In addition to this list, there follow a number of others that list the abandoned railroad rights-of-way, and end-to-end driving directions for the longer canals, which cross-reference the sites by subject.

Finally, it should be noted that the story of New England's forgotten relics is always changing. The author welcomes any suggestions or additions to this to be used in later editions of this book. Letters may be sent to the author care of New York Graphic Society, 34 Beacon Street, Boston, Massachusetts 02106.

Connecticut

Avon. *Farmington Canal remains*. See Canals list.

Bakersville. *Steadman's Mill*. From traffic light on Rt 25, go E and turn at 1st left. Pass firehouse and descend on rd to Maple Hollow. Mill is across stream on left.
Old Tannery Building (ca 1850). At traffic light, Rt 25.

Baltic. *Textile mill complex*. Rt 97, E side of river.
Railroad station. Up hill from mill, opp side of Rt 97.

Boardman Bridge. *Old Charcoal burners' rds*. On Housatonic Range Trail. W off Rt 7 onto Rt 37. Walk N along trail from Rt 37. This 1½-m section of trail to Squash Hollow Rd follows old charcoal rds.

Botsford. *Wooden RR water tank*. At station.

Bristol. *H. C. Thompson Clock Co*. Small factory bldgs. Woodland St just off Farmington Ave.

Bulls Bridge. *Bulls Falls iron furnace* (1826–86). Outer wall is partial rubble, inner wall whole. Sluiceway wall along bank. Take rd W off Rt 7 to covered bridge. Park on E side. Follow E bank of river S about 100 yds to furnace.

Burlington. *George Washington Turnpike*. SE off Rt 4 along S side of green. Continue straight to end of rd. Old pike continues as path.
Schwarzmann Mill (1796). Grist, saw, and cider mill. W from jct Rts 4 & 179 on Rt 4. Right (N) onto Vineyard Rd to mill.

Canaan. *Charcoal pits.* Scattered throughout Housatonic State Forest.

Chaplin. *General store.* Opp church. Unoccupied since 1930s.

Cheshire. *Farmington Canal remains.* See Canals list.

Clarks Falls. *Houses.* In town on Rt 216.
> *Gristmill.* Operating. Open 1–5:30 Sundays. On Rt 216.

Collinsville. *Collins Ax Company.* Large complex of buildings and power canals.
> *Railroad bridge and abandoned trackage.* Over river by Collins Co.

Cornwall Bridge. *Dudleytown (1747–1920). Deserted settlement.* E on Rt 4 from jct Rts 4 & 7. 1st right onto Dark Entry Rd. Park at end of rd and follow trail up ravine. Map available at general store in Cornwall Bridge.
> *Railroad Station.* Off Rt 7, below bridge.

Cornwall Hollow. *Meetinghouse.* Small, Greek style. W side Rt 43.
> *Charcoal pits.* W off Rt 43 onto Yelping Hill Rd. Ascend rd .6m to Appalachian Trail. Walk trail N to pits located just S of ridge.

Deep River. *Mill* on Milldam and Pond. N on Rt 9A. Right at "Beauty Boutique" sign just S of town line. Adjoins a small fieldstone bldg now a beauty salon.

East Brooklyn. *Millworkers' housing.* City block of adjoining brick duplexes. From Rt 6 turn S onto S. Main St, drive E toward river, then S onto Tiffany St. Houses on right at end of st.
> *Gasholder house.* Follow above directions; at end of Tiffany St turn left across field, stop at gate. Gasholder house straight ahead btwn factory and river.

East Canaan. *Beckley Iron Furnace (1847–1923).* S from center on Lower Rd to furnace by river. Dam upstream.

East Thompson. *Depopulated farming area.*
> *House.* E of Raceway.
> *House.* In center on East Thompson Rd.

East Windsor (community of Scantic). *Milestone.* "X mild to the Hartford Cout-Hof 1765" (sic). Moved from Post Rd to Scantic Academy bldg (Rt 140).

Ellsworth. *Farmhouse.* Partially collapsed. Rt 4 near top of hill, E side. Town was once a charcoal burners' camp.

Fairfield. *Windmill.* 3015 Bronson Rd. Take exit 21N off Conn. Turnpike.

Falls Village. *Power canal (built 1849–51).* 3 levels, 1m long with stone arch over rd, like a thick castle wall against side of hill. Originally built to transform Falls Village into a great industrial town like Lowell, Mass. Built without mortar and as a result never successful due to leaks. On Main St. W off Rt 126.

Farmington. *Farmington Canal remains.* See Canals list.

Gilman. *One-room schoolhouse.* Corner Stanton Rd and old main rd btwn Colchester and Norwich. Edges road on hillside by stream.

Granby. *Newgate Prison and Copper Mine.* E on Rt 20, 2nd left (N) after RR tracks.
> *Farmington Canal remains.* See Canals list.

Granby Station. *Old railroad depot* and nearby double-outhouse, identically painted in RR company colors. Rt 189 S at RR tracks.

Haddam. *Charcoal pits.* In Turkey Hill section of Cockaponset State Forest.

Hampton. *Milestone.* Stolen by Deacon Nathaniel Mosley, used as his tombstone in 1788. The stone later fell over and the buried end was found to read "R. Hand Road to Boston Left Hand Rd. to Worcester." From Rt 97 at N end of village, take right (E) onto Hammond Hill Rd. Cemetery on N side, E of river. Stone is lying flat in NW corner at 2nd row of graves uphill from large oak tree in swamp.

Hartland Hollow. *Deserted settlement.* Mill and house foundations. N off Rt 20 at N end Barkhamsted Reservoir. Follow old stage rd to bridge. Left are mill foundations. Up hill are farm foundations.

Hattertown. *Schoolhouse.* Across pond, E side of "green."

Hebron. *Wells Woods. Deserted settlement.* Cellar holes. E on Rt 66, right onto
  Hunt Rd for .5m, then left onto Wells Woods Rd to stone walls enclosing old
  foundations of hand-cut granite.
  Town pound. W on Rt 66 to bottom of hill, left onto Chestnut Hill Rd.
  Park by bridge. Pound is downstream on private property.
  Gay City (1796–1860). *Deserted mill town.* Cellar holes. In Gay City State
  Park.
Huntsville. *Buena Vista Iron Furnace* (1847–56). On Hollenbeck River off Rt 63.
Kent Furnace. *Iron furnace of Monitor Iron Works* (1826–92). Now maintained
  by state.
Lakeville. *Iron furnace salamander* (1762), *cannonball from Salisbury Furnace.*
  By old RR station off Rt 41 S.
  Ore beds and iron mines. Now flooded. N side of Rt 44 W of town.
Lebanon. *Town pound.* W from center on Rt 207 for 1m. On N side opp high
  school.
Ledyard. *Up-and-down sawmill.* Restored and operating. Rt 214 E of center at
Lime Rock. *Iron furnace* (1825–84). N on Old Furnace Rd from Rt 112 W of
  Historic District.
  raceway. Furnace on private property on E side near top of rd.
Litchfield. *Prosperous hill town.* Has weathered declines and still stands as a town
  of beautiful churches and colonial mansions.
  Milestone. "33m to Htfd, 102m to NY, J Strong, AD 1787." Rt 25 ½m W
  of center. On N side in front of Litchfield Savings Bank.
Lower City. *Deserted manufacturing settlement.* A few bldgs and foundations.
  Upper City and Little York. Vanished manufacturing towns.
Macedonia. *Charcoal pit.* In Macedonia Brook State Park. On Appalachian Trail
  in sag between Cobble and South Cobble mts.
  Charcoal pits. In Macedonia Brook State Park. On Orange Trail.
  Old Poughkeepsie–Hartford Stage Rd. On Appalachian Trail btwn Rt 341
  and Macedonia Brook Rd.
Mansfield. *Sawmill bldg.* Skeleton and chimney, 2 stories. On Old Turnpike Rd
  off Rt 44A, E side of Fenton River.
Mechanicsville. *Ruins of old textile mill complex.* 2-story powerhouse with high
  arched windows resembling gothic church ruins. Sluicehouse and dam at N
  end, best seen from RR tracks. From Rt 12 turn onto "Old Rt 12," park at
  P.O. Cross tracks to complex.

Millington Green. *Deserted settlement.* Cellar holes. Once a thriving lumber town.
  W of Millington on Rt 82 at N end of Devil's Hopyard State Park.
Milton. *Houses.* .5m N from center on Shear Shop Rd. Also N side Great Hill
  Rd, .5m W of turnoff for Mohawk Pond.
Montville. *Fieldstone factories.* Along Rt 163 W of Connecticut Turnpike.
Moodus. *Old textile mill bldgs* (built 1830s–40s). 1st mill at base of hill, jct
  Rts 149 & 151. 2nd mill halfway up hill from 1st, behind houses.
Mount Carmel. *Farmington Canal remains.* See Canals list.
Mystic Seaport. *Ropewalk and ropemaking equipment.* Museum exhibit. A section
  of the Plymouth Cordage Company's now-dismantled walk.
New Hartford. In Nepaug State Forest: *Satan's Kingdom.* Old bandit hideout (late
  18th century). *Charcoal pits.* On Valley Outlook Trail NE of Rome Spar
  Outlook.
New London. *Old Town Mill* (1650, rebuilt 1712). Restored mill with operating
  waterwheel. 32 Mill St.
  Schooner hull and other ship hulls. Rt 32 north past Coast Guard Academy.
  Turn right (E) onto Mohegan Ave, then left onto Naumkeag Ave. Descend
  to shipyard. Left (N) on dirt rd just before shipyard gates. Hulls along
  shoreline just above shipyard.
New Preston. *Gristmill.* Restored. On East Aspetuck River at falls.

Noank. *Hulls of two 4-masted schooners: Alice L. Pendleton* (1918), lumber carrier; *Guilford Pendleton* (1918). At Noank Shipyard at Morgan Pt.

North Ashford. *Stagecoach inn.* At center, W off Rt 171 at church. .25m to inn on N side.

North Canton. *Small church* (1872). By North Canton Methodist Church, which replaced it as congregation grew.

North Granby. *Schoolhouse.* E off Rt 189 at library. 1m to school on N side.

North Stonington. *Depopulated farming area.*

Norwich. *Railroad shops, roundhouse, and turntable bldgs.* Red brick, in partial use by light industry companies. Opp 64 N Main St (Rt 12).

Orcuttsville. *Wooden factory bldgs.* Rt 190 & RR tracks.

Plainville. *Farmington Canal remains.* See Canals list.

Robertsville. *Foundation of Richard Smith's Iron Furnace* (1770). E off Rt 8 to jct of Sandy Brook and Still River.

Rockville. *Classic upland mill town.* Mills now converted to other industries.

Rocky Hill. *Milestone.* "Hartford/6-M/Turnpike/Runs to Saybrook/35 Miles/Granted 1802." At 74 Old Main St.

Salisbury. *Triphammer of Mt Riga Furnace.* In front of town hall.
    Mount Riga Furnace (1810–48). Across from church on Rt 44 follow sign to Mt Riga. Continue up hill onto dirt rd to sign for cemetery at dam. Park; follow W side of stream down to furnace.
    Charcoal burner's roads. On Mt Riga, crossing Appalachian Trail N of Lion's Head; also crossing Bald Peak Trail E of Lion's Head.
    Charcoal pits. Mt Riga on Bald Peak Trail.

Sharon Valley. *Iron furnace* (1825–98). Behind ballpark.

Shelton. *Short canal and locks* (ca 1860s).
    Upper Locks. N on Howe St to Riverview Park. Locks at dam below.
    Lower Locks. At N end of factories lining river at center.

Simsbury. *Tuller's Grist Mill.* Restored. On Rt 167 E of center.

Southford. *Small wooden church.* N corner jct Rts 67 & 188.

Staffordville. *Church.* On Rt 19 below top of hill along Furnace Brook.
    Wooden row houses. Beside church.

Sterling. *Town pound* (1722). Large. 1m E of village.

Suffield. *Enfeld Falls Canal.* See Canals list.
    Farmington Canal remains. See Canals list.

Terryville. *Factory waterwheel.* Rt 6 W from center, N side approx house no. 455.

Thompson. *Brandy Hill Baptist Church* (1809). Rt 193 N from center to Brandy Hill.

Totoket. *Tanbark crushing circle*(?). Now a garden in front yard. Rt 80 E of Totoket Rd. On N side at Rolling Acres (approx house no 414).

Union. *Operating brick charcoal kilns.* N on Rt 171 from jct Rts 171 & 190. Large works on right (E).

Vernon Center. *Milestone* (1801) "VI:M.T.C.H." (6m Tolland Court House). N side Rt 30, just E jct Rts 30 & 85.

Versailles. *Textile mill complex.* Mansard-roofed. E side outlet Versailles Pond.
    Houses. River Drive. Workers' dwellings.

Voluntown. *Shetucket Turnpike.* E on Rt 165 from jct Rts 49 & 165 (E of Voluntown). Old pike leaves Rt 165 to N at first path E of jct.

Washington. *Shepaug RR tunnel.* S from Washington on Rt 199. Right (W) onto Curtis Rd (opp Nichols Hill Rd). Drive to "T." Turn left (S) to tunnel.

Wauregan. *Church.* Millworkers' church. Rt 205 uphill from river.
    Sluicegate house. Rt 205. NE side of Quinebaug River Bridge.

West Stafford. *C. P. Bradway Machine Shop.* Off Rt 190 onto Krol Rd opp fire station to weathered clapboard bldg beside stream.

Wilsonville. *Schoolhouse* (ca 1830). Corner Wilsonville and Pompeo rds, E of
   Rt 12.
   Mill. E side of Rt 12. Fieldstone and wood. Appears to be a stone gristmill
   expanded for industry.
Windsor. *Milestone.* "Hartford: IX Miles." Rt 159 N, opp 912 Palisado Ave.
Windsor Locks. *Enfield Falls Canal.* See Canals list.
Winsted. *Gilbert Clock Works.* Large complex of deserted factory bldgs.
   Rt 8 N of green.
Woodbridge. *Cement kilns.* From exit 59 Wilbur Cross Parkway take Rt 69 N.
   1st kiln in woods on hillside across fields just S of house no 1978. 2nd kiln
   farther N at corner of Dillon Rd.
Woodstock. *Depopulated farming area*

Maine

Allagash Wilderness Waterway. *Eagle Lake and West Branch RR* (ca 1930).
   Steam locomotives, roadbed, tramway, trestle. At State Forestry Camp btwn
   Eagle & Chamberlain lakes.
   Gas-powered Lombard log haulers. At Churchill Depot, downriver from
   Churchill Lake.
   Both sites accessible only by boat.
Bath. *Winnigance tidal-powered sawmill.* Still operates. From Bath take Rt 209 S
   to village of Winnigance at bridge over inlet. Sawmill in woods on left after
   bridge. Good view from Rt 209 N of village.
   Percy and Small Shipyard. 4 bldgs and shipways, being restored. Schooner
   yard. 451 Washington St.
Blue Hill. *Bisbee Copper Mine.* Smelter furnace. 1½m SW of Blue Hill on Rt 15.
Boothbay Harbor. *3 schooner hulls.* All decayed. *Courtney C. Houck* (1913)
   4-masted. *Edna M. McKnight* (1918) 209 ft, 4-masted. At West Harbor on
   road to Southport (Rt 27).
Cherryfield. *Cherryfield Mine* (1878). E on Rt 1. Right at Forest Station. Ascend
   hill to mine and shafthouse.
Dexter. *Gristmill* (1818). Restored.
Dover-Foxcroft. *Lime kiln and quarry* (ca 1875). From Foxcroft Golf Course
   walk N to kiln.
East Lebanon. *Little River Grist, Shingle, & Clapboard Mill.* Restored. From Rt
   202 take Little River Rd S to mill by bridge.
East Raymond. *House.* Rt 85 at crest of hill, E side, N of town hall.
East Vassalboro. *Turbine-powered sawmill.* Operating. Rt 32.
Hancock County. *Northern section, depopulated area.*
Harborside. *Cape Rosier Mine* (1881–1958). Buildings standing. N of village;
   on E side just before inlet.
Jefferson. *Town pound* (1826). Circular, 30-ft diam, 8 ft high. On S side Rt 126,
   1m E of Rts 213 & 126 jct.
   Sawmill. Water-powered. E side of town on Rts 126 & 206.
Katahdin Iron Works (1840s–90s). *Iron furnace, charcoal kilns.* Now a state park.
Kennebec County. *Depopulated farming area.* NW corner.
Limerick. *Hill farmhouse.* On old Limerick–Newfield Rd. From Limerick take
   Rt 11 S. Take 1st right after cemetery on W side. House on N at crest of hill.
Medomak. *5-masted schooner. Cora F. Cressey* (1902), 273 ft. From Bremen,
   take Rt 32 S to Keene Neck Rd. Turn left onto rd and follow to end; turn
   left at Audubon Camp and park at shore. Ship 200 yds N.
Moody. *Milestone* (1769). On E side "Old Post Rd" off Rt 1.
Naples. *Cumberland & Oxford Canal remains.* See Canals list.

Nobleboro. *Schoolhouse.* White wood. Rt 1 N, on NW side.

North Edgecomb. *Church.* Small wood. On old main rd paralleling Rt 1. Church
    at top of hill.

North Parsonsfield. *House.* Rt 160 opp general store.
    Baptist Church (1854). Rt 160 N on E side.
    Schoolhouse. Blazo School. Rt 160 N at bend.
    Seminary Bldgs. Rt 160 N at bend.

North Shapleigh. *Schoolhouse.* Restored.

North Windham. *Cumberland & Oxford Canal remains.* See Canals list.

Orrington. *Town pound.*

Parsonsfield. *Parsonsfield Union Church.*
    Schoolhouse. By church.
    Farmhouse. On rd SE from church .25m. Rambling, with barns.
    Town pound. Middle Rd. Turn E to Province Lake on rd just below church.
    Pound on right (N), .5 m.
    Cemeteries. By roads throughout town.

Pembroke. *Iron furnace and mine* (1828). On Rt 1.

Phillips. *Sandy River and Rangely Lakes* RR. Roundhouse and Station. 2 foot
    gauge RR.

Piscataquis County. *Southwestern towns, depopulated area.*

Porter. *Meetinghouse of the Bullockites Sect* (1818–24). From Rt 25, ascend rd
    by general store N. Continue N to 2nd right near crest of hill. Meetinghouse
    on left.
    Town pound (1825). Just before meetinghouse on right side.

Rockland. *Lime kilns.* Front St by modern lime works.

Rockport. *Lime kilns.* 7 remain. On Rockport Harbor at mouth of Goose River.

South Acton. *Schoolhouse.* Dilapidated, NW side of "green."
    House. On Acton Corner–South Acton Rd.

South Windham. *Cumberland & Oxford Canal remains.* See Canals list.

Sullivan. *Sullivan Silver Mine and buildings* (1877–1910). Rt 1 W to Sullivan
    harbor. Park E side and take rd N to mine.

Thorndike. *Sawmill.* Restored. Rt 110 E.

Topsham. *Mill.* On Tabor River.

Union. *Canal lock remains* (1846–50). N on Rt 131 from jct Rts 17 & 131.
    1st right, E (.25m S of lake). Cross river to remains of upper lock of Georges
    River Canal.
    Farmhouse, barn and outbuildings. W on Rt 17 from jct Rts 17 & 131.
    2m W to farm on N side.

Warren. *Canal lock remains* (1796, rebuilt 1846, abandoned 1850). N from jct
    Rts 90 & 131, pass school; at bend, continue straight onto dead-end rd to
    river. Park and descend to river and lock remains.

West Newfield. *Water-powered sawmill.* Operating. Jct Rts 11 & 110.

Wiscasset. *4-masted schooners. Hesper* (1918) & *Luther Little* (1917). On
    shoreline just S of causeway over inlet.

Massachusetts

Allston. *Milestone.* "6 Miles Boston, 1729." On E side Harvard St btwn
    Brighton and Commonwealth aves.

Assonet. *Mill turbine.* Rt 79 N of center. On W side in parking lot opp Mill St.

Attleboro Falls. *Gasholder house.* NW corner Elm & Mt Hope sts.

Bancroft. *Berkshire Tissue Mills* (1894). Depopulated town. Also unused houses,
    meetinghouse, school, & offices.

Barre. *Town pound.* Common St. S from "green" .25m on rise on left.

Bass River. *Windmill.* Willow St.

Billerica. *Middlesex Canal remains.* See Canals list.

Blackstone. *Houses.* On "green" off Rt 122. N end of town.

    Large school. Wooden. On "green" off Rt 122.

    Sluicegate house. Has hand-operated gearing. Park at bridge over power canal on Rt 122. Descend to canal on NE side. House just upstream.

    Blackstone Canal remains. See Canals list.

Bondsville. *Methodist church.* Rt 181. South Main St, on E side. Old textile town.

Boston. *Large gasholder house.* Brick. Domed roof. On corner Mass. Ave and Gerard St, just S of Boston City Hospital at entrance to Southeast Expwy.

Boxford. *Restored gristmill.* Small. From center drive E. Left on Mill Rd. In an interesting complex of old sluiceways and power equipment.

    Sawmill. Take Depot St (marked "To Rowley") opp 1st Cong Church. Sawmill on left at pond.

Brookfield. *Milestones of Old Post Rd.* Rt 9.

Byfield. *Milestone (1708).* At Governor Dummer Academy. S side rd, opp "green" at 4-rd jct.

Cambridge. *Milestone (1734, revised 1794).* Near Cambridge Common in Old Burying Ground.

Canton. *Milestone (1786).* On Rt 138, in SW corner of cloverleaf with Rt 128.

Charlestown. *Ropewalk (built 1832–37).* In U.S. Navy Yard. Stands at edge; can be seen from st beneath Tobin Bridge.

Charlton. *Town pound.* From Rt 31 at center take Muggett Hill Rd E to pound behind cemetery.

Chatham. *Windmill (1797).* Restored. Operates daily ex Tues in July & Aug 9–4:30. Off Shattuck Place.

Chelmsford. *Middlesex Canal remains.* See Canals list.

Chelmsford Center. *Mill.* Restored. Rt 4 S, then E onto Mill St. Red bldg in hollow on right.

Cheshire. *Lime kilns.* Off Lanesboro Rd, W side of reservoir S of town.

Chester. *Depopulated mining town.* Once large emery producer.

    Workers' houses. At center.

    Store (1921). At center.

    Railroad roundhouse. Brick, 6 stalls. S side of tracks at W end of town. Once sheltered extra locomotives to aid trains over top of Berkshires.

Clinton. *Railroad trestle.* 2nd highest in New England. By reservoir dam, Rt 70.

Concord. *Abandoned farming area.* In Estabrook Woods Preserve.

Cordaville. *Gutted brick factory.* Along RR tracks W of Rt 85.

Dalton. *Large mill.* Rt 8 N, on left.

Eastham. *Windmill (1793).* Restored. Open late June–Sept 15 daily 10–5, Sun 1–5. Free. Opp town hall.

Easthampton. *Farmington Canal remains.* See Canals list.

Egremont. *Lime kilns.* Perpetual. From Sheffield take Rt 7 N. Left onto Lime Kiln Rd. Becomes unpaved at West Rd. Continue short distance on Lime Kiln Rd to pump shed and telephone pole at rd entering from right. Park. Kilns in brush to right (N).

Farnumsville. *Blackstone Canal remains.* See Canals list.

Fiskdale. *Schoolhouse.* From center, S on Holland Rd. 1m to school on W side.

Gloucester. *Dogtown (1719–1830). Deserted settlement.* Cellar holes. From interchange 11 on Rt 128, take Rt 127 N. Take 2nd right onto Reynard St, left at end of st onto Cherry St, then 1st right onto Dogtown Rd. Park here and continue on foot down dirt rd to Dogtown.

Groton. *Milestones (1780s).* Erected by Oliver Prescott. Stones of slate 4–5 ft high. Take main st E of village to small "green" at jct Old Ayer Rd. Stones opp "green" on N and S sides.

Hampden. *Brick charcoal kilns.* Remains and rubble. In wooded area in E part of town.

Hawley. *Abandoned farming area.* In Hawley State Forest.

Heath. *Schoolhouse.* On "green."

Hockanum. *Schoolhouse* (1840). Brick.

Hopkinton. *Town pound.* Collapsed. W on Main St, then left onto W Main St. Pound 100 yds on right.

Housatonic. *Great manufacturing mill.* Brick. Along tracks. N end of town.
   Millworkers' apartment house. Long multistoried bldg with separate entrances for each family. Rt 183 just S of town.
   Power house. On river N on Rt 183.

Jamaica Plain. *Milestone* (1735). N corner of "green" at Center and South sts.

Leverett. *Town pound.* Circular. N on Montague Rd. Pound on left opp elementary school.

Lowell. *Pawtucket Canal and locks* (1822–23, rebuilt 1840s). Guard locks, NW of corner Broadway and Clare St. Swamp locks, E of Dutton St and Rt 3A interchange. Lower locks, SE of corner Central and Prescott sts.

Lunenburg. *Town pound* (ca 1750).

Martha's Vineyard. *Town pound.* N side of rd btwn Gay Head and Chilmark.

Medfield. *Town pound.* Rt 27.

Medford. *Tidal lock in Mystic River.* From Medford Sq, take Rt 16 S one block to river. Lock on E.

Middleton. *Stucco mill.* Endicott exit Rt 95. 1st right onto Peabody St after crossing Ipswich River. Then left onto Mill St after again crossing river. Mill on right. *Ironworks site* (1708–90). Next to mill.

Millville. *Blackstone Canal remains.* See Canals list.

Milton. *Milestones* (1823). W side Blue Hill Ave (Rt 138).
   Milestone (1734). Adams St, at E end of Hutchinsons Field wall.

Mount Holyoke. *Mt Holyoke House,* at summit.
   Driving wheel for tramway, above halfway house.

Nantucket. *Windmill* (1746). Prospect St. Built out of shipwrecks. Admission fee.

New Bedford. *Ropewalk.* Lambeth Rope Corp. Exit 4 off Rt 140 to Kings Hwy.
   N ¼m to 1893 ropewalk housing modern equipment, on L.

New Marlborough. *Hill town.* Beautiful, still-prosperous old hill town.

New Salem. *Depopulated hill town. Churches.* On green.

Northampton. *Farmington Canal remains.* See Canals list.
   Gasholder house. Crafts Ave behind City Hall.

North Attleboro. *Gasholder house.* Now a swimming pool salesroom. Elm St, one block N of East St.

North Billerica. *Middlesex Canal remains.* See Canals list.

North Easton. *Railroad station* (1881). Designed by H. H. Richardson.

North Leverett. *Abandoned farming area, cellar holes.* On Metacomet Trail S of Rattlesnake Gutter Rd.
   Operating brick charcoal kilns. Pioneer Valley Charcoal Works. E on N Leverett Rd. Right onto Coke Kiln Rd, then left after stream.
   Water-powered sawmill. Sawmill River Lumber Company. Operating.

North Uxbridge. *Crown and Eagle Mills* (1825, 1829). Large stone textile mills, also adjoining buildings: shops, offices, and warehouses. From Rt 122, E at light onto Hartford Ave. *Blackstone Canal remains.* See Canals list.

Norton. *Copper works slag heap* (abandoned 1910). S on Rt 140 to bridge. Field of slag on SE corner.

Osterville. *Windmill.* On Osterville Grand Island.

Pelham. *Depopulated hill town.*
   Cellar holes. Along Metacomet Trail.

Pembroke. *Town pound* (1824). On town hall lawn. Plaque.

Petersham. *Hill town.* Beautiful and still thriving.

Princeton. *Mt Wachusett Mountain House, cellar hole.* Near summit.

Richmond. *Richmond Iron Furnace* (1830–1923). Rt 41 S. Cross over small brook by garage. Park 100 yds farther, just past private rd. Descend wooded slope on E to brook and furnace.

Rowe. *Davis* (1882–1910). *Abandoned mining town.* Cellar holes of over 150 bldgs. From Charlemont take Rt 2 W. Turn N onto Legate Hill Rd. Ascend rd until it becomes dirt. Continue across slope on rd until it turns downhill. Small building on left is schoolhouse. Mine up dirt rd to left (E).

Rowley. *Milestones.* W side of Rt 1.

Roxbury. *Milestone, Parting Stone* (1744). Eliot Sq. Marked jct of Upper and Lower paths.

Sandwich. *Windmill* (1800). At Heritage Plantation. Moved from original site and restored.

    Dexter Gristmill (1654). Restored. Behind town hall. Open June 15–Oct 14 daily 10–5, Sun 1–5. Admission fee.

Saundersville. *Blackstone Canal remains.* See Canals list.

Shirley Center. *Town pound.* E side of "green" btwn church and grange.

Shutesbury. *Depopulated hill town.* Interesting center on hilltop.

    Town pound. On rd N from common at E side of church. On E side near base of hill.

Somerset. *Shipbuilding town.* Stone jetties and wharves along Taunton River.

Southampton. *Farmington Canal remains.* See Canals list.

Southborough. *Town pound.* Behind Southborough meetinghouse at center.

South Hadley Falls. *Hadley Falls Canal.* Converted to a power canal. Locks just below dam. Traces of bed along river N of Rt 202 bridge.

Springfield. *Wait Milestone* (1763). Presently in foyer of Springfield Armory Museum.

Stockbridge. *Gristmill.* Restoration. On grounds of Berkshire Playhouse.

Stoughton. *Railroad station* (1888). With clock tower.

Sturbridge. *Tantisques Lead Mine.* Honeycomb of shafts, deep cuts, and waste piles. (1638–1900). S on Rt 15/86. Take exit 2, continue S to Leadmine Rd. Right on Leadmine Rd ascending hill to sign for mine.

Sutton. *Town pound.* Totally overgrown. W of center on rd to Manchaug. Left side by town garage.

    Milestone (1771). 5 ft high. W on rd to Manchaug. At turn by school continue straight onto Boston Rd. Stone 1m farther on right.

Topsfield. *Abandoned farming area.* In Bradley W. Palmer State Park.

Townsend Harbor. *Spalding Grist Mill.* Restoration. Rt 119 E by dam.

    Factory. With Victorian tower. Rt 119 E just beyond gristmill.

Walpole. *Milestone* (1740). By town hall.

Warren. *Old Bay Path milestones.* Old Post Rd and Rt 67.

West Brewster. *Stony Brook Mill.* Gristmill restoration. Off Setucket Rd. Operates July & Aug. Wed, Fri, Sat, 2–5.

West Concord. *Large factory.* Brick. W on Rt 62, right side at Assabet River.

Westfield. *Farmington Canal remains.* See Canals list.

Westminster. *Town pound.* Academy Hill. Built 1799, moved ca 1810.

West Otis. *Church.* Brown, small, barnlike. From Rt 23, turn S on Town Hill Rd. Bldg 100 yds on left (E).

West Stockbridge. *Pit and walls of railroad roundhouse* (1838). Short distance up right-of-way from abandoned RR crossing on Rt 41.

    Lime kilns. Along old RR right-of-way S of town.

Westwood. *Town pound* (1700). On Rt 109 .5m W of Rt 128, exit 59W.

West Yarmouth. *Baxter Gristmill* (1789). Restored. Off Rt 28.

Whately. *Town pound* (1771). Low stone walls. W off main st opp town hall onto West St. Up hill to pound on N side.

Whitinsville. *Great stone textile mill.* Below dam opp library.

Williamstown. *Old Boston–Albany Post Rd.* Rt 2 W to old path continuing straight from main st.

Brick charcoal kiln. From Boston–Albany Post Rd hike Taconic Crest Trail
  S .5m. After crossing field turn W 150 ft to kiln.
Wilmington. *Middlesex Canal remains.* See Canals list.
Woburn. *Middlesex Canal remains.* See Canals list.
Worcester. *Railroad station.* Large ornate station. Crumbling. Franklin St.
Woronoco. *Brick charcoal kiln.* Westfield Mountain. On property of Berkshire
  Chapter Appalachian Mountain Club. On Trail along Dam Brook.

New Hampshire

Acworth. *Depopulated hill town.*
Alstead Center. *Town pound.* Rt 12A.
Ashland. *Ashland Paper Mills.* Brick factory buildings. Along stream W side of
  town.
  Railroad station and depot. Rt 3B, S end of town.
Auburn. *Town pound* (1853). Rt 121 S on E side. .5m N of Longmeadow church
Bartlett. *Railroad roundhouse.* Now highway garage. Wooden. SE of RR crossing
  on Rt 302 W of town.
Bow Center. *Town pound.*
Canaan Center. *Small mill atop stream.*
  Schoolhouse.
Center Effingham. *Schoolhouse.* Rt 153 S.
Chester. *Town pound* (1804). Rt 121 N, on W side. About 100 yds N of
  Candia Rd.
Claremont. *Perfecto Grain Mill* (mid-1800s). Large classic grain mill in dingy
  area of town. Corner Main & River sts.
  Covered wooden railroad bridges (1905, 1906). Rt 103 E along Sugar River.
Clinton Village. *Two barnlike small mills.* From Antrim take Rt 31 uphill. Turn
  left where Rt 31 takes a sharp right. Mills on left at stream. Town is classic
  example of a small river valley manufacturing village forming a transitional
  stage between farming area on heights and large industrial factories in valley.
Concord. *Gasholder house* (1888). Off S Main St, just below jct Rts 3 & 30.
  Best seen from RR overpass Rt 3.
Contoocook. *Covered wooden railroad bridge* (1889).
Cornish. *Schoolhouses.* In Center Cornish, & N of South Cornish on Rt 120.
Danbury. *Depopulated farming town.* Clustered around old RR line. Old center
  has desolate feel.
Dublin. *Town pound.* NE corner town cemetery at tip of Dublin Lake.
Dunbarton. *Town pound.* Rt 13 N .5m.
Durham. *Town pound.* Quarried granite. Rt 108 E of center at Durham Point Rd.
East Andover. *Farmhouses.* Rt 11 E.
East Derry. *Up-and-down sawmill.* Restored. State-owned.
East Grafton. *Small wooden mill.* Tub/turbine gearing in basement. From Rt 4,
  turn N onto rd to E Grafton. Ascend hill to mill on left by river.
Fabyan. *Fabyan House railroad station and depot.* Ornate station of old White
  Mountain resort hotel.
Franconia. *Franconia Iron Furnace* (ca 1810–1850). Jct Rts 18 & 117, W side
  of river S of bridge.
  Ore Hill Iron Mine. Rt 117W up hill past Sugar Hill. Then left (S) onto
  Easton Rd. Continue to abrupt right-angle turn. Turn left onto unpaved
  Toad Hill Rd. Ascend rd, stopping at clearing on left where rd drops off
  to right. Walk up trail leading NW from clearing .25m to mine. Mine is a
  100-ft-deep slit from 4–10 ft wide passing beneath trail.
Freemont. *Mill at falls.* Exeter River.

Gilmanton. *Town pound*. Rt 107 S .5m.
    Church. Rt 107 N approx 4m from center. On E side, S of grange.
Glenn House. *Mount Washington Summit Road Toll House* (1860). By stream
    at base of toll road.
Goffstown. *Schoolhouse*. Rt 13 N up hill to corner of Snook Rd, on left.
Greenville. *Railroad trestle*. Highest in New England. Spanning Souhegan River.
Hampton. *Gristmill*. Restored. Mill Pond Lane off High St.
Hampton Falls. *Milestone*. E side Rt 1 opp "green."
Harrisville. *Restored upland textile town*. Cheshire mills and boardinghouses.
Haverhill. *Abandoned farming settlements*. In hills to E.
Hill. *Murray Hill Schoolhouse*. From Rt 3A of Hill turn W on rd to Hill
    Center. Continue past Hill Center to open view on heights with schoolhouse
    on N side and vista of mountains beyond.
Hillsboro. *Contoocook Woolen Mill*. Beautiful wooden mill. With additions it
    looks like a great snail. Rt 149, on river.
    Wooden railroad bridge. N of Rt 149, bridge over river. Only American
    covered RR bridge with sidewalk.
Lempster. *Depopulated hill town*.
    Small farmhouse. N edge of town.
Lincoln. *Trestle of East Branch & Lincoln Logging Railroad*. In Pemigewasset
    Wilderness spanning Bear Brook at jct Bondcliff & Wilderness hiking trails.
    Can be reached only on foot.
Lisbon. *Stone charcoal kiln* (ca 1860). Partially collapsed. Plaque on opp side of
    rd. Rt 10 N. On W side 2m N of jct Rt 117.
Livermore. *Deserted logging town*. Now overgrown. In Crawford Notch on
    Sawyer River Rd.
Lyman. *Depopulated farming town*.
Lyme. *Abandoned farming settlements*. In hills to E.
Lyndeborough. *Town pound* (1774). Next to church.
Maplewood. *Railroad station*. Completely overgrown by woods. From Rt 302 at
    E end of golf course turn N onto Maplewood Hill Rd. Drive approx 100
    yds to woods at edge of golf course. Station on left (W) about 100 ft in
    woods just opp large barn on right.
Marlow. *Farmhouses*. On rd W to E Alstead.
    Wooden mill. Clerestory roof. Being restored. On Rt 123 E, at Abbot Brook
    and Cold Spring Pond.
Merrimack. *Canal lock remains*. On grounds of Budweiser brewery.
Milton. *Town pound*. Circular. Rt 16 opp town house 2m N of Milton.
Monadnock. *Monadnock Mountain House*. Ruins and cellar hole on hiking trail
    halfway up S side of mountain.
North Hampton Center. *Milestone*. Set in wall on Post Rd W of center.
North Haverhill. *Lime kiln*. At Lime Kiln Campgrounds. Follow signs from center.
North Weare. *Country store*. By sawmill S side of center.
    Victorian house. N side E of center.
Northwood Narrows. *General store*.
Penacook. *Town pound*.
Pike. *Small industrial mill*. At falls, Rt 25.
Quinntown. *Deserted settlement*. Cellar holes. From Orfordville, take Rt 25A E
    to Jacobs Brook. Turn right onto dirt rd along brook. Ascend rd to Quinn-
    town at Appalachian Trail.
Richmond. *Depopulated farming area*. Houses, cellar holes. Along Metacomet
    Trail N of Rt 119 in Grassy Hill area.
Roxbury Center. *Abandoned hill town*. Cellar holes.
Rumney. *Town pound*. Quincy Rd.
Salisbury. *Depopulated farming area*. Rts 4 & 127.

South Acworth. *Small interval early manufacturing town.*
    Church. S over bridge.
South Lee. *Harvey's Mill* (1725). Grist- and sawmills. W on Rt 152 from jct
    Rts 152 & 125, to North River.
Wakefield. *Town pound.* On dead-end rd N of post office.
Wilmot. *Schoolhouse.* Decayed and crumbling. From Wilmot take rd N 3m to
    White Pond and Camp Wilmot. School on W side btwn rd and pond.
Wilton. *Frank J. Moors Sawmill.* Take Rt 101 W from jct Rts 101 & 31 for 1m.
    Mill on left (S) across wooden bridge. Also dam upstream of rectangular
    granite ties laid in steps.

Rhode Island

Ashaway. *Town pound.* On Chase Hill Rd .75m SW of Bradford Ashaway Hwy.
    S side at 1st hillcrest.
    Ropewalk. Unused. 714 ft. On property of Ashaway Line and Twine
    Manufacturing Co.
Block Island. *Hotel.* SE part of island near site of razed Ocean View Hotel.
Carolina. *Deserted mill complex.* Factories and houses. Rt 12 at Beaver River,
    W side by stream and along dirt rds N & S of stream.
Chepachet. *Town pound* (1749). Trapezoidal. Rt 102 S 1m below jct Rts 102 &
    44 on left side at corner of Pound Rd.
Exeter. *Gristmill.* Rt 102 W, opp golf course.
Foster Center. *Town pound.* On South Killingly Rd W from Foster Center. On
    left (S) in marsh at bottom of hill. Brook runs through corner.
Hope Valley. *Town pound.* N side Skunk Hill Rd, 1m W of Arcadia Rd.
    Mill, dam, and power equipment. S to pond at left on Hope Valley Rd.
Jamestown. *Windmill.*
Kent-Washington counties. *New London Turnpike.* From Hope Valley to exit 7
    Rt I-95.
Lime Rock. *Lime kilns.* Perpetual kiln & colonial open draft kiln. From jct Smith
    Rd & Louqisett Pike, take pike short distance N, kilns in woods on left (W)
    just after quarry pool and before 1st house on right.
    Perpetual kiln. On Smith Rd just E of Rt 146. On N side beside flooded
    quarry.
    3-draft colonial kiln. From Rt 146 going N take Sherman Ave exit. Park at
    2nd dirt rd to right (S). Walk 100 yds down dirt rd to kiln on right.
Lonsdale. *Moffit Mill.* Wooden mill. Rt 123 N, .5m N of Arnold House. On E
    side by Moshassuck River Bridge.
    Blackstone Canal remains. See Canals list.
Narragansett. *Deserted ferry landing town of South Ferry.* Stone walls, cemetery,
    and church. Scenic Rt 1A N to South Ferry Rd on right.
Nooseneck. *Hopkins Mill.* Early textile mill. Rt 3 & Nooseneck River. E side in
    hollow. Clerestory monitor with ventilation stacks from use as a cattle barn.
    Mill bldg. W side Rt 3 & Nooseneck River, opp Hopkins Mill.
Pawtucket. *Slater Textile Mill & Museum.* Early textile manufacturing area
    now in slump.
Portsmouth. *Windmills.* Rt 114 S toward Newport.
Potter Hill. *Mill complex.* Long line of mill buildings built from early to late
    18th century. W side Pawcatuck River.
    Millworkers' houses. On side rds E & W of mill.
Richmond. *Town pound.* 8 ft high. "In use." On right side (E) of Nooseneck Rd
    .75m N of jct Rts 112 & 138.
Rockville. *Yawgoog Line & Twine Ropewalk* (1851). Factory bldg, 100 ft; rope-
    walk, 600 ft. Rt 138 E on N side, just beyond post office.

Shannock. *Early wooden textile mill*. Rt 91 W. Pass beneath RR overpass. Mill upstream from bridge on side rd S. Also powerhouse in stream.

Usquepaugh. *Kenyon Corn Meal Company Gristmill*. Operating. Visitors: Sat, Sun 12–5.

West Gloucester. *Fieldstone and wood factory/mill*. W on Rt 44. N side just after pond before Conn-RI border.

White Rock. *Schoolhouse*. Large red brick, from Victorian era. On White Rock Rd btwn Westerly DPW & White Rock Mill.

Woodville. *Textile/factory complex*. Millworkers' houses, cinderblock factory and power canal. Opp milldam, on S side.

Woonsocket. *"Remnants" mill*. Jct Main St and Harris Ave. Tall textile mill with different-style additions.

Wyoming. *Wooden mill bldg*. Barnlike with 2 cupolas. Rt 3 at Wyoming–Hope Valley Bridge. In brush on NW side.

Vermont

Bellows Falls. *Gristmill*. In center by power canal.

Bennington. *Remains of 2 iron furnaces*. From jct Rts 7 & 9, take Rt 9 E for 2m to furnaces on left (N).

Brattleboro. *Estey Organ Company*. Once-great New England industry.

Bridgewater. *Woolen mill of Vermont Native Industries (1825–1973)*. Large wooden mill. Closed because of inability to meet EPA pollution standards. *Wooden timber dam*. In river upstream of mill.

Burlington. *Lake Champlain railroad trestle*. NE of Burlington on lake. Stretches from Colchester Point to South Hero Island.

Chippenhook. *Small fieldstone mill*. Shell only. Tub/turbine gearing remains in basement.

Clarendon. *2-story white wooden schoolhouse*.

Clarendon Springs. *Clarendon Mineral Springs Resort Hotel (1834)*. Red brick with white wooden porches and columns.

Concord. *Small wooden mill building*. Off Rt 2 E of town. At turn for Concord Corners, descend to river past burned factory and cross river to red 2-story mill on SE.

Dorset. *Small mill with iron waterwheel*. Restored. On Hollow Rd. S from center on Rt 30 to left (E) by Harrow House. Take left here and continue across bridge. Bear right after bridge, then left. Mill downhill from hairpin in rd.

East Charleston. *Schoolhouse*. Rt 105 N. Left at road descending to elementary school. Continue past modern school across stream to little schoolhouse with small bell tower in field on right. Very scenic.

East Clarendon. *Kingsley's Gristmill*. Tall gristmill. In gorge upriver from covered bridge. Best seen from trail along opp bank.

East Dorset. *South Village Iron Furnace*. Rt 7 S from East Dorset 1m to 1st right (W). Then 1st left onto old Rt 7. Pass lake on right. Just S of dam on right by house is furnace.

Forestdale. *Iron furnace (1810)*. From jct Rts 53 & 73, take Rt 53 N. Then take right onto Furnace Rd. Where rd curves S, park and follow path E into woods. Furnace a short distance on right. Furnacetop can be seen from behind Highway Dept Garage on Rt 73.

Glastenbury. *Deserted settlement*. Cellar holes. Along Appalachian Trail NE of Bennington.
Hotel ruins and right-of-way for trolley line. Now surface rubble.
Charcoal kilns. Upstream from hotel foundation.

Hancock. *General store*. SW corner jct Rts 100 & 125.

Hartland. *Turbine equipment.* Rt 5 S across covered bridge. Equip by bridge on
SW bank.

Heartwellville. *Old Stage Road.* Now U.S. Forest Service Trail. 10m over Green
Mountains from Heartwellville to Appalachian Trail at Congdon Camp
(Dunville Hollow), then to Burgess Rd in Bennington.

Island Pond. *Avery's Gore.* Deserted settlement area. Now overgrown.

Jericho. *Large gristmill.* Rt 15 W on Browns River.

Kent's Corner. *Sawmill.*

Manchester Center. *Wooden mill.* At falls by jct Rts 7 & 30.

Manchester Green. *Mount Equinox Resort Hotel.* Mineral spa. Large wooden
bldgs. Main part temporarily closed. Bldgs on E side in long disuse.

Middlebury. *Stone manufacturing mill.* Mill St.

Montgomery. *Avery's Gore.* Abandoned settlement area. Overgrown. Disenfran-
chised 1963.

Mount Holly. *Hill farm settlement.*
    Cook farmhouse. Victorian house on right by turn at crest of hill. From
    Rt 103 turn N to Mt Holly.

Northfield. *Woolen mill.* Closed by inability to meet EPA pollution standards.

North Montpelier. *Large wooden mill.* On stream below reservoir dam.

North Pomfret. *Depopulated farming area.* Cellar holes along Appalachian Trail.
    Kings Highway. Old colonial highway. On Appalachian Trail by Bunker Hill.

Pittsford. *Granger's iron furnace* (1828–45+). By sawmill on Furnace Brook NE
of Pittsford Mill.

Pomfret. *Old hill settlement.* Cellar holes along paths in hills.

Readsboro Falls. *Sawmill.* Behind houses in gorge. Extremely scenic.

Rochester. *Talc mine.* Rt 100 S. On E side rubble of bldgs and step cuttings can
be seen along hillside.
    Emerson lime kiln. From jct Rts 73 & 100, take Rt 100 S for 2.5m. Turn
    right onto side rd. Continue for .5m. Kiln on left.

St. Albans. *Railroad repair shops.* Mid-19th-century architecture.

Somerset. *Abandoned settlement.* Cellar holes. From Searsburg go E on Rt 9, then
left (N) onto Somerset Reservoir Rd. Continue N to site.

South Pomfret. *Depopulated hill farms.* Cellar holes along trails in woods.

South Reading. *Early map manufacturing settlement.* Now without industry.
    In upland ravine.
    House. Decayed. In center by rd S over stream.

South Strafford. *Elizabeth Copper Mine* (closed 1958). *Complete copper works.*
    Take rd continuing straight up hill at SE end of town where Rt 132 bends
    left. Ascend to works and mine at end of paved road.

Swanton. *Wooden railroad bridge.* S of Swanton on Missiquoi River.

Tinmouth. *Depopulated farming area.*
    Dutch-roofed farmhouse. Rt 140 just E of center on N side.
    Farmhouse. 1m S on old main st, E side.

Troy. *Boston & Troy Iron Furnace* (1838). From jct Rts 100 & 101, take Rt 100
E .5m. Then left (N) on rd along stream to bridge 1m. Park. Furnace is
W along stream.

Vergennes. *Large gristmill.* W along Otter Creek.

Vershire. *Ely Copper Mine and deserted mining town.* Rubble and cellar holes.
    From W Fairlee drive W on rd following stream. Continue to large rubble-
    filled clearing. Mine in woods to N. Note tram embankments N of clearing.
    House in woods W of clearing.

Warren. *Sawmills.* In gorge just S of center.

Weathersfield Center. *Town pound.* By church.

West Barnet. *Mosquitoville.* Depopulated settlement. In swampy area S of Harvey
Lake at jct of rds from S Peacham and W Barnet.

West Charleston. *Depopulated small manufacturing settlement.* Small mill bldgs
    and houses in town.
West Glover. *Keene's Corner & Slab City.* Abandoned farming settlements.
    Cellar holes.
Weston. *Bowl Mill.* Gristmill museum.
Wheelock. *Caledonia Spring House.* Mineral spa. Large brick house. Rt 122 on E
    side N of town hall.
Whitingham. *Sawmill.* 3 stories, semicollapsed. On Rt 100, E side of town on N
    side across field.
    Sadawga Springs Hotel. 19th-century mineral spa. 3-story wood with overhang
    on 1st floor. Doors opening off each floor. In center on Rt 100 at NE
    corner downhill & opp side st from general store/post office.

Site List The Longer Canals

Rather than listing the longer canals in sections under separate towns,
each canal is listed from end to end as a whole for the ease of those wishing
to explore it. For those who wish to visit individual remains, this list
constantly refers to basic landmarks by which one can orient oneself.

Farmington Canal

Completed 1835. 80m from New Haven, Conn., N to Northampton, Mass.
Mount Carmel, Conn. *Canal bed and lock remains.*
    From Mt Carmel N, the canal's remains are easily detectable. S of this point,
    modernization has obliterated almost everything.
    Begin at Rt 10 N at Mt Carmel center. N to Todd St on left. Take Todd St
    short distance to RR tracks. Park. Dry bed of canal parallels tracks on
    W side. Return to Rt 10.
    Take Rt 10 N to next left, Shepard Ave; turn onto Shepard to see water-
    filled canal stretching N. Return to Rt 10.
    Follow Rt 10 N to Cheshire–Mt Carmel line and there turn left onto Sanford
    Rd. Descend to RR tracks. Park. Remains of an old lock can be found in
    woods, SW corner Sanford Rd & tracks.

Cheshire. *Canal lock, canal bed, locktender's house. Turning pool. Embankment.*
    N of lock off Sanford Ave along tracks is a long stretch of water-filled canal.
    Return to Rt 10.
    Follow Rt 10 N and turn W on Brooksvale Rd (Y intersection). Descend to
    tracks and park. Follow tracks S to lock in perfect condition, turning pool
    for canal boats to tie up out of traffic, and locktender's house. Note also
    RR bridge built while canal was still operating. Return to Rt 10.
    Continue N thru Cheshire to Johnson Ave, last rd W before Milldale. Turn
    onto Johnson Ave and drive .3m to point where rd becomes steep. Turn
    right onto dirt rd. This is dry canal bed. Follow rd N to embankment over
    Tenmile River. Canal bed is 60 ft above river.

Plainville. *Water-filled canal section.*

    Take Rt 10 N to jct Rts 10 & 72 in Plainville. Turn W onto Rt 72. At Washington St (3rd light) turn left (S) and drive 5 blocks to canal section preserved in Norton Park. Return to Rt 10 and drive N.

Farmington. *Aqueduct abutments, feeder canal.*

    At Farmington center cross river on Rt 4 W. After bridge, take Town Farm Rd N, 1st rd on right. Continue past golf course, stop and park by woods N of Farmington Club. On hillside, right, is dry bed of feeder canal that brought water from the Farmington River at Unionville to fill Conn section of the canal. Follow feeder canal E along slope to river to main canal bed and abutments of the canal aqueduct over the Farmington River, the sole remains of a 280-ft trough across the river. Return to car and drive N to Avon.

Avon. *Water-filled canal section.*

    Take Rt 10 1.5m N of Avon to sign identifying water-filled canal section near RR crossing. Follow Rt 10 N through Simsbury.

Granby. *Canal embankment across field.*

    On Rt 10 N of Simsbury, just before Granby line, turn right (E) onto Farren Rd and continue past Simsbury airport. At end of Farren Rd, turn left (W) onto Floydsville Rd. Drive .25m to treeline with 15-ft-high canal embankment in trees.

Suffield. *Water-filled canal.*

    Return to Rt 10 and drive N to Granby center. At green, turn right (E) onto Rt 20 and then take 1st left (N) at corner of green onto Hungary Rd. Follow Hungary Rd 2m to quarried face of Manitook Mountain on left (W). On right by RR tracks is water-filled section of the canal. Park here and follow tracks N to water-filled canal at S end of Lake Congamond. Return W to Rt 10 and drive N to Westfield, Mass.

Westfield, Mass. *Feeder canal.*

    In Westfield are the remains of the feeder canal that ran from the Westfield River S of Woronoco to meet and fill the northern section of the Farmington Canal at a spot near the Westfield Exit of the Mass Turnpike.

    From Westfield take Rt 10/202 N over Westfield River, then take 1st left (W) onto Pochassic Rd. Continue W, keeping to rd along river's edge. In about 2m a rd enters on right; after this point the dry bed of the feeder canal will begin to be seen on slopes to right (N). Cross bridge at 2.5m from Rt 10; now feeder canal can be distinctly seen on right. Feeder's jct with river can be seen by continuing W to RR tracks, parking, and following tracks NW.

Southampton. *Lockwall, canal storehouse, dry bed.*

    Returning to Rt 10, continue N 6m to RR crossing 1m S of Southampton. Park by house, SW corner Rt 10 & tracks, once a storehouse for boats on canal. Walk S on tracks short distance to lockwall alongside tracks. Tracks are built on canal bed. Return to car and drive N through Southampton. 1.5m N of center on hillside, right, opp "Canal Bowling," the dry bed of the canal can be seen cutting across hillside.

Easthampton. *Water-filled canal bed, storehouse.*

    Continue N on Rt 10 to Easthampton. N of green, descend to river. On right (E) of bridge and on S side of pond is a building once a canal storehouse.

    Continue N on Rt 10 1.5m, turn right (E) onto O'Neill St, just S of Easthampton-Northampton line. At .25m, O'Neill St crosses water-filled canal section.

Northampton. *Reconstructed northern terminus of canal.*

    Continue N on Rt 10 through Northampton to point near Rt 10 & Damon Rd where town has covered over a dump and redug the canal's northern terminus with the Conn River for the Bicentennial.

Enfield Canal

Completed 1829. Still in use although primarily a power canal.
  5m from Windsor Locks N to Suffield, Conn.
Windsor Locks. *Canal and set of three locks.*
  Off Rt 159 just N of Rt I-91. Flight of 3 locks. 90 ft long, 20 ft wide,
  lifting boats 10 ft each. Separated by 50-ft pools for passing.
  Canal continues N through town. Note rings in canal wall W side just N of
  S end of canal, for tying up boats. The banks are of stone and cement,
  making this the only New England canal able to withstand wakes of steam-
  powered boats without its banks being washed away.
Suffield. *Aqueduct, northern lock.*
  From Windsor Locks drive N on Rt 159, crossing RR tracks into Suffield.
  1m beyond tracks cross bridge. Take 1st right (E) onto Paper St. Descend
  to end of paved rd. Park. Follow rd to stream. 100 yds downstream is
  Stony Brook Aqueduct, 104 ft long.
  Return to Rt 159 and continue N to Rt 190 jct. Just S of jct take road E
  to river. Park and walk to riverbank and northern lock.

Blackstone Canal

Completed 1828. 45m from Providence, R.I., NNW to Worcester, Mass.
Lonsdale, R.I. *Four-mile section of water-filled canal.*
  From jct Rts 122 & 123, take Rt 123 W downhill to bridge. Canal passes
  beneath. This section is in almost perfect condition, although on N side can
  be seen factories built directly over canal. This section stretches N to
  Quinnville before it merges with the Blackstone River near the Rt 116 bridge.
  To see another part of canal section drive N on Rt 122 to Berkeley. Turn
  left (W) and descend to river past Berkeley airport. Cross bridge over
  river to find water-filled canal paralleling river.
  Other short sections of this canal are in R.I., but they are unrecognizable
  as they have been converted to power canals.
Blackstone, Mass. *Water-filled section of canal.*
  The next section of canal of any size lies on the state line. Drive N on Rt 122.
  After entering Blackstone, take 1st left (W) onto St. Paul St and pass
  town hall. Just beyond, a bridge crosses canal with rds N & S along its banks.
  Return to Rt 122 and continue through center to high bridge at N end of
  town. Below passes another canal section, converted to a power canal. On
  N side a sluicegate house straddles the canal. To S is site of locks that
  lowered boats into slackwater section of river.
Millville. *Canal lock.*
  Continue NW on Rt 122 to town of Millville. Turn left (SW) at center
  and cross bridge. Beneath SW side of bridge are remains of locks where
  descending boats exited a slackwater section of river.
  Continue across bridge, ascending hill to church at 3rd left. Turn left and
  drive to end of st. Park and descend to riverbank. Here is a perfectly
  preserved canal lock, minus doors. S of lock is old towpath along riverbank.
North Uxbridge. *Mile long canal section, towpath embankment built up along
  lakeshore.*
  Return to Rt 122 and drive N through Uxbridge to traffic light at Hartford
  Ave in North Uxbridge. Turn right (E) onto Hartford Ave, drive up over
  hill and down slope to 1st bridge. Park.
  S of bridge can be seen a mile-long section of canal stretching in a straight
  line to Rt 16 E of Uxbridge. On N side of bridge, along W bank of lake,

can be seen the towpath embankment in the lake snaking along the shoreline to create the canal out of the lake's edge.
Farnumsville. *Water-filled canal section.*
    Return to Rt 122 and drive N to Farnumsville. Turn left (W) at factory,
cross bridge, and park at 2nd bridge .25m beyond. Beneath passes a water-
filled canal section.
Saundersville. *Water-filled canal section.*
    Return to Rt 122 and drive N to jct Rts 122 & 122A. Drive 1.5m NW on
Rt 122A, then turn right (NE) onto Pleasant St. Drive .3m across RR
tracks to bridge. River passes on left; canal section passes beneath.

Middlesex Canal

Completed 1804. 22m from Boston NW to Lowell, Mass.
Woburn. *Water-filled canal sections. Replica of an old canal boat.*
    Begin at exit 39 of Rt 128. Take Rt 38 S .5m to Central Sq. Turn right (W)
opp Wyman School, and drive a short distance to canal channel.
    Return N on Rt 38 to traffic circle; on N side take right onto Alfred St.
Immediately on left is long section of canal extending N into North Woburn.
Wilmington. *Canal bed, aqueduct remains, boulder with towline grooves.*
    Continue N from Woburn on Rt 38 to Wilmington Town Forest. Turn left
into forest and park at end of paved rd beside ball park. Walk short distance
down dirt rd to dry canal bed crossing left to right. Turn right (N) to
abutments and central pier of the Maple Meadow Aqueduct.
    Retrace steps and continue S in canal bed. Note towpath bank on left, berm
bank on right. Soon the canal bends left around the side of a hill. Go
around bend until the straight portion of the canal can be seen farther on.
Then begin to look along towpath bank on left for the 4-ft boulder grooved
from the towlines pulled across its horizontal face.
    Return to car and drive on Rt 38 to Wilmington Shopping Center just N
of Rt 129 jct. Take 1st rd left (W) at N end of shopping center. Cross bridge
over tracks and see an overgrown canal section on N side. Continue straight
to stop sign. Turn right onto Shawsheen Ave–Rt 129. Drive N to 1st rd
right (E). Turn and drive to end of rd. Park and follow canal along tracks
to small granite shelves along stream that are the remains of the Lubber
Brook Aqueduct.
Billerica. *Abutments and pier of Shawsheen River Aqueduct.*
    Return to Rt 129 and drive N to town line at Shawsheen River. Immediately
on right are remains of Shawsheen River Aqueduct.
North Billerica. *Water-filled canal section, towpath embankment into Concord
    River, floating towpath anchor rings, guard lock.*
    Continue on Rt 129 N toward North Billerica. At the jct where Rt 129
turns W and Rt 3A turns N, drive N on Rt 3A. Turn right (E) onto 2nd
rd right, Lowell Ave. Follow Lowell to village and keep to left at center to
cross bridge over Concord River. Follow rd around river to point on E side
where deep cut of canal channel passes beneath rd. Park.
    Follow canal to river where towpath embankment stretches out into river.
Return to car and retrace route back across bridge by milldam to small
bridge just beyond. Park.
    Below passes canal. On N side of rd in millyard are covered remains of a
guard lock. This did not raise or lower boats but simply protected canal
N of this point from damage by eddies from the river. On opp side of rd
at SE corner of canal and river is a large flat stone with two iron rings
attached. These rings anchored the floating towpath that once stretched
across the river to meet the towpath embankment on the far side.

Chelmsford. *Tollhouse.*

Return to jct Rts 3A & 129; take Rt 129 NW to Chelmsford. Tollhouse in center by town hall.

Cumberland & Oxford Canal

Completed 1830. 20.5m from Portland, Me., N to Sebago Lake, with additional lock between Sebago and Long lakes.

South Windham. *Canal sections, lock remains.*

From bridge at South Windham take main st E. Turn left (N) onto River Rd. Continue N on River Rd and take left (W) onto Newhall St. Descend to river, cross bridge, and park on W side. NW of millpond can be seen a short canal section with its towpath embankment built up into pond. S across rd is a long dry stretch of the canal.

Return to River Rd and continue on it N. After descending to cross a brook, turn onto the next rd left (W). Cross river on wooden bridge. Park on W side. Here are dry sections of the canal paralleling river. Walk S on old towpath by riverbank. In the bed on canal banks are iron shafts and wooden debris from the old locks. Where the towpath ends stand the remains of the Lower Kemp Lock. Four piers rise from the lock site and beneath the water can be seen the timbers and fieldstone walls of the 80-ft-long, 10-ft-wide lock.

North Windham. *Eel Weir power canal.*

Return to River Rd and drive N to North Windham. Turn onto Rt 35 W and drive to girder bridge. Passing beneath the bridge is the Eel Weir canal, a long section of the C&O Canal now used to produce hydroelectric power.

Naples. *Songo locks.*

Return to North Windham and take Rt 35 N to signs for Sebago Lake State Park. Enter park and drive to lock, still in use, on Songo River. It is not the original lock of 1830, but a cement replacement built in 1911.

Site List Abandoned Railroad Rights-of-Way

This list of the longer abandoned lines and those abandoned in the last fifteen years gives the end-points of each line by towns within each state. They can be traced out on the map in Chapter 19 or on a road map. Remember that for the most part the shorter lines follow a straight path, while the longer lines usually follow rivers and pass through intermediate cities.

Connecticut   Amston-Colchester, Berlin-Middletown, Bethel-Litchfield, Botsford-Bridgeport, Branchville-Ridgefield, Canton-Simsbury, Canton Center-Poquonock, Farmington-Salisbury, Melrose-Rockville, Meriden-Waterbury,

North Bloomfield-West Suffield, Oneco-Plainfield, Portland-Thompson, Torrington-Winsted

Maine   Albion-Wiscasset, Bemis-Canton, Derby-Greenville, Harmony-Hartland, Harrison-Hiram, Lewiston Junction-Livermore Falls, Lisbon-Rangely, Portland-Salmon Falls, Portland-Sanford, Salmon Falls-York Beach, Skowhegan-Waterville

Massachusetts   Ashburnham-Gardiner, Athol-Ludlow, Attleboro-Taunton, Barre Plains-Clinton, Billerica-Concord, Dennis-Provincetown, Douglas-Franklin, Easthampton-Greenfield, Easthampton-Mount Tom, Easton-Taunton, Fitchburg-Sterling, Mansfield-Taunton, Millis-West Medway, Northampton-Williamsburg, Palmer-Winchendon, Richmond-West Stockbridge, Shelburne Falls-South Deerfield

New Hampshire   Claremont-Concord, Milford-Hollis

Rhode Island   Coventry-Greene, Wood River Junction-Woodville

Vermont   Anthony-Bennington, Brattleboro-South Londonderry, Leicester-Whiting

Site List By Subject, with Suggestions for Further Exploration

In addition to the sites listed in this book, there are many more to be found by the careful explorer. For those interested in specific subjects, the bibliography can provide a wealth of information. For those who want to see what else they can discover in a particular territory, the suggestions given before each subject list should help.

The explorer should refer to any local histories written about his area and should also consult the WPA state guidebooks first written in the 1930s. Some have lately been revised and are excellent. Other current editions are merely abridgments of the original. For these, the first editions, however outmoded, are still more useful.

Roads and milestones

Compare the maps in Wood's *Turnpikes* to state and topographical maps. The old turnpike roads will appear on the modern map as "side roads" off or paralleling present highways. They will take an almost straight line across the countryside, while the modern road swings left and right to pass through towns and population centers that appeared after the old turnpikes were built.

The milestones of Connecticut and eastern Massachusetts have been well catalogued in the books listed in the bibliography. Finding others is chancy. The best prospects lie in following old county roads and turnpikes. The explorer should keep a sharp lookout in the vicinity of large colonial houses that may have once been taverns, at crossroads, and in colonial-era towns, especially near the village green.

Connecticut   Burlington, East Windsor, Hampton, Litchfield, Macedonia, North Ashford, Rocky Hill, Vernon Center, Voluntown, Windsor
Maine   Moody
Massachusetts   Allston, Brookfield, Byfield, Cambridge, Canton, Groton, Jamaica Plain, Milton, Rowley, Roxbury, Springfield, Sutton, Walpole, Warren, Williamstown
New Hampshire   Glenn House, Hampton Falls, North Hampton Center
Rhode Island   Kent-Washington counties
Vermont   Heartwellville, North Pomfret

Canals

In addition to the sites listed here are the less spectacular remains of the longer canals, the dry beds and banks, that can still be identified. For those interested in following a canal end to end, the U.S. Department of the Interior Geological Survey topographical maps show where the canal beds still exist, and they have identified vanished portions of the old routes with a dotted line. These maps are available in map stores, large stationery stores, or by writing to the U.S. Geological Survey, Washington, D.C. 20242, and asking for the indexes for the states desired.

The short river canals can also be located, as they were always in the general vicinity of a falls. For the most part, however, they have been long abandoned and floodwaters have removed all but trace remains, masonry, or the shallow canal bed; or they have been converted to power canals and their original characteristics are hard to distinguish.

Connecticut   Avon, Cheshire, Farmington, Granby, Mount Carmel, Plainville, Shelton, Suffield, Windsor Locks
Maine   Naples, North Windham, South Windham, Union, Warren
Massachusetts   Billerica, Blackstone, Chelmsford, Easthampton, Farnumsville, Lowell, Medford, Millville, Northampton, North Billerica, North Uxbridge, Saundersville, Southampton, South Hadley Falls, Westfield, Wilmington, Woburn
New Hampshire   Merrimack
Rhode Island   Lonsdale

Rural farming areas

Tour the backroads in hilly upland areas. Especially in the vicinity of still-farmed, large river valley areas, and large old mill towns.

Except in the areas where suburbs have grown up, any upland area will yield cellar hole remains, stone walls, and overgrown fields. One must get some distance from cities and tourist areas before lately abandoned houses will be found.

Off the road, many of the New England hiking trails (see Bibliography) follow now overgrown farm roads and offer excellent prospects for exploration.

Connecticut   Cornwall Bridge, East Thompson, Ellsworth, Hartland Hollow, Hebron, Litchfield, Milton, New Hartford, North Stonington, Woodstock
Maine   East Raymond, Hancock County, Kennebec County, Limerick, North Parsonsfield, Parsonsfield, Piscataquis County, Union
Massachusetts   Concord, Gloucester, Hawley, New Marlborough, New Salem, North Leverett, Pelham, Petersham, Shutesbury, Topsfield

New Hampshire   Acworth, Danbury, East Andover, Haverhill, Lempster, Lyman, Lyme, Marlow, Quinntown, Richmond, Roxbury Center, Salisbury
Vermont   Glastenbury, Island Pond, Montgomery, Mount Holly, North Pomfret, Pomfret, Somerset, South Pomfret, Tinmouth, West Barnet, West Glover

Schools, churches, stores, and other community buildings

The suggestions here are basically the same as for rural farming areas. For glimpses of old hill towns, seek out towns on maps with the word "Center" in their names. Many one-room schoolhouses can be expected to be found in backwoods areas, especially in Maine, where school consolidation is still going on.

Connecticut   Chaplin, Cornwall Hollow, Gilman, Hattertown, North Canton, North Granby, Southford, Staffordville, Thompson, Wauregan, Wilsonville
Maine   Nobleboro, North Edgecomb, North Parsonsfield, North Shapleigh, Parsonsfield, Porter, South Acton
Massachusetts   Bancroft, Blackstone, Bondsville, Fiskdale, Heath, Hockanum, New Salem, Rowe, West Otis
New Hampshire   Canaan Center, Center Effingham, Cornish, Gilmanton, Goffstown, Hill, North Weare, Northwood Narrows, South Acworth, Wilmot
Rhode Island   Narragansett, White Rock
Vermont   Clarendon, East Charleston, Hancock

Town pounds

Many more pounds than those listed here lie forgotten and overgrown across the New England countryside. For those in search of others, the pounds were usually located outside of the old town center, somewhere between .25 to .75m. Unless there was only one road through the town, the pound was usually built not on the main road, but on the second most important road into the village.

Connecticut   Hebron, Lebanon, Sterling
Maine   Jefferson, Orrington, Parsonsfield, Porter
Massachusetts   Barre, Charlton, Hopkinton, Leverett, Lunenburg, Martha's Vineyard, Medfield, Pembroke, Shirley Center, Shutesbury, Southborough, Sutton, Westminster, Westwood, Whately
New Hampshire   Alstead Center, Auburn, Bow Center, Chester, Dublin, Dunbarton, Durham, Gilmanton, Lyndeborough, Milton, Penacook, Rumney, Wakefield
Rhode Island   Ashaway, Chepachet, Foster Center, Hope Valley, Richmond
Vermont   Weathersfield Center

Village mills

The old mills are easiest to find when renovated for commercial purposes, as they are well advertised. Hardest to find are the mills forgotten and in disrepair. A number have been compiled by the Historical American Building Survey, and by the magazine, *Old Mill News*, published in Wiscasset, Maine.

For the most part, however, mill hunting is the work of touring many small river valleys in the hope of a chance discovery. The low rate of discovery in this activity is greatly offset by the beautiful scenery of these valleys.

The best chance of finding a mill lies in following streams that are not so small that the mill could not expand its works during the nineteenth century, or so large that the mill has likely been carried away by floodwaters. Floodwaters also had their effect on the narrower ravines, yet wide river valleys often had their mills torn down by farmers who found the mill property valuable farming land.

Follow streams that are from 10 to 20 feet wide located in steep valleys with flat floors 100 to 200 feet wide. These streams offered the best protection from floods but they were not so attractive that they were worth clearing for large farms.

Connecticut Bakersville, Burlington, Clarks Falls, Deep River, Fairfield, Hartland Hollow, New London, New Preston, Simsbury
Maine Dexter, East Lebanon
Massachusetts Bass River, Boxford, Chatham, Chelmsford Center, Eastham, Middleton, Nantucket, Osterville, Sandwich, Stockbridge, Townsend Harbor, West Brewster, West Yarmouth
New Hampshire Canaan Center, Claremont, Clinton Village, East Grafton, Freemont, Hampton, Marlow, South Lee
Rhode Island Exeter, Jamestown, Lonsdale, Portsmouth, Usquepaugh
Vermont Bellows Falls, Chippenhook, Concord, Dorset, East Clarendon, Jericho, Manchester Center, Vergennes, Weston

Sawmills and lumbering

The directions for locating sawmills are similar to those given for finding the gristmills. In New Hampshire, Vermont, and Maine, many sawmills, now gas- or steam-driven, still operate in buildings originally set up to be water-driven.

Connecticut Burlington, Ledyard, Mansfield, Millington Green
Maine Allagash Wilderness Waterway, Bath, East Lebanon, East Vassalboro, Jefferson, Thorndike, Topsham, West Newfield
Massachusetts Boxford, North Leverett
New Hampshire Ashland, East Derry, Lincoln, Livermore, South Lee, Wilton
Vermont Kent's Corners, Readsboro Falls, Warren, Whitingham

Tanneries

The old buildings of the tannery trade have all but disappeared. The objects that stand the best chance of survival are the tanbark crushing circles, yet these can quickly vanish beneath a few years' underbrush.

The best chance of locating these is for local historians to research and identify the tannery sites in their towns and then visit them to dig and explore.

There is also a great possibility that many crushing circles are known, but their owners have never realized their true nature.

Connecticut Bakersville, Totoket(?)

Resorts

Many of the great old resorts now out of business have either burned down or have been taken over as meeting places by nonprofit organizations. The Vermont mineral spring hotel sites can be found in the *Vermont Life* article cited in the bibliography.

Hotel remains can be found near the summit of almost every high New England mountain lying outside the Green Mountain–White Mountain belt.

Massachusetts   Mount Holyoke, Princeton
New Hampshire   Monadnock
Rhode Island   Block Island
Vermont   Clarendon Springs, Glastenbury, Manchester Green, Wheelock,
   Whitingham

Mining

The many mines of New England are listed in the guides in the bibliography.
As they are intended for rockhounds, there is a greater emphasis on minerals to be
found than on descriptions of structures. However, the guides do give a compre-
hensive list of sites.

Connecticut   Granby
Maine   Blue Hill, Cherryfield, Harborside, Sullivan
Massachusetts   Chester, Norton, Rowe, Sturbridge
Vermont   Rochester, South Strafford, Vershire

Iron furnaces

Most furnaces have been identified, especially those with remains. For those
interested in local exploration or in identifying mines and bog ore sites, the
bibliography gives the necessary sources.

Connecticut   Bulls Falls, East Canaan, Huntsville, Kent Furnace, Lakeville,
   Lime Rock, Robertsville, Salisbury, Sharon Valley
Maine   Katahdin Iron Works, Pembroke
Massachusetts   Middleton, Richmond Furnace
New Hampshire   Franconia
Vermont   Bennington, East Dorset, Forestdale, Pittsford, Troy

Kilns

For other lime kiln sites, see the mineral guides.
   For charcoal pits, exploring the old trails in the hills around the iron furnace
sites will usually prove fruitful. Look for a 6-inch-deep circular trench approxi-
mately 15 feet in diameter. Usually the flora within the circle differs from its
surroundings. Digging will usually uncover charcoal pieces near the surface.

Connecticut   Boardmans Bridge, Canaan, Cornwall Hollow, Haddam, Mace-
   donia, New Hartford, Salisbury, Union, Woodbridge
Maine   Dover-Foxcroft, Katahdin Iron Works, Rockland, Rockport
Massachusetts   Cheshire, Egremont, Hampden, North Leverett, West Stock-
   bridge, Williamstown, Woronoco
New Hampshire   Lisbon, North Haverhill
Rhode Island   Lime Rock
Vermont   Glastenbury, Rochester

Textile mills

Many scenic mills still in use can be located through the bibliography. For the
explorer, the *Davison's Textile Blue Book* contains an excellent map showing all
New England mill towns.

Connecticut   Baltic, East Brooklyn, Hebron, Mechanicsville, Moodus, Rockville, Versailles, Wauregan
Massachusetts   Blackstone, North Uxbridge, Whitinsville
New Hampshire   Harrisville, Hillsboro
Rhode Island   Carolina, Hope Valley, Nooseneck, Pawtucket, Potter Hill, Shannock, Woodville, Woonsocket, Wyoming
Vermont   Bridgewater, Northfield, North Montpelier

Manufacturing

Most early industries grew in the cities of western Connecticut, southeastern Massachusetts, and the area around Providence, R.I. A good turn-of-the-century industrial site list can be found in the books published by the Davison Publishing Company that are similar to their *Textile Blue Book* but cover other topics.

Connecticut   Bristol, Collinsville, Falls Village, Lower City, Montville, Orcuttsville, Staffordville, West Stafford, Wilsonville, Winsted
Massachusetts   Assonet, Bancroft, Cordaville, Dalton, Housatonic, Townsend Harbor, West Concord
New Hampshire   Ashland, Claremont, Clinton Village, Pike, South Acworth
Rhode Island   West Gloucester, Woodville
Vermont   Brattleboro, East Clarendon, Hartland, Jericho, Middlebury, South Reading, Vergennes, West Charleston

Gasholder houses

No published list exists and there is no way to find others. These are all municipal plants; however, others that might remain will probably be found in large industrial complexes, where they were built to supply factory power and were later left standing or renovated to new uses.

The only way to locate these is to know what they look like and keep an eye open for them.

Connecticut   East Brooklyn
Massachusetts   Attleboro Falls, Boston, Northampton, North Attleboro
New Hampshire   Concord

Coastal schooners

Derelict ships are a familiar sight along the New England coast. Few, however, reach the age of the schooner derelicts. Ship remains can be seen in the scrapyards of the larger New England coastal towns.

Another class of remains are those driven ashore by storm and soon buried by shifting sands. The outer half of Cape Cod has many such wrecks, whose wooden ribs periodically appear and disappear from shifting dunes. Other wrecks lie underwater and can be located on coastal navigation charts. These await the inquisitive SCUBA diver.

Connecticut   New London, Noank
Maine   Bath, Boothbay Harbor, Medomak, Wiscasset
Massachusetts   Somerset

Ropewalks

There is little chance that there are any others than those listed below. However, for those interested, consult the Davison Publishing Company annuals on the cordage trade.

Connecticut   Mystic Seaport
Massachusetts   Charlestown, New Bedford
Rhode Island   Ashaway, Rockville

Railroads

Railroad relics lie virtually everywhere in New England. For the most part they take the forms of stations, depots, and old rights-of-way. Old rolling stock has been either scrapped or sold to railway museums. The best way to seek out the old lines is to compare the lines shown in the map in Chapter 19 with current state tourist maps that show lines in use today. For those touring these old lines, there will invariably be a "Depot St." in each town where one can find the old station.

The list below is only a small section of New England's railroad remains and is for the most part a list of the more unusual or scenic remains. See also the Abandoned Rights-of-Way list.

Connecticut   Baltic, Botsford, Collinsville, Cornwall Bridge, Granby Station, Norwich, Washington
Maine   Allagash Wilderness Waterway, Phillips
Massachusetts   Chester, Clinton, North Easton, Stoughton, West Stockbridge, Worcester
New Hampshire   Ashland, Bartlett, Claremont, Contoocook, Fabyan, Greenville, Hillsboro, Lincoln, Maplewood
Vermont   Burlington, St. Albans, Swanton

Bibliography

In addition to the books cited in the reference notes, there are a number of other books about specific sites or general subjects. Those listed below are some of the more interesting. They are noted in order of chapter subject.

Introduction

Adams, James T. *The Founding of New England*. Boston, 1921.
————. *Revolutionary New England, 1691–1776*. Boston, 1923.
————. *New England in the Republic, 1776–1830*. Boston, 1926. These three books are probably the best general New England histories.
American Guide Series. State guidebooks to interesting and historical sites. First published in the 1930s, written by the Federal Writers' Project of the WPA. A number of volumes have been revised and reprinted in the 1970s. These are the most complete guidebooks available which deal with the states and their tourist attractions. Some of the modern revised editions are rather poor.
National Register of Historic Places, 1972. Washington, D.C., 1972 (and later supplements). Lists historical sites of all states, most of which are restored or preserved by historical organizations.

1 The New England Landscape

Jorgensen, Neil. *A Guide to New England's Landscape*. Barre, Mass., 1971. Very readable overall study of New England's landforms and vegetation.

2 Paths, Post Roads, and Turnpikes

Dwight, Timothy. *Travels in New York and New England*. New York, 1821. Many later reprints. Journals of New England in the 1790s. Especially interesting in comparison to Madame Knight's experiences.
Earle, Alice M. *Stage Coach & Tavern Days*. New York, 1901.
Green, Samuel A. "Old Milestones Leading to Boston," *Massachusetts Historical Society Proceedings* 42 (1908–9). Lists milestones of eastern Massachusetts, especially those in greater Boston.
Holbrook, Stewart. *The Old Post Road*. New York, 1962. Popular history of Boston Post Road.
Jenkins, Stephen. *The Old Boston Post Road*. New York, 1913. A history of the towns along the way.
Jones, Herbert G. *The King's Highway from Portland to Kittery*. Portland, 1953. Stage road along lower Maine coast.
Journal of Madame Knight, 1704. New York, 1825. Heavily reprinted. A fascinating first-person account.
Marlowe, George F. *Coaching Roads of Old New England*. New York, 1901.

Covers routes across northern Massachusetts into New Hampshire and Vermont.

Mitchell, Isabel S. *Roads and Road-Making in Colonial Connecticut.* New Haven, 1933. Short work on the subject.

Parks, Roger N. *Roads and Travel in New England 1790–1840.* Sturbridge, Mass., 1967. A comparison to the Mitchell volume.

Sage, Henry P. "Ye Milestones of Connecticut," *Papers of the New Haven Colony Historical Society* 10 (1951). Exhaustive list of Connecticut's remaining milestones.

Wood, Frederic J. *The Turnpikes of New England.* Boston, 1919. Gives a short history of virtually every New England turnpike; also excellent maps.

3 The Canals

Clarke, Mary Stetson. *The Old Middlesex Canal.* Melrose, Mass., 1974.

Coomes, Z. "The Blackstone Canal," *Proceedings of the Worcester Historical Society* 1 (8) (April 1935).

Harlow, Alvin F. *Old Towpaths.* New York, 1926. Basic text on American canal building.

Harte, Charles R. *Connecticut's Canals,* 54th Annual Report, Connecticut Society of Civil Engineers. New Haven, 1938. Farmington and Enfield Canals.

———. *Engineering Features of the Old Northampton Canal,* 49th Annual Report, Connecticut Society of Civil Engineers. New Haven, 1933. Physical features of Farmington Canal.

Milliken, Philip I. *Notes on the Cumberland and Oxford Canal.* Portland, 1954. Available from the Canal National Bank of Portland, Canal Plaza, Portland, Me. 04111.

Roberts, Christopher. *The Middlesex Canal 1793–1860.* Cambridge, 1938. Economic study of canal and canal building.

4 The Farms on the Hills

Appalachian Mountain Club. *The A.M.C. Massachusetts and Rhode Island Trail Guide.* Boston, 1967.

———. *The A.M.C. White Mountain Guide.* These and the following guides are excellent for locating and exploring abandoned farming areas.

Appalachian Trail Conference. *Guide to the Appalachian Trail in Massachusetts and Connecticut.* Washington, D.C., 1968.

———. *Guide to the Appalachian Trail in New Hampshire and Vermont.* Washington, D.C., 1968.

Bidwell, Percy W. *Rural Economy in New England at the Beginning of the 19th Century.* New Haven, 1916. Reprinted, 1972. An excellent discussion of all phases of early rural life and business.

Black, John D. *The Rural Economy of New England.* Cambridge, 1950. A study of rural adjustment in the twentieth century.

Blanchard, Fessenden. *Ghost Towns of New England.* New York, 1960. Folksy, first-person account of visits to "cellar hole" towns.

Connecticut Forest and Park Association. *Connecticut Walk Book.* East Hartford, 1970. Hiking guide.

Eisenmenger, Robert W. *The Dynamics of Growth in New England's Economy 1870–1964.* Middletown, Conn., 1967.

Goldthwait, James W. "A Town that has Gone Downhill," *Geographical Review* 17 (4) (October 1927). Study of the population shifts in a group of rural New Hampshire towns.

Green Mountain Club. *Guide Book of the Long Trail*. Rutland, 1971. Hiking guide for Vermont's Green Mountains.

Rosenberry, Lois K. M. *Migrations from Connecticut After 1800*. New Haven, 1936.

————. *Migrations from Connecticut Prior to 1800*. New Haven, 1936. Both works are short and highly readable.

Stillwell, Lewis D. *Migration from Vermont*. Montpelier, 1948. Similar to Rosenberry but a larger work.

Wilson, Harold F. *The Hill Country of Northern New England 1790–1930*. New York, 1936. Reprinted, 1956. A must. Covers all stages of New England's rural hill life.

5 Rural Schools and Churches

Johnson, Clifton. *A Book of Country Clouds and Sunshine*. Boston, 1896. A series of articles and vignettes on the twilight of the hill farm communities in the 1890s.

————. *The Country School in New England*. New York, 1893. Folksy account of country school life.

————. *Old Time Schools and Schoolbooks*. New York, 1904. Recently reprinted. Excellent and exhaustive, extremely readable.

"Village Life in New England," *Littell's Living Age*, 1881, pp. 35–40. How a New England village changed between 1840 and 1880.

7 The Village Mill

Hamilton, Edward P. *The Village Mill in Early New England*. Sturbridge, Mass., 1964. Popular study of saw-, grist-, and fulling mills.

Old Mill News. Magazine published by the Society for the Preservation of Old Mills. P.O. Box 435, Wiscasset, Me. 04578. Up-to-date information on the fate of various mills.

Rawson, Marion. *Little Old Mills*. New York, 1935. Extremely readable story of early mills of all kinds.

Zimilies, Martha and Murray. *Early American Mills*. New York, 1973. The mills and their development with emphasis on New England. Heavy coverage of grist- and textile mills. Many pictures.

8 The Sawmills and the Lumber Industry

The works listed under Chapter 7 all contain sawmill information.

Belcher, Fran. A series of articles on White Mountain logging and logging railroads in *Appalachia* 33 (1960–61).

Pike, Robert. *Tall Trees, Tough Men*. New York, 1967. Nostalgic look at the story of New England lumbering.

Springer, John S. *Forest Life and Forest Trees*. New York, 1856. Traveling in the Maine woods in the 1850s.

9 The Village Tannery

Welsh, Peter C. *Tanning in the United States to 1850.* Washington, D.C., 1964. Good study of early tanning.

10 Mineral Springs and Mountaintop Resorts

Koier, Louise. "Those Wonderful Waters," *Vermont Life,* Summer 1957. Chronicles and lists all mineral spring hotel sites in Vermont.
Massachusetts Department of Natural Resources. *The Case of the Holyoke Range.* Boston, 1962. Short history of the Mount Holyoke Range.

11 Mining

Abbott, Callamer. *Green Mountain Copper.* Randolph, Vt., 1973. Fascinating account of Vermont copper industry, especially "Ely War."
Morrill, Philip, et al. *Maine Mines and Minerals,* 2 vols.
———. *Mineral Guide to New England.*
———. *Rhode Island Mines and Minerals.*
———. *New Hampshire Mines and Mineral Locations.*
———. *Vermont Mines and Mineral Locations.*
    All are available from Winthrop Mineral Shop, East Winthrop, Me. 04343. Exhaustive lists of mines and mineral locations. More emphasis on mineral deposits than aboveground remains.
Phelps, Richard H. *Newgate of Connecticut.* Hartford, 1876. Full history of mine and prison.
Ryerson, Katherine. *Rock Hound's Guide to Connecticut.* Stonington, Conn., 1968. Companion book to Morrill's series.

12 The Iron Industry

Allen, Richard S. "Furnaces, Forges, and Foundries in Vermont," *Vermont Life,* Winter 1956–57.
Annin, Katherine H. *Richmond, Massachusetts 1765–1965.* Richmond, 1964. Has a section chronicling efforts to keep the Richmond Furnace alive during the twentieth century.
Harte, Charles, and Keith, Herbert. *The Early Iron Industry of Connecticut.* 51st Annual Report, Connecticut Society of Civil Engineers. New Haven, 1935. Best work on the subject. Lists all sites of furnaces in Connecticut and adjoining New York and Massachusetts.
Lesley, John P. *The Iron Manufacturer's Guide to the Furnaces, Forges, and Rolling Mills of the United States.* New York, 1859. Information, location, and statistics on all iron furnaces of the 1850s and before.
Lure of the Litchfield Hills. Box 215, Collinsville, Conn. Semi-annual magazine. Has had many articles over the years on iron furnaces of Salisbury area.
Morrill, Philip, et al. *Maine Mines and Minerals,* 2 vols.
———. *Mineral Guide to New England.*
———. *Rhode Island Mines and Minerals.*
———. *New Hampshire Mines and Mineral Locations.*

———. *Vermont Mines and Mineral Locations.*
    All are available from Winthrop Mineral Shop, East Winthrop, Me. 04343.
    Ore, furnace and forge sites are listed.
Pynchon, W. "Iron Mining in Connecticut," *Connecticut Magazine* 5 (1899).
    Article in three parts.
Spargo, John. *Iron Mining and Smelting in Bennington, Vermont 1786–1842.*
    Bennington, 1938.
Swank, James M. *Statistics of Iron and Steel Production of the United States.*
    Washington, D.C., 1881. Much on colonial iron.

13 The Kilns

Dale, T. Nelson. *Lime Belt of Massachusetts and Parts of New York and Con-
    necticut.* Washington, D.C., USGS Bulletin 744, 1923.
Grindle, Roger Lee. *Quarry and Kiln: The Story of Maine's Lime Industry.*
    Rockland, Me., 1971. Best account of lime industry and lime ships.
Kemper, Jackson. *American Charcoal Making.* Washington, D.C., 1941. National
    Park Service study of one of the last charcoal burners in the Pennsylvania
    hills.
Morrill, Philip, et al. *Maine Mines and Minerals,* 2 vols.
———. *Mineral Guide to New England.*
———. *Rhode Island Mines and Minerals.*
———. *New Hampshire Mines and Mineral Locations.*
———. *Vermont Mines and Mineral Locations.*
    All are available from Winthrop Mineral Shop, East Winthrop, Me. 04343.
    Kiln sites are listed.

14 The Textile Industry

Davison Publishing Company. *Davison's Textile Blue Book.* New York, 1887–
    1933, annually. Lists all New England textile mills, with handy map of
    towns.
Devino, William S. *A Study of Textile Mill Closings in Selected New England
    Communities.* Orono, Me., 1966. What happens after the mills close.
Historic American Building Survey. *New England Textile Mills.* Washington,
    D.C., 1971. Specifications on a number of exemplary mills.
Zimilies, Martha and Murray. *Early American Mills.* New York, 1973. The mills
    and their development with emphasis on New England. Many pictures.

15 Manufacturing

Bishop, John L. *A History of American Manufactures from 1608 to 1860.* Phila-
    delphia, 1864. Reprinted, 1956. Traces history of all types of manufacture,
    many of which began in New England.
Collins Company. *A Brief Account of the Development of the Collins Company.*
    Collinsville, 1935. Company-sponsored history.
Estall, R. C. *New England: A Study in Industrial Adjustment.* New York, 1966.
———. *New England: A Study in Industrial Development.* New York, 1966.
Fuller, Grace P. *Introduction to the History of Connecticut as a Manufacturing
    State.* Northampton, Mass., 1915.

Le Blanc, Robert G. *Location of Manufacturing in New England in the 19th Century*. Hanover, N.H., 1969. Excellent account of the hows and whys of the shape of New England's industrial growth.

Paullin, Charles O. *Atlas of Historical Geography of the United States*. Baltimore, 1932. Treasurehouse of maps showing how many trades developed out of New England sites.

Ransom, Stanley A. "History of the William L. Gilbert Clock Corporation, Winsted, Connecticut," *Lure of the Litchfield Hills*, 1971, four-part series.

17 The Coastal Schooners

Kirkland, Edward C. *Men, Cities, and Transportation*. Cambridge, 1948.

Leavitt, John F. *Wake of the Coasters*. Middletown, Conn., 1970. First-person account of life on a coastal schooner.

Morgan, Charles S. *New England Coastal Schooners*. Salem, 1963. Short history with many illustrations.

Parker, W. J. L. "The Great Coal Schooners of New England 1870–1909," Maine Historical Association 2 (6) (December 1948). Story of the *Wyoming* and her sister coal carriers.

Tod, Giles M. S. *The Last Sail Down East*. Barre, Mass., 1965. Has exhaustive list of schooners, their specifications, and their travels.

18 The Ropewalks

Morison, Samuel E. *The Ropemakers of Plymouth: A History of the Plymouth Cordage Company 1824–1949*. Boston, 1950. Company history.

19 The Railroads

Baker, George P. *Formation of New England Railroad Systems*. Cambridge, 1937. Charts consolidation of New England railroad companies.

Bulletin of the Railway and Locomotive Historical Society, Harvard Business School, Boston. Published twice yearly. Good reading and great pictures.

Dunbar, Seymour. *A History of Travel in America*. Indianapolis, 1915. The basic text on American transportation.

Establishing Trails on Rights-of-Way. Washington, D.C., Department of the Interior, Bureau of Outdoor Recreation, 1971. Available from Superintendent of Documents, U.S. Government Printing Office, Washington, D.C. 20402. Lists trackage abandoned after 1960.

Harlow, Alvin F. *Steelways of New England*. New York, 1946. Exhaustive study, though hard to follow.

Kirkland, Edward C. *Men, Cities, and Transportation*. Cambridge, 1948.

Lindahl, Martin L. *New England Railroads*. Boston, 1965.

Rand McNally's Handy Railroad Atlas of the United States. Compare latest edition to map on page 159 to determine the latest lines abandoned.

Williams, Ernest W., Jr. "Looking Back. Fifty Years of American Railroading," *Bulletin of the Railway and Locomotive Historical Society* 125 (October 1971). Traces economic decline of railroads since 1920s.

Index

Sources of Illustrations

All illustrations not cited here are photographs taken by the author. Illustrations reproduced courtesy of the following sources:

American Antiquarian Society, *View of Worcester Massachusetts, Taken from Union Hill 1837–8* (C. P. Anderson, *Del.*, T. Moores, *Litho.*, Boston): 26; Bath Marine Museum, Bath, Me.: 141; Fran Belcher: 75; *Berkshire Eagle*, Pittsfield, Mass.: 103; Billerica Historical Society, Billerica, Mass., *View from William Rogers House*, watercolor by William Barton, 1825: 20 bottom; Boston Athenaeum, *Crown and Eagle Mills, Uxbridge, Massachusetts*, James Kidder, *Del.*, Senefelder, *Lith.* (Boston 1828–34): 118 top; and *Quincy Rail Road*, David Claypoole Johnson, Pendelton, *Lith.* (Boston): 150; Currier Gallery of Art, Friends' Fund, Manchester, N.H. *Clarendon Springs*, 1853 (James Hope): 83; Peabody Museum, Salem, Mass.: 138, 139; Railway and Locomotive Historical Society, Boston, Mass.: 153, 156, 161, 162, 163, 164 top, 190.

Illustration sources:

Armroyd, George, *Internal Navigation* (1830): 155; Bachelder, John, *Popular Resorts* (1875): 11; Barber, John W., *Connecticut Historical Collections* (1838): xiv, 90; Barber, *History and Antiquities of New England* (1842): 5; Barber, *Massachusetts Historical Collections* (1841): 25, 152; Bryant, William C., *Picturesque America* (1872): 12, 71, 102 top, 136; Coffin, Charles, *Building the Nation* (1882): 193; Collins Company, *Brief Account* (1935): 172; *Columbia Magazine*, Phila. (1789): 3; *Connecticut Magazine* (1899): 97, 102 bottom, (1903): 124; *Contributions of the Old Residents Historical Association, Lowell, Mass.* (1887): 19, 20 top, 24, 188; Coolidge, A. J., *History and Description of New England* (1859): x; Dearborn, J. W., *History of Parsonsfield* (1888): 48, 181; Dunbar, Seymour, *History of Travel in America* (1915): 7; *Encyclopaedia: A Directory of Arts, Sciences, and Literature* (1798): 147; Erving, Henry, *Connecticut River Banking Company* (1925): 187; *Every Saturday* (1871): 41, 74 left; French, H. W., *Art and Artists in Connecticut* (1879): 8; Frost, John, *Pictorial History of America* (1856): 70, 170; *Gleason's Pictorial* (1852): 148, 176; Goodrich, S. G., *Pictorial Geography of the World* (1840): 43; Greely, Horace, *Great Industries of the U.S.* (1872): 52, 60, 62 bottom, 125, 127, 128 top, 174, 182; *Harper's Monthly* (1856): 82, (1857): 91, (1860): 18, (1862): 131; *Harper's Weekly* (1869): 135, (1870): 40, (1873): 53 top, (1879): 22, 108; Hazen, Edward, *Popular Technology* (1850): 77; Hill, Frank, *Lowell Illustrated* (1884): 132; Hitchcock, Edward, *Geology of Massachusetts* (1841): 114; Hopkins, Livingston, *Comic History of the United States* (1880): 39; Jackson, Charles, *Geology and Mineralogy of New Hampshire* (1884): 92; Jackson, Charles, *Geological and Agricultural Survey of Rhode Island* (1840): 110 left; Jenkins, Stephen, *Old Post Road* (1913): 10; Johnson, Clifton, *Country School in New England* (1893): 53 bottom; *Katahdin Iron Works* (1863): 101; Kobbe, Gustave, *New Jersey Coast and Pines* (1889): 107; Knight, Charles, *English Encyclopaedia* (1861): 145, 146, 197; Knox, Thomas,

Underground World (1882): 157; Curtis, Ann Lampton, and Sierra, Dorothea: 2, 6, 21; *Mt. Holyoke* (brochure ca. 1870): 84, 85; *1900 Summer Excursions Via Fitchburg Railroad* (1900): 159; O'Callaghan, Peter J., 62 top, 94, 112; Pepper, John, *Boys Book of Metals* (ca. 1880): 110 right; Phelps, Richard, *Newgate* (1876): 89; *Scribner's Monthly* (1877): 72; Springer, John, *Forest Life and Forest Trees* (1956): 73, Stebbins, L., *80 Years Progress of the United States* (1867): 38; Taylor, W. Cooke, *Handbook of Silk, Cotton and Woollen Manufactures* (1843): 116; U.S. House Report 341, April 2, 1830, *Farmington and Hampshire Canal Company*: 28; *Universal Magazine*, London (1751): 80; Warner, Charles F., *Picturesque Hampshire* (1890): 9; Wood, *Turnpikes* (1919): 16, 168; *Yankee Notions*, New York (1857): 42, 154.